USING

BUSINESS

BASIC

Wilson T. Price

Merritt College, Oakland, California

Holt, Rinehart and Winston

New York   Chicago   San Francisco   Philadelphia
Montreal   Toronto   London   Sydney   Tokyo
Mexico City   Rio de Janeiro   Madrid

To my wife Jean
and the success of
JP Designs

Library of Congress Cataloging in Publication Data

Price, Wilson T.
  Using business basic.

  Includes index.
  1. Basic (Computer program language) 2. Business—
Data processing. I. Title.
HF5548.5.B3P75 1983   001.64'24   83-189
ISBN 0-03-063176-9

Printed in the United States of America

Published simultaneously in Canada

    5 6   039   9 8 7 6 5 4 3

CBS COLLEGE PUBLISHING
Holt, Rinehart and Winston
The Dryden Press
Saunders College Publishing

Contents

Preface

Virtually every Basic book that comes on the marketplace is described as using structured programming techniques. For most of them the use of structured methods is relegated to lip service. A few do a good job of sticking to the three basic structures (sequence, selection, and looping) in presenting solutions to programming examples. However, the nature of Basic makes it difficult to write programs that are truly structured. For instance, a Basic program of any substance that does not use a **GOTO** is difficult to imagine. Yet it *is* possible to incorporate use of the **GOTO** into a framework that achieves the goals of good program design and functions within the three basic components of structured programming. That is the top priority in this book.

This book is not one on learning Basic; it is one on *how to systematically solve business-related problems while learning Basic.* From the first page of the book the stress is on organizing a problem into logical components: *program modularization.* Heavy emphasis is placed on breaking problems into components and then programming the components relatively independently of one another. Programming methods used in this book draw heavily on proven techniques now widely used in structured Cobol programming. For instance, in business data processing, there is a wide class of problems that can be broken down to three main modules:

Initialization module
Processing module
Termination module

Normally, the processing module (which may consist of multiple submodules) is repeatedly executed until there is no more data to process. To this end, the **PERFORM** is commonly used in Cobol. Programs in this book use a similar approach with the **GOSUB** statement. In fact, the **GOSUB** is a central focus from almost the very beginning.

This significantly reduces the need for using the **GOTO** statement. Overall, specific constraints are placed on use of the **GOTO**. In a nutshell, it must be used within the limit that every routine or sequence of statements has a single entry point and a single exit. Of course, there are a few exceptions to this which are necessitated by the nature of Basic. Needless to say, good judgment must be used in every situation; after all, the objective is to learn good programming methods *not* to contrive program structure solely for the purpose of being able to say, "Look, it is structured."

Overall, the attempt has been to make this a student's book. Some of its important features are:

1. In all programming examples, modularization is emphasized. This is especially important to the beginning student when covering advanced topics where example programs necessarily become much larger than earlier examples. Not only does modularization provide the student with examples that are easy to follow but it illustrates programming techniques that are critical to writing good, readable, and easy to maintain programs.

2. For most of the main developments, this book remains within the constraints of minimal Basic and attempts to address the lowest common language denominator. Needless to say, there are numerous exceptions to this (where appropriate). For instance, Chapter 5 deals with files and Chapter 6 with the **PRINT-USING**. In such cases, the emphasis is on concepts as much as on particular forms.

3. Emphasis is placed on using structured techniques and minimizing use of the **GOTO** statement. Since Basic does not include true block **IF-THEN** and **IF-THEN-ELSE** structures, this concept is simulated to maintain good structured techniques.

4. Each new topic is introduced through and oriented around a simple example. Each example is described in detail, its implications are discussed, it is solved, and important features of the solution are discussed. The progression is always from the concrete to the abstract.

5. As a rule, example programs are kept short, with primary focus on the topic being introduced. For the beginning student it is felt that the value of an example program or sequence in illustrating a concept is inversely proportional to the amount of code that is extraneous to that particular concept.

6. Each chapter includes "mind-jogger" exercises within the chapter; the answers to these exercises are at the end of the chapter. The intent is to provide a reinforcement vehicle for important concepts. In many cases they relate the significant point(s) concerning an example program and give the student a better insight to some of the fine points. The student should be urged to complete each exercise as it is encountered and then refer to the answer to be certain of comprehending it.

7. The book contains four appendixes which include reserved words, the ASCII character set, and summaries of Basic commands, statements, and functions. These summaries include differences between the forms discussed in this book and the comparable forms of the Apple, Radio Shack, and IBM microcomputers.

Concerning the topical organization of this book, the detailed table of contents speaks for itself. However, some important points may not be evident from this list.

First, Chapter 1 presents a prewritten program complete with a "data file" in the form of a set of **DATA** statements. The first student assignment should be to key this program into the computer and run it. A "do it because it works" approach is to be used here. This provides a basic framework on which to hang the beginning concepts a student needs: interacting with the computer, the distinction between entering and running a program, the distinction between commands and statements, and other principles. Fundamental elements of the language structure are brought out using this same example program in Chapter 2.

Second, the concept of data files is stressed throughout the book—first in approaching the **DATA** statements as forming a "file", then with the actual disk files themselves. Using sequential files is described in Chapter 5 in order to take advantage of the file capabilities of many versions of Basic. However, for any classroom environment in which data files are to be used at the earliest possible time, Chapter 5 could be covered following Chapter 3 (or even Chapter 2).

Third, Chapter 11 consists of three independent components: string manipulation (above and beyond that introduced in Chapter 6), user-defined functions, and menu control. Any of these topics can be introduced at virtually any point in the book (beyond the first few chapters) in order to meet the particular objectives of a given course.

Acknowledgments

My first expression of thanks must go to my students who have provided me with many of the ideas in this book and who have endured some of my "less than successful" experiments. A very close second for my appreciation goes to Jack Olson, one of my colleagues at Merritt College. It was only after much harassing by him (over a long period of time) that I finally conceded to the fact that commonly used Cobol techniques for implementing structured methods could be used fruitfully in Basic. I consider myself fortunate to have him as a friend, colleague, and "sounding board."

Individuals who influenced this book through their contributions to its predecessor *Elements of Basic-Plus Programming* include Richard Bidleman, George Grill, Peter Simas, Norman Sandak, Robert van Keuren, and Robert Wilson.

Careful typing and proofing by Kathie Kane made life immensely easier for me. In my own programming, I seem to be frustratingly error prone. Two very conscientious students, Alan Claypool and Mark Seeman, took great care in checking my programs in an effort to bail me out.

Finally I wish to thank users of my books who have taken their valuable time to send me their reactions, observations, and critical remarks; many of them are reflected in this book. I will sincerely appreciate any and all comments about this book. They may be sent to me at Merritt College, 12500 Campus Drive, Oakland, CA 94619.

Wilson T. Price

Introduction

OBJECTIVES

To many, the computer and its terminology are very foreign. Furthermore, the rigorous way of thinking imposed by programming has a tendency to throw many people for a loss. The purpose of this introduction is to provide the basis on which to begin learning the discipline of programming. Concepts and topics about which you will learn in this chapter are as follows:

1. The basic notion of what programming a computer is all about. This is illustrated by a simple analogy.
2. The principles of top-down design. Very large and complex problems can often be nearly impossible to comprehend. However, if broken down into small, independent components (modules), they are easily understood.
3. The fact that structured programming is basically a set of rules for solving programming problems. The use of flowcharts, which are pictorial representations of the program logic, is described.
4. The computer itself, called *hardware.* The modern computer consists of input and output devices (for getting information in and out of the computer), memory, a control unit, and auxiliary storage.
5. Programs that make the computer work for us, commonly referred to as *software* systems. Specialized systems for controlling the computer are called *operating systems* and provide for automatic control of the computer.

Basic Concepts of Programming

A STORY OF SUCCESS To gain a little insight into the world of the computer, let us consider the story of a very bright college student who had a strong dislike for conventional "work." When faced with the prospect of financing his college education, he decided to do so by playing the horses—a means of earning an income which he considered infinitely superior to pumping gas or washing dishes. Since his hobby had long been horse racing, he had an extensive file of information on the horses that generally raced at the local tracks. This file consisted of a set of 5 × 7 cards: one for each horse. Each card showed the past record of the horse (including best running times), information on how well the horse did under various weather conditions, and so on.

The information file was the key to the student's success. Prior to each weekend, he would select from his file the record of each horse running that weekend. Armed with this stack of cards, a summary form, a pencil, his brilliant mind, and his system, he would sit down to work (Figure 1). His system consisted of a series of calculations which gave each horse a performance score between 0 and 100. Past experience had shown that the horse with the highest score in each race was usually the winner.

Figure 1   A human computer system

The procedure the student followed was simple:

1. Take the next card from the set of data cards.
2. Calculate the HPS (Horse Performance Score) for that horse.*
3. Record the horse's name and score on the summary form.
4. Go back to step 1 and repeat the sequence for the next horse.

The summary form then provided the student with all of the information he would need at the track that weekend.

Eventually the student became bored with the horses, but not before finishing college. He then put his (by then) computer expertise to use and obtained a challenging, well-paying job in programming.

HORSE RACING AND COMPUTER PROGRAMMING   Now what has all of this to do with computer programming? To answer that, let us consider the following.

First, it illustrates a data processing application. *Data processing* is a very common term which can be defined as the processing of raw data (information) to obtain useful results. In the story, the raw data was supplied by the 5 × 7 cards, the calculations comprised the processing, and the summary sheet represented the useful results.

Second, the set of 5 × 7 cards consisted of the same components as data to be used by a computer. The student had a *file* of *data*. This file consisted of a set of *related records*. Each record contained several *pieces of information* about a particular horse. In data processing terminology, each piece of information is called a *field*. The notions of file, field, and record are

---

*What is involved in this step? We can assume that many detailed calculations are required. Since the formula was a closely guarded secret, only the student knew what the exact procedures were.

illustrated for the horse racing example in Figure 2(a). It is important to recognize that data to be used by a computer contains the same three components: files, records, and fields. For example, a file of employee payroll records which a company uses to pay its employees is illustrated in Figure 2(b). As with the horse racing example, you can see that the file consists of a set of related records (employee master records). Each record contains information about one specific element of the file (one employee). The in-

Figure 2   Files, records, and fields.

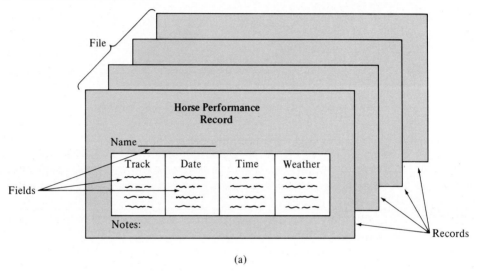

(a)

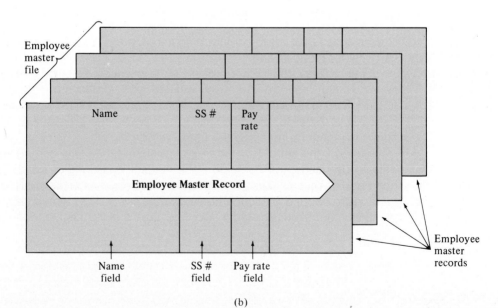

(b)

formation on each record is divided into fields. Each field contains one piece of information about the employee: the Name field contains the employee's name, the Pay Rate field contains the employee's pay rate, and so on. Most data going into a computer or coming out of a computer consists of files, records, and fields.

Third, the sequence of steps carried out by the student in processing his data is very similar to the manner in which a computer operates. That is, one performs a sequence of steps (such as the following) one after the other.

1. Read next record.
2. Calculate the HPS.
3. Record the results.
4. Return to step 1.

Now you might wonder about how to calculate HPS (step 2). Is the computer so smart that it knows what to do without being told in detail? The answer is NO!! Just as we cannot do the horse racing calculation without being told exactly what has to be done, so the computer cannot do any desired calculation without being told exactly what to do. The computer is capable of some pretty amazing things. But it has no intelligence and no judgment, so it cannot decide what has to be done. This brings us to the First Law of Programming:

If you want the computer to do a particular thing, you must tell it in exacting detail to do that particular thing.

The corollary of the First Law can be stated as:

If you don't tell it, it won't do it.

The second corollary is:

The computer will do what you tell it to do, even if you don't mean it.

For most people, learning to program means learning to be precise.

WRITING COMPUTER PROGRAMS If you accept the fact that you must tell the computer exactly what to do, you are probably wondering *how* to do it. Let us consider this question in two parts: (1) How do you figure out what you want the computer to do? (2) Once you have figured out what you want it to do, how do you tell it to do it? The *how* is what this book is all about—to learn the answers to these questions. Basically there is a very simple procedure to follow in writing any computer program:

1. *Define the desired results.* Analyze the problem to see what useful results, or output, are required. Decide on exactly the information which the computer is to output.

2. *Examine the input data.* Does it contain everything you need to produce the desired output? If the needed data is not there in exactly the desired form, can you combine some of the input fields to produce the desired output? If the answer to one of these questions is "yes," you can go ahead. However, if the answer to both questions is "no," you do not have the necessary input data to produce the desired output.

3. Devise an overall plan (sometimes called an *algorithm*) for converting the input data into the desired output. A number of techniques are commonly used for this purpose, including structured flowcharts (described later) and pseudocode.

4. Express the solution in a language which the computer can understand. This is called "coding the program"; this book involves coding programs in the Basic language.

Many students dislike the preliminary work of clearly defining and solving the problem. They prefer to get right to the coding. These students usually find, however, as the problems become more complicated, that the program cannot be coded until the solution algorithm has been developed; the flowchart is a convenient way to express the algorithm. This brings us to the Second Law of Programming:

The longer you spend on defining your output and developing your overall solution, the faster the programming task will go.

The corollary to the Second Law is:

Resist the urge to code!!!

Top-Down Program Design

WHAT IS TOP-DOWN DESIGN? The top-down approach to problem solving basically involves beginning with the broad, overall problem and breaking it down into two or more relatively independent components. As a rule, components are divided according to the *function* they perform. For instance, it might be possible to consider a particular problem as consisting of:

- Edit the data and verify its accuracy
- Perform calculations
- Write an output report

The next step would be to inspect each of these components and determine if it reasonably could be broken down further. For example, the first function might be further broken down as:

- Edit the data and verify its accuracy
    Edit data
    Verify accuracy
    Process invalid data

The nature of this operation gives us the clue to the name *top-down design*. That is, we start at the top (the overall) and work successively downward until we have the original (large) problem broken down into a set of manageably sized *modules*. One very important facet is that, when using this technique, we first concern ourselves with the *what* and ignore (at least initially) the *how*. In other words, we simply figure out *what* we must do before we begin working on how to do it. This may sound like the obvious way to handle a problem— *and it is*. However, it is astonishing how frequently beginning programmers cannot figure out what is to be done and so they select a particular area of the problem and begin programming it. This is sometimes referred to as a bottom-up approach and involves nibbling away in the hope that the overall solution will appear magically during the process. More often than not, it does not happen. In fact, if the problem is one of any magnitude, you can almost guarantee that the result will be a disastrous mess. One of the most important rules of programming is:

Think first, program later.

AN EXAMPLE OF TOP-DOWN ANALYSIS To illustrate the top-down technique, let us consider how to approach the task of computerizing a company payroll application.

Example 1
The Eagle Manufacturing Company wishes to computerize its factory payroll operation. Factory employees are paid according to a complex formula which includes such factors as hours worked, job classification, employee seniority, and the company's profit in the preceding fiscal quarter. The calculations include tax computations, accumulation of year-to-date figures, and provisions for voluntary deductions. All input and output records have already been defined by the systems analyst; all that remains is to write the program.

To apply the top-down design technique to this problem, the first step would be to portray the overall program in terms of its functions, which is done in Figure 3(a). Notice that no details are given at this point as to how the program will accomplish its results. The entire program is represented as a single box, and its function is to convert the input data into the desired output.
    The next step is to expand the one-box representation. The expansion is shown in the *hierarchy chart* of Figure 3(b). This expansion may seem to

Figure 3   Top-down
program design—
Example 1.

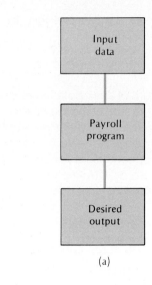

(a)

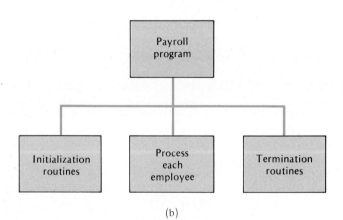

(b)

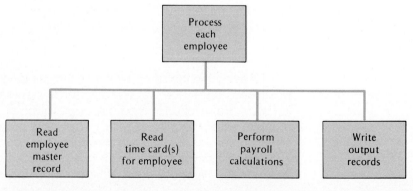

(c)

belabor the obvious. It may seem trivial and pointless; but it is not. The whole objective of top-down program design is to permit the programmer to specify the contents of the program one step at a time, with each step being a simple expansion of the previous one. Again, there is no concern with the content of the boxes. The question, "What does the term *Initialization Routines* include?," not only is not answered; it is not even asked. At this point in the program development, it is sufficient to know that an initialization routine will be required, and to provide a place for it. Note that the lines connect the lower boxes to the upper box to show that they make up the functions performed by that box. Note also that there is no designation of the sequence in which blocks are executed. The purpose of the chart is simply to show what has to be done by each component of the program.

The procedure continues with the expansion of one of the new boxes. The initialization and termination boxes cannot yet be expanded because their functions are dependent on the main part of the program, so the next task is to expand the "Process Each Employee" block. Figure 3(c) illustrates the basic expansion. Here again the same principles appear: simple statements, horizontally aligned, of what the box is to accomplish, with no specific details as to how anything is to be done.

The reader, at this point, may be questioning the significance of all of this. It is simply this: Very few human minds can grasp all of the details and relationships of a complex computer program. The mind, however, can deal very competently with a small portion of the program, or with a large portion of it broken down into a number of small parts or functional blocks. Top-down program design, then, is nothing more than a technique for taking a large problem, dividing it into a few basic elements, subdividing each element into subelements, and so on until the problem has been broken down into pieces of manageable size.

Further expansion of Example 1 might then involve breaking the "Perform Payroll Calculations" box down into regular pay computations, overtime pay computations, deduction computations, and so on. Only when the entire problem has been clearly defined as a complete set of reasonably sized modules should the programming begin.

Structured Programming

INTRODUCTION Once a problem has been broken down into basic components, or individual *modules,* then the programming may start. The first step is to define the *program logic;* that is, now that the *what* has been defined, the *how* must be determined. For instance, each person's Social Security deduction will be calculated until the deduction reaches a certain maximum, then it will be discontinued. Similarly, which voluntary deductions will be calculated for each employee and what are the methods used in the calculation? This brings us to the topic of *program logic.*

Structured programming can be defined as *a set of formalized rules for coding programs.* In general, structured techniques are applicable to virtually all languages. However, the languages most commonly used today (Cobol, Basic, and Fortran) were not designed with structured methods in mind. Although additions have been made to make them more compatible with structured methods, they leave something to be desired from this point of view. On the other hand, the Pascal language was designed specifically as a structured language. Thus, in using structured methods, the programmer should be realistic and keep in mind the language to be used.

But regardless of the language being used, top-down principles and structured techniques can be implemented with great benefit. For instance, we can think of the payroll program as consisting of a main routine (module) that controls or *calls* the needed submodules. This notion is illustrated in Figure 4, which is virtually identical to the hierarchy chart of Figure 3(b). This representation shows that each of the three "second-level" routines is controlled by the main routine. Actually this brings us close to consideration of the program logic and the next topic: flowcharting.

Figure 4   Main routine controlling "sub" routines.

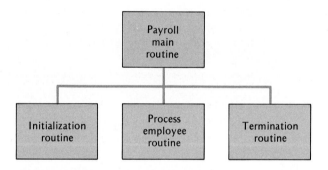

FLOWCHART SYMBOLS   One of the most commonly employed methods of representing program logic involves the use of diagrams called *flowcharts.* With the advent of top-down design and structured techniques, many in programming felt that flowcharts were no longer necessary, if not totally useless. However, the key to using any tool, including flowcharts, is careful planning. If flowcharts are used in conjunction with structured techniques, they are very valuable in illustrating program logic.

The blocks in a hierarchy chart illustrate general functions to be performed and their relationship to one another. Flowcharts also use a block representation, but they differ from hierarchy charts in two important respects:

1. They illustrate logic flow—that is, the order in which operations are carried out. For instance, there is no indication in Figure 3(c) that if an employee has not worked (no time cards), then payroll calculations will not be performed.

Figure 5 Flowchart symbols.

The *flow direction symbol* represents the direction of processing flow, which is generally from top to bottom and left to right. To avoid confusion, flowlines are sometimes drawn with an arrowhead at the point of entry of a symbol. Whenever possible, crossing of flowlines should be avoided.

The *processing symbol* is used to show general processing functions not represented by other symbols. These functions are generally those that contain the actual information-processing operations of the program. In the case of Basic, this is primarily arithmetic.

The *predefined process symbol* indicates a sequence of operations defined elsewhere. Since the code is not in the "main-line" portion of the program, these are sometimes referred to as "out-of-line" routines.

The *repetitive predefined process symbol* denotes an out-of-line routine which is executed repeatedly until occurrence of the indicated condition (as described above the broken line).

The *input/output symbol* is used to denote any function of an input/output device in the program. Both input and output are common to the computer terminal or, as we shall learn, to computer files.

The *decision symbol* is used to indicate a point in a program at which a decision is made to take one of two or more alternative courses of action. This symbol represents the selection structure.

The *termination symbol* represents any point at which a program originates or terminates. With normal program operation, such points are at the start and completion of the program.

One other symbol that will be of use is the *connector symbol*. Whenever a program becomes sufficiently complex that the number and direction of flowlines is confusing, it is frequently useful to utilize the connector symbol. This symbol represents an entry from, or an exit to, another part of the flowchart. It is also used to indicate a "juncture" point in the selection structure.

2. Differently shaped boxes are used to represent different types of operations. For example, an input operation is represented by a differently shaped box than a series of calculations.

The flowchart symbols used in this book are summarized in Figure 5 (see preceding page).

FLOWCHARTING As an illustration of flowcharting, let us consider a simplification of Example 1. The flowchart solution in Figure 6 consists of a set of flowcharts—one for each routine represented in Figure 4. Following are important points relating to these flowcharts.

1. Each routine has a single entry point and a single exit. This single-entry/single-exit concept is crucial to structured programming.

Figure 6   Modularized flowcharts.

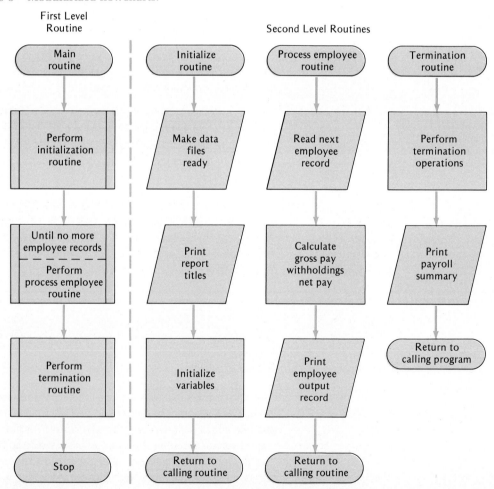

2. The sequence of operations is clearly illustrated. Processing will proceed from one box to the next. For instance, execution of the "Perform Initialization Routine" in the Main Routine causes the corresponding sequence to be carried out. That is, data files are made ready, then necessary titles are printed, then variables are initialized. After this is completed, control returns to the Main Routine.
3. The Process Employee Routine is carried out repeatedly until there are no more records. Figure 7 is another way of representing the repeated execution of this routine.

Figure 7   Repeated execution of a module.

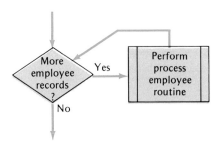

4. The Calculate box in the Process Employee Routine does not include any detail as to how the calculation is to be done. On the basis of the earlier discussion of payroll calculations, this would be likely to be done in one or more other modules (third level or lower).

When flowcharting a problem solution, we should never get too carried away with detail. For instance, if we were to print a series of report heading lines, we would label a single box as "Print Heading Lines." It would not be necessary to include a "Print Date" box, followed by a "Print Page Heading" box, followed by a "Print Column Headings" box, and so on. Too much detail sometimes can cause us to "lose sight of the forest for the trees."

STRUCTURED PROGRAMMING CONSTRUCTS In 1966, two computer scientists, Bohm and Jacopini, presented a paper in which they laid the basis for structured programming. In their paper, they proved mathematically that any computer program can be flowcharted using combinations of three basic constructs: *sequence, selection,* and *looping.* Figure 8 includes segments of the payroll flowcharts to illustrate these constructs.

THE REALITIES OF PROGRAMMING IN BASIC All of this theory can sound just great *until* we start programming in a language such as Basic, which was not specifically designed for structured programming methods. However, these techniques and Basic *are* compatible within limits when good judgment is used. One of the first places where a problem arises with Basic is knowing when there are no more data records.

Figure 8   Structured programming constructs.

The *sequence* (*process*) construct which consists of successive operations carried out on an unconditional basis.

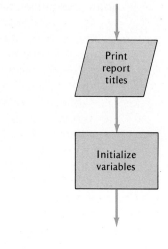

The *selection* construct which selects either of two operations to be carried out.

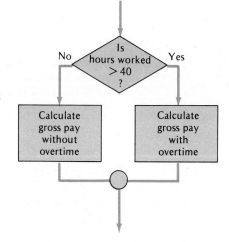

The *looping* construct which states that an operation is to be repeated as long as a certain condition exists.

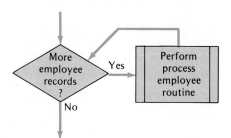

For instance, let us assume that we are to process a payroll data file manually. Then in executing the loop of Figure 8, upon processing the current employee record, we would look to see if there were another employee record in the file. If there were, we would process it; if not, we would continue to the next operation. With some versions of Basic, it is possible effectively to ask, "Is there another record?" However, with most Basics, the only way to tell is by attempting to read the next record and discovering that there is none. The problem with this is that it produces an error condition which may terminate the program. One method of avoiding this problem is to follow the last valid data record with a special *trailer record* for which the program can search. For instance, let us assume that each record of our employee file includes a 4-digit employee number. Then our file might appear as illustrated in Figure 9. In this case, the trailer record has an "employee number" of 9999. Needless to say, it is merely a dummy record, it has no valid employee data, and it should not be processed as a data record. Its sole function is to mark the end of the data file. It is commonly referred to as an *end-of-file* (or simply *EOF*) record.

Figure 9   A trailer record in a file.

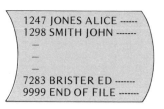

```
1247 JONES ALICE ------
1298 SMITH JOHN -------
  —
  —
  —
7283 BRISTER ED -------
9999 END OF FILE -------
```

In the Process Employee Routine of Figure 8, we see the steps:

Process Routine
　　Read the next record
　　Do the calculations
　　Print the results

Since we will be using a trailer record, the following slight variation of this procedure is necessary.

During Initialization
　　Read first record

Process Routine (executed repeatedly until trailer record)
　　Do the calculations
　　Print the results
　　Read the next record

Although this approach might appear to make a simple operation clumsy, it is quite convenient. We should note that it involves, in a sense, a "look ahead to the next record" approach. Figure 10 is a simplified flowchart representation which contrasts these two methods. This technique forms the basis for programming in Basic.

Overall these structured methods, coupled with top-down design, represent powerful programming tools and are widely used in business and industry.

Figure 10
Read–process–write
loops.

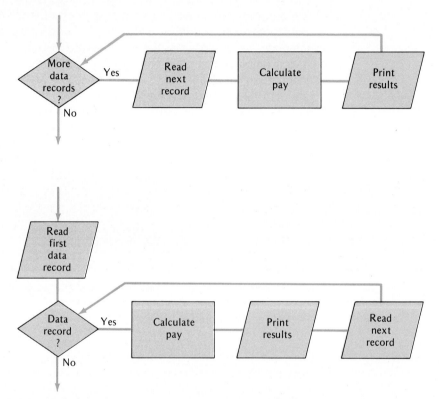

Computer Hardware

A computer is a tool which we can use to process information and obtain results. Computers do not themselves solve problems; we do. We write programs of instructions telling the computer what to do. Then it will accept information, or *data,* perform required operations on that data, and provide the results we need. Every computer system consists of two fundamental components: *hardware* and *software.*

Hardware is the physical portion of the computer system. For use within this book, we shall consider the basic components of the computer to be those illustrated in Figure 11.

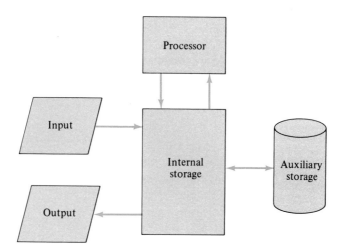

INPUT/OUTPUT As the name implies, *input* units allow us to enter data into the computer for processing. A wide variety of devices are used for input, including keyboard type terminals, and machines which read data from punched cards, magnetically encoded checks, and even handwritten documents.

Results of the machine computations are made available to us through *output* devices. These include printers which print full lines and even pages at a time, video display units, and audio devices.

Most systems which use Basic are designed around *terminals* that perform both input and output. Information is entered into the computer via a typewriter-style keyboard. Some terminals print the results on paper, much as an ordinary typewriter does (called *hard-copy* devices). Cathode-ray tube terminals display the results on a television-like screen (called *soft-copy*).

PROCESSOR The processor is the computer's "electronic control center." Here instructions are carried out for bringing information into the system, performing computations, making decisions, and producing results.

INTERNAL MEMORY Internal memory is used for temporarily holding programs of instructions and data that are currently being operated upon. The memory of any computer is a highly organized storage area. In most computers, the basic unit of memory is called the *byte*. Each byte has its own individual address and is capable of storing one character (letter, digit, or special character such as a dollar sign). Thus in order to store the phrase

This is a line.

the computer would use exactly 15 consecutive bytes of memory. Note that in addition to the letters, this line includes three spaces and a period. Similarly, the Social Security number

123456789

would occupy 9 bytes, but if stored with "normal" punctuation as

123-45-6789

it would occupy 11.

On the other hand, if numeric quantities are to be entered and used in calculations, they are converted to a special *floating-point binary* form which always requires a group of 4 bytes.* Thus the numbers

187601, 8.37519, −1, 0, 652

could be entered into the computer as numeric quantities and each would require exactly 4 bytes when stored in its encoded form.

Fortunately for the casual programmer, there is no need to be concerned with this detail. The computer keeps track of where everything is stored. When we bring a new quantity into memory, we give it a name and Basic stores it for us. We can then retrieve it or change it simply by using its name. If we are using numeric data, code conversion is done automatically by the Basic system.

In the broad sense, memory holds two general types of information. First, it holds data quantities which are being used in calculations (much like the memory of a pocket calculator). Second, it holds the program of instructions which tell the computer what to do. These come from the Basic programs such as those we will be writing from this book. Our Basic programs will allow us to bring data into memory, to manipulate it, and to print it out. Special control commands will allow us to move programs into and out of memory.

AUXILIARY STORAGE

Where internal memory retains programs and data which are currently in use, auxiliary storage is used for long-term retention of both programs and sets of data. Auxiliary storage can best be thought of as equivalent to a large file cabinet capable of storing huge quantities of information. As a rule, the capacities of auxiliary storage devices are many times those of internal memory units.

The words *memory* and *storage* are often used interchangeably. However, in this book, the word memory will refer exclusively to internal "working" memory (which is commonly considered part of the processor, or *central processing unit,* as it is often called).

---

*Actually this is only part of the story. Most computers also can handle whole-number quantities (integers) which occupy 2 bytes; many also handle double-precision floating-point quantities which occupy 8 bytes.

Computer Software

The word *software* is used to describe programs of instructions which make the computer work. On a broad basis, software is divided into two general types: user-written programs (such as those we shall write from this book) and operating system programs. Our programs will describe the data we want the machine to process, the operations to be performed on that data, and the results we wish to receive. On the other hand, operating system programs are really a basic component of the overall computer system itself. It is these programs which supervise the operations of the computer and ensure that various tasks are carried out properly.

The key to the operating system and most modern computers is the *supervisor* program (sometimes called a *monitor* or *executive* program). The supervisor remains in memory at all times and maintains control, directly or indirectly, while the computer is in use (see Figure 12). In addition, the operating system consists of programs for performing such chores as automatically maintaining records and keeping track of what is stored in auxiliary storage (the libraries). The overall nature of the supervisor as it relates to the computer is illustrated in the schematic representation of Figure 13.

**Figure 12 The
supervisor in
memory.**

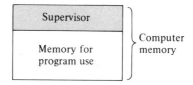

Figure 13 Animated representation of an operating system. (*From J.K. Rice and J.R. Rice, Introduction to Computer Science; copyright 1969 by Holt, Rinehart and Winston. Used by permission.*)

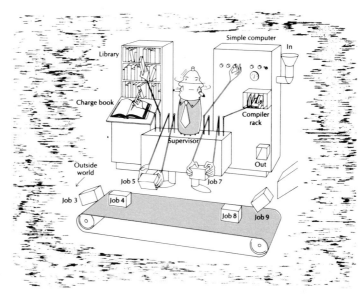

TIMESHARING Through the use of operating systems and special hardware features of the modern computer, the total amount of useful work performed (throughout) has been greatly increased over earlier systems. One widely used technique for serving multiple users at the same time is called *timesharing*.

Generally speaking, timesharing refers to the allocation of computer resources in a time-dependent fashion to several programs, simultaneously in memory. The principal notion of a timesharing system is to provide a large number of users with direct access to the computer for problem solving. The user thus has the ability to "converse" directly with the computer for problem solving (hence the terms *conversational* or *interactive* computing). In timesharing, the basic consideration is, in a sense, to maximize the efficiency of each computer user and keep her or him busy.

Figure 14 illustrates the notion of a time-shared system. Each user has her/his own communications terminal, portion of memory, and auxiliary storage. In timesharing, the processor time is divided among the users on a scheduled basis. Each program will be allocated its "slice" of the processor time (commonly measured in fractions of a second) according to some predetermined scheduling basis, beginning with the first program and proceeding through the last. Upon completing the cycle, it is begun again so that an individual user scarcely realizes that someone else is also using the computer.

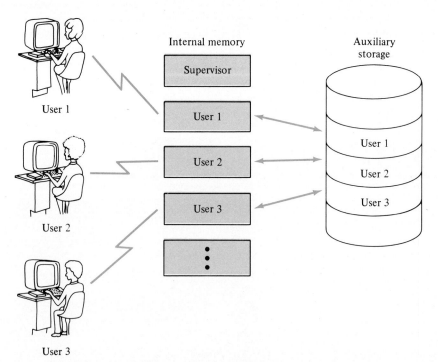

**Figure 14
Timesharing
environment.**

CHAPTER 1

Running a Program

OBJECTIVES

After a computer program has been written, it must be entered into the computer and then run. This involves considerable "interaction" with the computer. The objective of this chapter is to acquaint you with the "how" of using the computer for entering and running programs. You will learn how to:

1. Gain access to the computer via a terminal (log-on) and terminate a "session" (log-off).
2. Enter a program into the terminal.
3. Run a program which has been entered.
4. Make corrections to a program already entered.

The vehicle for this is a simple bookstore inventory calculation. The necessary Basic program is prewritten (Figure 1-4 in this chapter); details of how each statement of the program works is postponed until Chapter 2. Remember, the objective of this chapter is merely to learn how to interact with the computer.

Fundamental Principles of Basic

A BOOKSTORE INVENTORY   Let us assume that we work for a bookstore with a large stock of books and that keeping a check on the number of each title in stock has become a problem. In view of the fact that the bookstore management is very backward regarding modern inventory techniques using the computer, we decide to prepare a simple demonstration program to show what can be done. Before we can do the programming job, we must first figure out what results we want from the computer, and then determine if the necessary data is available. After some digging, we decide to prepare a simple demonstration program to process one book as a sample. To be complete, we formally define the job as follows:

Example 1-1

A one-record book inventory file contains the following.

    Book identification number
    Book title
    Inventory balance at beginning of month
    Copies received during the month
    Copies sold during the month
    Copies lost or destroyed during the month

Prepare a program which will calculate a new book balance. Printed results must include appropriate headings and the following information about the book.

Book identification number
Book title
Inventory balance at beginning of month
Updated inventory balance

We can see that the operations are relatively simple; the processing sequence involves reading a data record, performing the calculations, then printing a line. The calculations are:

New balance = old balance + copies received
− copies sold − copies lost and destroyed

In view of the fact that this program is to be used to demonstrate simple inventory processing to the bookstore manager, we elect to use one of the records from the inventory file. Following is the data which will be incorporated into the test case.

Book number	4451
Title	Modern Math
Old balance	453
Received	150
Sold	313
Lost	2

Expected results from the computer processing run are shown in Figure 1-1.

Figure 1-1 Expected output from inventory run.

BOOK NUMBER	BOOK TITLE	OLD BALANCE	NEW BALANCE
4451	MODERN MATH	453	288

PROCESSING COMPLETE

OVERALL LOGIC OF THE PROBLEM

The logic of this problem solution is virtually identical to that of Figure 6 of the Introduction. However, since it is somewhat simplified as a concession to our first attempt, the process routine is executed only once. We see this in the set of flowcharts in Figure 1-2.

ACTIONS TO BE TAKEN

We have now *defined* the problem and devised a *solution* to it. At this point, we could follow our simple sequence of instructions and perform the inventory calculations manually. However, the intent of this book is to learn computer programming, so let us proceed in that direction. Let us consider the actions to be taken in three general steps.

Figure 1-2   A set of flowcharts for Example 1-1.

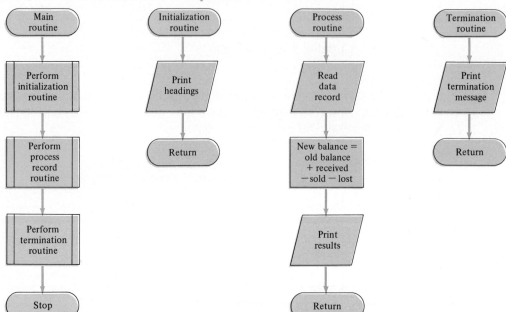

1. We must write the computer program. This involves converting the English interpretation of our problem into instructions which tell the computer what to do. In Basic, these instructions are called *statements*. Thus a Basic *program* is made up of individual *statements*.

2. We must enter the Basic program into the computer and save it for later use. During the entering phase, the computer is *not* performing our inventory calculations; it is merely accepting our program. In effect, we are interacting with the operating system of the computer. In this respect, we tell it what we wish to do through the use of *commands*. These are *not* the same as statements.

3. At our request, the computer runs our program. It carries out the action requested by each program statement (*executes* the statement) and produces the results which our program is designed to yield.

These steps and corresponding principles are illustrated in Figure 1-3. Because of the nature of interactive programming, the beginner often finds the distinctions between commands and statements and between entering and running a program confusing. You should study Figure 1-3 carefully since it will be referred to in describing how to use Basic on the computer.

With this background, let us see how the program of Figure 1-4 fits into the scheme of things. The similarity to ordinary English makes the function of this program intuitively apparent. However, let us delay until Chapter 2 the exact meaning of each statement in the program. Thus we can assume that

Figure 1-3   Preparing and running a program.

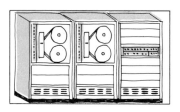

Step I	Step II	Step III
ACTION	*ACTION:*	*ACTION:*
You write the program.	You enter program into computer.	You have the computer run the program.
OCCURRENCE:	*OCCURRENCE:*	*OCCURRENCE:*
You convert the English statement of the problem to a computer program of instructions. This action is independent of the computer.	You interact with the operating system of the computer through use of *commands* and thereby enter the program into the computer.	The computer carries out the directions of each statement in the program. (The computer *executes* the program.)
END RESULT:	*END RESULT:*	*END RESULT:*
A set of instructions (Basic *statements)* telling the computer how to perform inventory calculations.	The program (of statements) now resides in the memory of the computer.	The inventory calculations are performed and the results are printed.

step I (Figure 1-3) has been completed and we are ready to enter the program into the computer (step II). In other words, we are ready to interact with the computer by way of the operating system.

EXERCISE

1.1 What is the difference between a statement and a command?

Accessing the System

THE TERMINAL KEYBOARD In using an interactive language such as Basic, the user "converses" with the computer via a terminal. The terminal may be a hard-copy device or it may be a CRT. In either case, input to the computer is via a typewriter-style keyboard such as that shown in Figure 1-5. As information is entered through the keyboard, it is transmitted to the computer and also printed by the terminal (hard-copy units) or displayed on the screen (CRTs). We should note that in

Figure 1-4   Program
to process an
inventory record—
Example 1-1.

```
100   REM   EXAMPLE 1-1
110   REM   PROGRAM TO UPDATE AN INVENTORY
300   REM
1000 REM MAIN ROUTINE
1010      GOSUB 2010
1020        REM INITIALIZATION ROUTINE
1030      GOSUB 3010
1040        REM PROCESS ROUTINE
1050      GOSUB 4010
1060        REM TERMINATION ROUTINE
1070      STOP
1080 REM END OF MAIN ROUTINE
1090 REM
2000 REM INITIALIZATION ROUTINE
2010      PRINT 'BOOK', 'BOOK', 'OLD', 'NEW'
2020      PRINT 'NUMBER', 'TITLE', 'BALANCE', 'BALANCE'
2030      PRINT
2040      RETURN
2050 REM END OF INITIALIZATION ROUTINE
2060 REM
3000 REM PROCESS ROUTINE
3010      READ B, T$, O, R, S, L
3020      LET N = O + R - S - L
3030      PRINT B, T$, O, N
3040      RETURN
3050 REM END OF PROCESS ROUTINE
3060 REM
4000 REM TERMINATION ROUTINE
4010      PRINT
4020      PRINT 'PROCESSING COMPLETE'
4030      RETURN
4040 REM END OF TERMINATION ROUTINE
4050 REM
9000 REM **DATA RECORD**
9010      DATA 4451, 'MODERN MATH', 453, 150, 313, 2
9999      END
```

Figure 1-5 special attention is called to certain of the keys. These are referred to throughout this chapter.

In this book, certain symbols and conventions are used to illustrate interaction with the computer.

Convention	Meaning
Password	Unshaded computer printout is information printed by the computer.
RUN	Shaded computer printout is information which is typed from the keyboard by the user.
(cr)	Indicates the Carriage Return key, which must be depressed upon typing information into the computer.

Figure 1-5   Typical terminal keyboard.

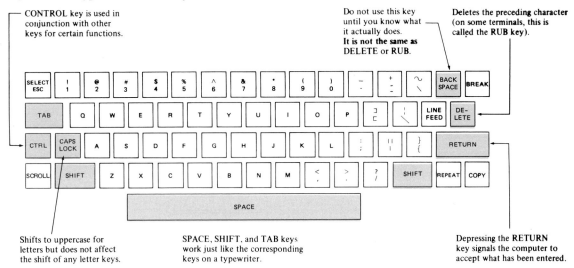

CONTROL key is used in conjunction with other keys for certain functions.

Do not use this key until you know what it actually does. **It is not the same as DELETE or RUB.**

Deletes the preceding character (on some terminals, this is called the **RUB key**).

Shifts to uppercase for letters but does not affect the shift of any letter keys.

SPACE, SHIFT, and TAB keys work just like the corresponding keys on a typewriter.

Depressing the **RETURN** key signals the computer to accept what has been entered.

LOG-ON The user of a personal computer (microcomputer) normally is the sole user of the machine at any given time. However, for a timesharing computer to which many users have access, some method is needed to maintain order. You would not be very happy, for instance, if you spent several hours working on a program and then someone else wiped it out. Timesharing systems resolve this problem by assigning each user an *ID code* or a separate *account* and an individual password for access to the system. To use the computer, an exacting procedure must be followed for logging on. Log-on procedures vary considerably from one computer to another, but most of them have two things in common: the request for an ID code or account number, and a password. The log-on procedure illustrated in Figure 1-6 is typical. Once you have

Figure 1-6   The log-on procedure.

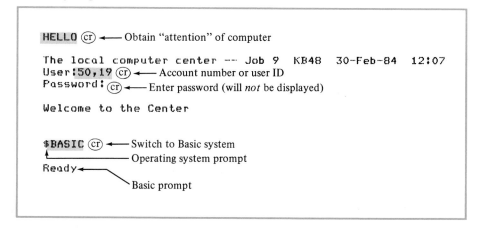

HELLO (cr) ◄—— Obtain "attention" of computer

The local computer center —— Job 9 KB48 30-Feb-84 12:07
User:50,19 (cr) ◄—— Account number or user ID
Password: (cr) ◄—— Enter password (will *not* be displayed)

Welcome to the Center

$BASIC (cr) ◄—— Switch to Basic system
◄———————— Operating system prompt
Ready ◄————————
◄————— Basic prompt

logged-on to a timesharing system or turned a microcomputer on, most computers are under the control of the operating system. If you wish to work in Basic, then you must give some directive to the computer to switch over to Basic. This has been done in Figure 1-6.

Whether you are functioning under the operating system or Basic, and whether you are using a timesharing system or a microcomputer, the computer signals that it is ready with a *prompt*. When referring to Figure 1-6, we see the $ used as the operating system prompt and the word *Ready* used as the Basic prompt. This system tells you two things: (1) whether or not you are in Basic, and (2) that the computer is waiting for you to enter something through the keyboard. Different versions of Basic use different prompts (for example, the right angle bracket > and the exclamation mark ! are commonly encountered). Examples in this book will use the word Ready; you should find out what the prompt is in the system which you will be using. In any event, when you receive the Basic prompt, the Basic system is awaiting a Basic command which will tell it what to do.

Entering and Running a Program

CREATING
A NEW PROGRAM
Now let us proceed to step II of Figure 1-3; that is, entering the program of Figure 1-4 into the computer. Assuming that we are logged-on to the system (Figure 1-6), the command **NEW** is used to tell the system that we wish to enter a new program. Then we may proceed to enter the program, statement by statement, as if we were typing at a typewriter. This is shown in Figure 1-7. In order to become familiar with the computer, enter the program into your account exactly as shown in Figure 1-7. Remember that after you enter each statement (or command), you must press the RETURN key. (On some keyboards, this is labeled the ENTER key.) You should double check the statement to make certain it was entered correctly. If it was not, the easiest way to handle it is simply to reenter the entire statement.

Upon completing the entering operation, you may run the program. It is of utmost importance to recognize that the computer does not perform the operations required by the program as the program is being entered. That is, after the entering task is finished (step II, Figure 1-3), no calculations of the new balance or anything else have been performed. These calculations are part of step III and are carried out only when the program is run.

Figure 1-7   Entering
a new program—the
NEW command.

```
NEW
New file name---INVEN ◄── Note: Some systems do not ask for
                                the program name at this point.
Ready

100   REM   EXAMPLE 1-1
110   REM   PROGRAM TO UPDATE AN INVENTORY
300   REM
1000 REM MAIN ROUTINE
1010      GOSUB 2010
1020        REM INITIALIZATION ROUTINE
1030      GOSUB 3010
1040        REM PROCESS ROUTINE
1050      GOSUB 4010
1060        REM TERMINATION ROUTINE
1070      STOP
1080 REM END OF MAIN ROUTINE
1090 REM
2000 REM INITIALIZATION ROUTINE
2010      PRINT "BOOK", "BOOK", "OLD", "NEW"
2020      PRINT "NUMBER", "TITLE", "BALANCE", "BALANCE"
2030      PRINT
2040      RETURN
2050 REM END OF INITIALIZATION ROUTINE
2060 REM
3000 REM PROCESS ROUTINE
3010      READ B, T$, O, R, S, L
3020      LET N = O + R - S - L
3030      PRINT B, T$, O, N
3040      RETURN
3050 REM END OF PROCESS ROUTINE
3060 REM
4000 REM TERMINATION ROUTINE
4010      PRINT
4020      PRINT "PROCESSING COMPLETE"
4030      RETURN
4040 REM END OF TERMINATION ROUTINE
4050 REM
9000 REM **DATA RECORD**
9010      DATA 4451, "MODERN MATH", 453, 150, 313, 2
9999      END
```

Note: Indent statements to set apart
one module from the other. On most
systems, the TAB key can be used.

Figure 1-8   Running a program—the RUN command.

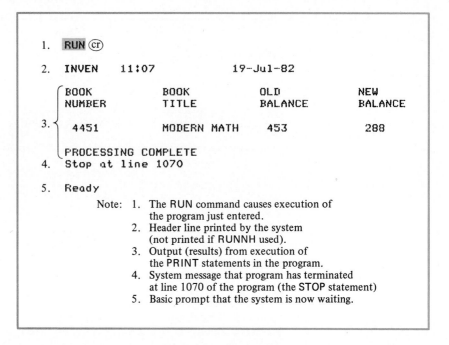

1. `RUN` ⓒⓡ

2. `INVEN    11:07              19-Jul-82`

3. {
```
    BOOK            BOOK            OLD             NEW
    NUMBER          TITLE           BALANCE         BALANCE

    4451            MODERN MATH     453             288

    PROCESSING COMPLETE
```
}

4. `Stop at line 1070`

5. `Ready`

Note:
1. The RUN command causes execution of the program just entered.
2. Header line printed by the system (not printed if RUNNH used).
3. Output (results) from execution of the PRINT statements in the program.
4. System message that program has terminated at line 1070 of the program (the STOP statement)
5. Basic prompt that the system is now waiting.

RUNNING THE PROGRAM   Once the program has been entered, we can run it using the **RUN** command as illustrated in Figure 1-8. When execution of the program is complete (that is, when the data has been processed), the system returns to the Ready state, to await our next command. Notice in Figure 1-8 that the computer prints the program name, the time of day, and the date. This is called the *header line* and in most Basics can be omitted by typing **RUNNH** instead of **RUN**. If your program output (designated as 3 in Figure 1-8) is not exactly the same as that in Figure 1-8, then you have made a mistake somewhere. How to correct an error in a program is the topic of the next section.

EXERCISE

1.2 What do you think would happen if you logged-on and immediately typed in **RUN** (before entering a program)?

Making Corrections to a Program

INSERTING AND DELETING LINES   One of the useful features of Basic relates to the fact that the system always keeps statements in order according to line numbers. For instance, let us assume that we left our statement 3020 when keying in the program. Upon noticing our error, we could simply key in the omitted statement as illustrated in Figure 1-9. The system would automatically place the statement in its proper position, as shown in the figure.

Figure 1-9   Inserting a statement.

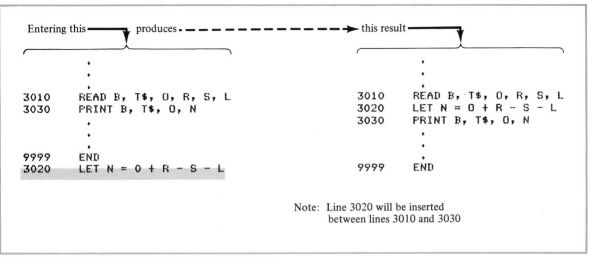

Note: Line 3020 will be inserted
between lines 3010 and 3030

Figure 1-10   Inserting an omitted statement.

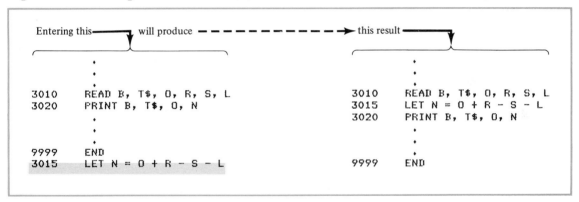

Sometimes, in writing a program, we will forget a statement and only realize our omission after the program has been entered. This is no problem since the statement can be inserted later between two existing line numbers, as shown in Figure 1-10. Now we see the value of incrementing line numbers by 10.

Sometimes we may need to delete a statement from a program. This is easily done simply by typing only the line number, and then hitting the return key. (The TRS 80 requires that you use the **DELETE** command—refer to Appendix III.)

Figure 1-11 illustrates a very subtle error. Statement 3020 has been misnumbered as 9020 and will end up some place other than where it belongs. The remedy shown in Figure 1-11 involves deleting the incorrect line and adding the correct one.

ERRORS
AND ERROR
CORRECTION

Try as we might to eliminate errors, some will always creep into a program. In general, they can be classified in two broad categories: syntax errors and logic errors. The Basic language consists of a very concise set of rules for writing statements. Any statement which does not follow those rules is said to have a *syntax* error. For instance, consider the following:

```
3030    PRINT C, B, O, N
7000    GOTO 210
```

entered incorrectly as

```
3040    PRIMT B, T$, O, N
7010    RETURN TO 210
```

In statement 3040, **PRINT** is misspelled, and knowing the "rules" for writing statements, the system will respond with an error indication. In some computer systems, the error and a corresponding message will be given as soon as

Figure 1-11   Deleting and inserting a statement.

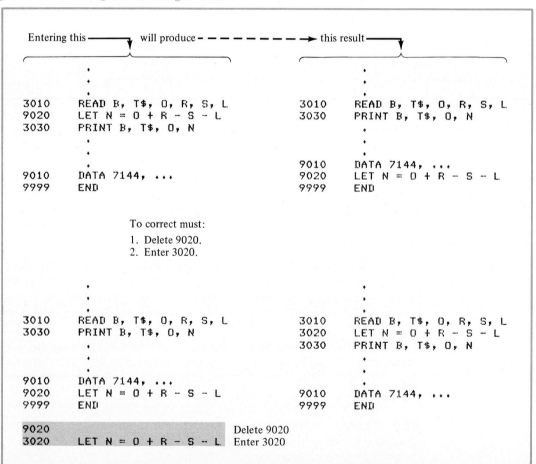

Figure 1-12   A syntax error message.

```
      Error condition and                                    Corrected version
      corrective action
            •                                                      •
            •                                                      •
            •                                                      •
      3020    LET N = O + R - S - L                           3020    LET N = O + R - S - L
      3030    PRIMT B, T$, O, N                               3030    PRINT B, T$, O, N

      ?Illegal verb at line 3030

      Ready

      3030    PRINT B, T$, O, N



      Note: On some systems the error is detected
            and the message printed immediately upon
            entering the line.  On others it is detected only
            upon running the program.  In both cases the
            corrective action is the same:  reenter the
            statement.
```

the statement is entered. With others, the error is detected and the message given when the program is run and the computer attempts to execute the statement. Similarly, statement 7010 should be **GOTO**; we must use the exact forms defined in the language, not our own variations. The sequence of events of entering and correcting these errors is illustrated in Figure 1-12.

As a rule, the system is very helpful in detecting syntax errors. However, logic errors are a completely different story. For instance, if in the inventory problem we accidentally added the copies sold rather than subtracted them, we would have

```
3020      LET N = O + R + S - L
```

rather than the correct

```
3020      LET N = O + R - S - L
```

Here we have an error in our *logic* and the system has no way of recognizing what we mean. It would be up to us to check everything carefully and reenter a corrected version of the statement.

LISTING A PROGRAM Often when we are making corrections to a program, what we see typed at the terminal or printed on the screen is confusing. For example, after making the corrections shown in Figure 1-11 (lower left), it is usually convenient to see the program as it actually exists (lower right). This is easily done using the command **LIST**. That is, typing **LIST** (followed by depressing the RETURN) will cause the latest form of the program on which we are working to be printed (or displayed) on the terminal.

EXERCISE

1.3 You have just finished entering a complete program and realize that you forgot a statement which belongs between lines 150 and 160. How would you enter it and get the computer to put it in its proper place?

Ending a Terminal Session

Upon completing your session with the computer, you must *sign off* (or *log-off*). This is especially important if you have your own account in the computer. If you do, then you will probably have one or more programs which you are saving (saving programs is described in Chapter 2). If you simply walk away from the terminal leaving it logged-on, then others can use your account. They might change or destroy your programs or use up your allotted computer time, if your computer center limits the time you can have.

A typical log-off procedure is shown in Figure 1-13. In this case, the user simply typed the keyword **BYE** and that terminated the session. Some systems use the word **OFF**; they both accomplish the same thing. Needless to say, if you are using a microcomputer on which it is not necessary to log-on, then it will not be necessary to log-off.

Figure 1-13   Logging off.

```
BYE (cr)
Saved all disk files; 64 blocks in use, 936 free
Job 12 User 59,7 logged of KB44 at 28-Mar-83 15:42
System RSTS V7.1-11 MERCOMPFAC-FCCD
Run time was 3.4 seconds
Elapsed time was 13 minutes
Good afternoon
```

ANSWERS TO PRECEDING EXERCISES

1.1 Commands are used to tell the operating system what you wish to do (they allow *you* to control the computer). Statements are used to form programs and are carried out only when your program is entered and run (they allow the *program* to control the computer).

1.2 The computer would have no program to run and so would do nothing; try it on the terminal to see for yourself.

1.3 Give it a line number of 155, then key it in. The Basic system automatically places it in its proper position according to the line numbers.

PROGRAMMING ASSIGNMENT

1.1 Enter and run the program of Figure 1-7.

CHAPTER 2

A Subset of Basic

OBJECTIVES

The focus of Chapter 1 was on how to interact with the computer. To this end, we used a prewritten program and paid no attention to why it worked. In this chapter, you will learn a subset of the Basic language which will allow you to write some simple programs. Important principles in this chapter are:

1. The overall structure of a program.
2. Line (statement) numbers and how they are used.
3. The importance of using remarks within a Basic program.
4. The principles of Basic variables and constants.
5. Input and output methods.
6. How to perform computations in Basic.
7. Transferring control within a Basic program.

To these ends, the following statements (which are used in Figure 1-4) are described.

DATA
END
GOSUB
LET
PRINT
READ
REM
RETURN

In addition, the general handling of programs (saving them, deleting them, and so on) is described.

Fundamental Principles of Basic

THE PROGRAM OF EXAMPLE 1-1   For convenience, the inventory program of Figure 1-3 (Chapter 1) is repeated here as Figure 2-1 (note that some additional lines have been added). By comparing the program statements with what we know of the problem requirements and the flowchart of Figure 1-2 (Chapter 1), we can surmise the following.

```
READ B, O, R, S, L          Read input data

LET N = O + R - S - L       Calculate new balance

PRINT C, B, O, N            Print results
```

One feature of the Basic language is that each program statement begins with a verb which directs the computer to carry out some action. This charac-

Figure 2-1   Program to update an inventory.

```
100   REM   EXAMPLE 1-1
110   REM   PROGRAM TO UPDATE AN INVENTORY
120   REM   INPUT QUANTITIES AND NAMES ARE:
130   REM     B - BOOK NUMBER
140   REM     T$- BOOK TITLE
150   REM     O - OLD BALANCE                    Descriptive remarks are
160   REM     R - COPIES RECEIVED                merely for the convenience
170   REM     S - COPIES SOLD                    of the programmer. The
180   REM     L - COPIES LOST AND DESTROYED      computer ignores them.
190   REM   CALCULATED QUANTITIES AND NAMES ARE:
200   REM     N - NEW BALANCE
300                                          REM ─── Indent REM here and at
1000 REM MAIN ROUTINE                            other points to give
1010      GOSUB 2010                             "white space" between modules.
1020      REM INITIALIZATION ROUTINE
1030      GOSUB 3010                          Main program
1040      REM PROCESS ROUTINE                 module
1050      GOSUB 4010
1060      REM TERMINATION ROUTINE
1070      STOP
1080 REM END OF MAIN ROUTINE
1090                                     REM
2000 REM INITIALIZATION ROUTINE
2010      PRINT "BOOK", "BOOK", "OLD", "NEW"
2020      PRINT "NUMBER", "TITLE", "BALANCE", "BALANCE"   Initialization: print
2030      PRINT                                            headings
2040      RETURN
2050 REM END OF INITIALIZATION ROUTINE
2060                                     REM
3000 REM PROCESS ROUTINE
3010      READ B, T$, O, R, S, L                  Process
3020      LET N = O + R - S - L                      Read data record
3030      PRINT B, T$, O, N                          Calculate new balance
3040      RETURN                                     Print results
3050 REM END OF PROCESS ROUTINE
3060                                     REM
4000 REM TERMINATION ROUTINE
4010      PRINT
4020      PRINT "PROCESSING COMPLETE"             Termination
4030      RETURN
4040 REM END OF TERMINATION ROUTINE
4050                                     REM
9000 REM **DATA RECORD**
9010      DATA 4451, "MODERN MATH", 453, 150, 313, 2 ─── Book data record
9999      END
```

teristic, and many other important concepts of Basic, are illustrated by the program of Figure 2-1. The important features which it will reveal are:

1. Line or statement numbers in Basic.
2. Remarks in the Basic program.
3. Basic constants and variables.

4. Basic expressions.
5. Input and output capabilities.
6. The **LET** statement.
7. The transfer statement.
8. The **end** statement.

In the following sections of this chapter, we shall study each of these features and relate them to the fundamental principles of Basic.

LINE NUMBERS   Each line which we see in the program of Figure 2-1 is called a *statement* and has a *statement number,* commonly called a *line number,* associated with it. Whenever we write a program in Basic, we must assign a unique line number to each line we enter into the computer. Furthermore, these line numbers must be selected so that they fall in the order in which we want the computer to consider each statement. Within each module, we see that each line number is 10 greater than the preceding one. However, in progressing from one module to the next, there is a large jump. There are no rules in Basic that require such grouping. The important thing is that each line number be greater than the one preceding it. In this example, line numbers are used to indicate (to the programmer) different portions of the program. In general, incrementing by 10 or more is a common practice since it allows space to insert additional statements later if a program must be changed. In general, these numbers may be chosen by the programmer; in Figure 2-1, they could just as well have been 50, 100, 150, and so on. The only restriction is size. All versions of Basic have a restriction on the largest number which can be used as a line number. Depending upon the system, it may be 9999, 32767, 99999, or some other value. Examples in this book will adhere to the 9999 limit. You should find out what the maximum is on your computer.

REMARKS IN BASIC   By placing **REM** at the beginning of the statement, that entire line may be used by the programmer for descriptive comments. Although the remarks line is ignored by Basic during the running of the program, it still will be printed or displayed with the program. The remarks included in this program adequately describe the purpose of the program. *The value of using extensive remarks in a program cannot be overemphasized.* Programmers commonly find that they must modify or expand an extensive program after completing it and progressing to another job. Even though they have written it themselves, much of the program can be very confusing unless remarks are used liberally.

Some systems allow the word **REM** to be replaced with an exclamation mark (!); others allow use of the single quote(') to serve the same purpose.

EXERCISES

2.1 Which types of statement entries in a Basic program do not require line numbers?

2.2 How is a descriptive remark indicated in a Basic program?

VARIABLES Upon inspecting the program statements in Figure 2-1, we see input, calculations, and output. Together with descriptive remarks, statement 3010 almost explains itself:

```
3010      READ B, T$, O, R, S, L
```

That is, we are directing the computer to read data into storage for the *variables* B, T$, O, R, S, and L (book number, book title, old balance, and so on).

The term *variable* has much the same meaning in Basic as in algebra; it is a symbolic name given to a quantity that may change in value during the running of a program. Each variable in a program will be assigned by the Basic system to some internal storage area into which a number may be stored. In Figure 2-1 we see the following variable names used to represent the designated quantities:

Variable	Field
B	Book identification number
T$	Book title
O	Old inventory balance
R	Number received
S	Number sold
L	Number lost
N	New inventory

Although in this example program, each variable is presented by a single letter, variable names are not, in general, so restricted.

In general, variable names may consist of one letter or one letter followed by a single digit. In some versions of Basic, variable names may consist of many letters (up to 30 or 40). Long variable names are highly desirable because they provide better documentation of what is occurring than do one- or two-character names. For instance,

```
NEWBAL = OLDBAL + RECEIVED - SOLD - LOST
```

provides a far better description (to us) regarding what is taking place than does

```
N = O + R - S - L
```

However, in the interest of being compatible with systems which are limited, examples in this book will use one letter or one letter and one digit. (The one exception in Figure 2-1 is T$; the nature of this variable is described in the next section.) By this one-letter or one-letter and one-digit criterion, the following are examples of valid and invalid choices for variable names.

Valid	Invalid	Reason
A	2N	Letter must be first
Z	JR	May not be two letters
B3	X25	Only one letter and one digit allowed
N9	6	Cannot be a single digit
B8	C+	Only letters and digits allowed

When selecting names for program variables, the choice should always be made so that the name describes the quantity it represents. This is usually difficult when operating within the domain of two-character names. If your system has a more extensive capability, then *use it.*

NUMERIC AND STRING VARIABLES
In a loose sense, data can be considered in two broad categories: that upon which arithmetic can be performed, and that upon which arithmetic will not be performed. For instance, hours worked by an employee will be totaled and then multiplied by the pay rate. Data upon which we do arithmetic is called *numeric data.* On the other hand, the employee name, or even the employee Social Security *number,* will not be involved in any arithmetic operations. Data such as this (which may consist of letters, digits, or even special characters) is commonly referred to as *string data.* String data can be read into a program in exactly the same way as numeric data. However, it is imperative that the system "know" whether a particular variable will be used to store numeric or string data. In Basic, *string variables* are defined in exactly the same way as numeric variables, except that they are indicated as such by adding the character $ at the end of the name. Thus, in statement 3010, the system recognizes the variables B, O, R, S, and L as numeric variables and T$ as a string variable. Within a given program, it is possible, for example, to use C for a numeric variable and C$ for a string variable. C and C$ are two distinctly different names.

Any data quantity read into a numeric variable must be a valid numeric quantity. On the other hand, a string data quantity may include letters, digits, and special characters (for instance, the hyphen, period, or slash). In other words, virtually anything can be validly processed as string data.

VARIABLES IN STORAGE
Each numeric variable used in a program will cause the Basic system to reserve one storage area into which a number may be stored. Thus the program of Figure 2-1 would require seven storage areas, one for each of the variables used. Each such storage area may contain one number at any given time. However, we can easily change the contents of a storage area by placing a new number in it, either by bringing in a new data value through an input operation or by performing a calculation. Prior to execution of any program, the Basic system sets all numeric variables to zero. Then execution of the program places values in them as needed. For instance, let us consider the data record for which this program is written:

Book number   4451
Old balance   453
Copies received   150
Copies sold   313
Copies lost   2

The contents of the assigned storage areas would appear as shown in Figure 2-2.

Figure 2-2 Memory contents.

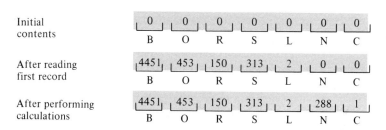

	Initial contents	After reading first record	After performing calculations
B	0	4451	4451
O	0	453	453
R	0	150	150
S	0	313	313
L	0	2	2
N	0	0	288
C	0	0	1

String variables are handled in a slightly different manner—but the overall appearance to the programmer is the same. That is, the information stored in a string area variable can be changed just as readily as that in a numeric variable.

EXERCISES

2.3 Which of the following variable names are invalid by the criterion used in this book?

    B   73   R4   SD   Q1298   4C

2.4 What value is stored in each variable of a Basic program prior to execution of the program?

Input/Output Operations

THE DATA STATEMENT   Throughout this book, emphasis is focused on the processing of data files. The simple program of Example 1-1 is quite contrived in that it involves processing only one data record. For an actual application, there would be many records to process. Furthermore, each time the processing run is made, the data stored in the inventory file will be different. In a disk-oriented computer system, the output of a run would probably be a printed report and an updated inventory file. In a tape-oriented computer system, it would be the report and a new inventory file with updated data. It is important to recognize that a data file and a program to process the file are usually two separate entities and are stored separately.

The Basic language, however, has a feature which allows data for a program to be included as part of the program itself. Although this is not practical for most actual applications, it is very convenient for the beginner who is learning Basic. This involves a special statement called the **DATA** statement. As we see in the program of Figure 2-1, the **DATA** statement is included following the program of instructions. As with all Basic statements, the **DATA** statement is preceded by a line number. The keyword **DATA** is then followed by a list of quantities which represent the input data to be processed. We can see that adjacent fields in a **DATA** statement are separated by a comma. If it helps to make the program more readable, one or more blank spaces may be inserted whenever appropriate. String data (the second field in the **DATA** statement) is enclosed within quotes. This may not be necessary but it represents a "safety" feature. When the program, including all **DATA** statements, is brought into storage for a run, the fields from each **DATA** statement (if there are more than one, which is usually the case) are placed, in order, into a *data pool*, one field after the other. Upon execution of the program, these fields will be available for processing.

THE READ STATEMENT Data which is stored in the data pool is made available to the program for processing by the **READ** statement. For example:

```
3010     READ B, T$, O, R, S, L
```

This statement will cause the computer to bring the next six fields of data from the data pool into storage, placing the first in the storage area reserved for **B**, the second in the area reserved for **T$**, and so on. If there is additional data in the **DATA** pool (more **DATA** statements), the execution of this statement a second time will cause the next six fields to be brought into storage. This procedure is illustrated in Figure 2-3. Each time the **READ** statement is executed in a program, a new set of data values will be brought into the program. If a **READ** is executed and no more data remains, the program will be terminated automatically. Thus, using the example data for the program of Figure 2-1, if the Process Routine were executed a second time, the program would "crash" at line 3010 (the **READ**). In this example, the Termination Routine would never be executed.

EXERCISE

2.5 Following is a **READ** statement, which will be executed repeatedly, and a sequence of **DATA** statements. What will be read into the listed variables with each execution of the **READ**?

```
150     READ A, B
  .
  .
  .
210     DATA 25,13
220     DATA 281,16,37,48,122
230     DATA 53
240     END
```

Figure 2-3   Reading data from the data pool.

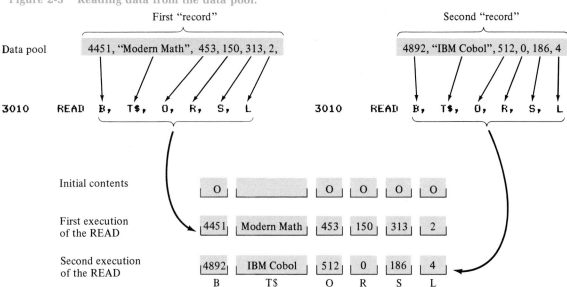

THE PRINT STATEMENT   The results of running the program of Figure 2-1 are repeated here in Figure 2-4. As we can see, the statement

```
3030     PRINT B, T$, O, N
```

will cause the current values in storage areas reserved for the variables **B**, **T$**, **O**, and **N** to be printed.

Figure 2-4   Sample output for Example 1-1.

```
BOOK            BOOK            OLD             NEW      ⎱ Heading printed by
NUMBER          TITLE           BALANCE         BALANCE  ⎰ lines 2010 and 2020

 4451           MODERN MATH     453             288      Detail line printed by statement 3030
                                                         Blank line and
PROCESSING COMPLETE  ◄──────────────────────────────── termination message printed
                                                         by statement 4020
```

Whenever a variable name is listed in a **PRINT** statement, the current value of the variable will be printed. In contrast, fixed, descriptive information (such as the headings) also can be printed. For instance,

```
2010     PRINT "BOOK", "BOOK", "OLD", "NEW"
```

causes the first line of the heading to be printed. In other words, anything which is included in quotes will be printed exactly as quoted. Furthermore, quoted quantities and variable values can both be printed with the same **PRINT** statement. For instance, an example output from

```
2310    PRINT "BOOK NUMBER", B
```

might be the following.

```
 BOOK NUMBER    4451
```

Whenever a **PRINT** statement is included with nothing in its *list,* it results in a blank line (see Figure 2-4). This is very convenient for improving the readability of program output.

When the **PRINT** statement is used, as it is in this example, the output will be printed according to a predetermined fixed format. In this respect, we can think of the terminal as a typewriter with preset tab stops at positions 1, 16, 31, 46, and 61. Thus the value for **B** in statement 3030 will be printed beginning at position 1. The comma separating **B** and **T$** causes the terminal to tab over to position 16 where the value of **T$** will be printed, and so on. Each output field will be left-justified beginning with the corresponding tab position. (This is in contrast to normal data processing procedures in which numeric fields are right-justified and alphanumeric fields are left-justified.) If the output number is negative, it will be preceded by a minus sign. If it is positive, it will be preceded by a space. (This is the reason the headings and the numeric results are not exactly aligned in Figure 2-4.) Basic includes other provisions for output to enhance the appearance of printed results; we will study these concepts in Chapter 6.

EXERCISE

2.6 The following **PRINT** statement is executed.

```
400    PRINT N2, N4, N6
```

Where will each field be printed on the page?

Other Program Statements

ARITHMETIC OPERATIONS Computation with the computer in Basic involves (1) performing arithmetic operations on two or more quantities from storage, and (2) saving the result in a preassigned area of storage. For example, if we were to assume that the length and width of a rectangle have been read into storage, then the following **LET** statement would calculate the perimeter and store it in **P**.

```
LET P = 2 * (L + W).
```

Let us first direct our attention to the so-called *expression* which is located to the right of the equal sign. In Basic, the term *expression* carries much the same meaning as it does in algebra. In a nutshell, an arithmetic expression is any collection of variables and constants related by *arithmetic operators*. The five common operator symbols are:

addition	+
subtraction	−
multiplication	*
division	/
raising to a power	^ or **

Note that the first three symbols are identical to ordinary arithmetic; the * is used to denote multiplication. Since Basic requires that each operation be explicitly indicated, the computer form will appear slightly different from the equivalent algebra form, as further illustrated by the following.

Description	Algebra	Computer Language
Simple interest	$P + Prt$	P + P*R*T
Simple discount	$\dfrac{P}{1 - dt}$	P/(1 − D*T)

Whereas in algebra multiplication is commonly implied (for instance 2*w* means 2 times *w*), in programming languages the multiplication must be indicated by the operation symbol.

In general, the rules for performing the arithmetic operations (that is, *evaluating*) an expression are much the same for evaluating algebraic expressions. That is,

1. All expressions within parentheses are evaluated first.
2. Raising to a power (exponentiation) is next.
3. Multiplications and divisions are then performed.
4. Additions and subtractions are performed last.

The rule of performing multiplication and division operations before addition and subtraction is commonly referred to as the *hierarchy of operations*. As a simple illustration of this hierarchy rule, let us evaluate the expression:

A + B * C

given that values for **A**, **B**, and **C** are 25, 3, and 16 respectively.

25 + 3 * 16
25 + 48
73

With the hierarchy of operations, there are no ambiguities since the multiplication is performed *before* the addition.

The use of spaces in forming expressions is strictly up to the programmer. That is, spaces may be inserted for the purpose of clarity—note that the preceding interest and discount forms use spaces on each side of the addition and subtraction operators but not around the multiplication and division operators. This is done solely to clarify (to the programmer) the grouping of the various elements of the expression.

EXERCISE

2.7 Given the values **A** = 6, **B** = 22, and **C** = 2, evaluate each of the following.
   a. **A+B/C**
   b. **2*A+B/C**
   c. **2*(A+B/C)**

THE LET STATEMENT As we saw earlier, the **LET** has much the form of the ordinary equation in algebra.

```
LET P = 2 * (L + W)
```

However, the equal sign as used in Basic has a far different meaning than in algebra. In Basic, the equal sign says:

1. Using the currently stored data values, evaluate the expression to the right of the equal sign.
2. Place the result in the storage area indicated by the variable on the left.

Most versions of Basic currently in use allow the **LET** statement to be written with or without the word **LET**. Thus statement 3020 of Figure 2-1 could have been written in either of the following ways:

```
3020    LET N = 0 + R - S - L

3020    N = 0 + R - S - L
```

Example programs in chapters which follow will omit the word **LET**.

THE STOP STATEMENT Line 1070 in Figure 2-1 is

```
1070    STOP
```

Actually there is not too much to say about this statement. It does exactly as the name suggests: It terminates execution of the program.

In this case, the **STOP** is used to permanently terminate program execution. Sometimes, when attempting to get all of the errors out of a program (to debug the program), the **STOP** is used to halt execution temporarily at one or more points. The programmer can then examine contents of selected variables and, when ready, resume execution of the program by typing in **CONT** (continue).

EXERCISE

2.8 What would happen if the **STOP** statement at line 1070 were accidentally left out?

THE GOSUB
STATEMENT
To implement the technique of calling submodules from a main module, we need a tool which will allow us to perform operations illustrated in Figure 2-5.

Figure 2-5   A main
module controlling
submodules.

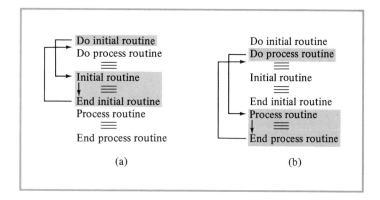

(a)   (b)

In (a) the line "Do Initial Routine" causes the sequence of statements in that routine to be executed. Upon completing the initialization, execution returns to the main module, and then progresses to the next step as illustrated in (b). From a programming point of view, we need a statement which allows us to jump to another statement. For efficient programming, we also need a statement which provides for a simple return from the submodule being "called" by the main module. The Basic statements which provide these features are the **GOSUB** and **RETURN**. Appropriate segments of the program from Figure 2-1 are repeated here in Figure 2-6. Following are the important features illustrated by this example.

1. The **GOSUB** breaks the normal progression from one statement to the next and causes execution to be transferred to another statement.
2. Prior to "departing," the **GOSUB** "remembers" its departure point (statement 1010 for the **GOSUB 2010**).
3. Execution of the submodule (beginning at line 2010) proceeds.
4. Upon reaching the **RETURN** statement, execution is returned to the statement following the calling **GOSUB**. In the case of **GOSUB 2010**, this is a remark line (1020), so execution falls through to line 1030.

Figure 2-6   The
GOSUB and RETURN.

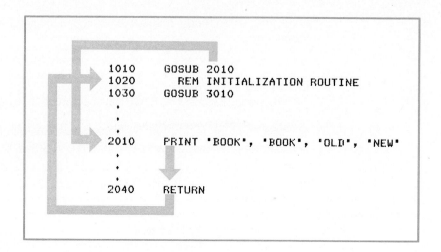

```
1010      GOSUB 2010
1020        REM INITIALIZATION ROUTINE
1030      GOSUB 3010
           .
           .
           .
2010      PRINT "BOOK", "BOOK", "OLD", "NEW"
           .
           .
           .
2040      RETURN
```

**THE END
STATEMENT**

Every program must include an **END** statement which has a line number larger than that of any other statement in the program. All programs in this book use 9999 for the **END**. You should find out what the largest line number is in your system and use that value as the line number of the **END**. This is not mandatory, but it is a good practice which prevents the error of numbering a statement in the program larger than the **END** statement. In Figure 2-1, the sole purpose of the **END** is to indicate to the Basic processor that no more statements follow. We should be aware that during execution of this program, the **END** statement does not play any role. That is, the various routines are executed until the **STOP** is encountered, at which point execution is terminated.

On the other hand, the **END** can also be used to terminate execution of a program. For instance, Figure 2-7 is a vastly simplified version of the inventory program. In this case, the **END** serves both to signify no more statements in the program to the Basic processor and to terminate processing after the printing operation.

Figure 2-7   Using the
END to terminate
processing.

```
100 REM THIS PROGRAM PROCESSES ON DATA
110 REM RECORD THEN TERMINATES ON THE
120 REM END STATEMENT
130 REM
200     DATA 4451, "MODERN MATH", 453, 150, 313, 2
210     READ B, T$, O, R, S, L
220     LET N = O + R - S - L
230     PRINT B, T$, O, N
9999    END
```

Saving Programs

At this point, you can begin writing and entering programs of your own. Often, as you progress to more difficult problems, you will find that you cannot complete the entry and testing of a program in one terminal session. Thus it will be necessary to "save" the program or portion of the program until your next session, which may be hours or days later. For this purpose, some type of "permanent" storage capability is needed.

TEMPORARY AND PERMANENT PROGRAM STORAGE Whenever the user signs on to an account, a temporary work area is set up within the internal memory of the computer. This temporary area is initially empty. As a program (or anything else, for that matter) is entered, it is held in this temporary portion of memory. When the session is terminated (by logging off), everything in that temporary area is lost. It is somewhat analogous to "borrowing" the use of a desk. When we first sit down, the desk top is clean. When we leave, someone comes in and cleans it by discarding everything which is there. In other words, the desk top is a work and temporary storage area. Let us carry this example one step further and assume that we have been provided a file cabinet for permanent storage of any work which we wish to save. This concept is illustrated in Figure 2-8. Anything we wish to save must be placed in the file cabinet before we leave or else it will be lost. If we must work on it at a later time, we can obtain it from the file and continue.

Figure 2-8 The concept of temporary and permanent storage areas.

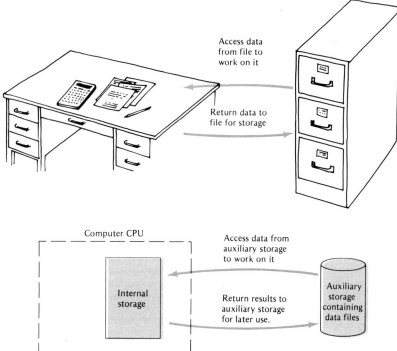

Access data from file to work on it

Return data to file for storage

Computer CPU

Internal storage

Access data from auxiliary storage to work on it

Return results to auxiliary storage for later use.

Auxiliary storage containing data files

This is exactly the situation which exists in a timesharing system (refer to the Introduction). The work space of internal memory corresponds to the desk top, and the disk storage corresponds to the file cabinet. If we would like to know what we have stored in the computer file, we simply type in the command **CAT** (abbreviation for catalog) and the system gives us a list as shown in Figure 2-9. (The format of the output from your computer will probably be slightly different.) Here we see that four programs **CUBE**, **PROB3**, **SALE**, and **MEAN** are stored on the disk under this account.

Figure 2-9   Getting a catalog listing—the CAT command.

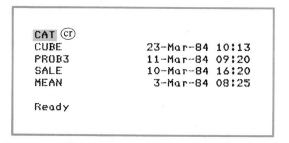

THE SAVE COMMAND

After we enter a new program, one of the first things we should do is to save it on disk. Most programmers have had the aggravating experience of entering and correcting a large program and then forgetting to save it before signing off. A typical timesharing session is shown in Figure 2-10. Here a new program (**INVEN**) is entered, saved (using the **SAVE** command), and run. In most microcomputers, it is necessary to include the name together with the **SAVE**. For instance, the **SAVE** command would be

SAVE INVEN   or   SAVE "INVEN"

THE OLD COMMAND

With a timesharing system, it is common practice to work on a program over the course of several sessions at the terminal. For instance, we might have sufficient time only to enter a program today but intend to return tomorrow to test it and make necessary corrections. Obviously we must save the program upon completing the entry. When we wish to retrieve it from disk storage at a later date, we must use the command **OLD**. (In some systems, this command is named **LOAD**. Check your installation to find out which it is.) This command causes the system to get the selected program from disk and load it into memory so that we may continue just as if we had never left. For instance, let us assume that we entered and saved **INVEN** during a previous session.

Figure 2-10   Using
the SAVE command.

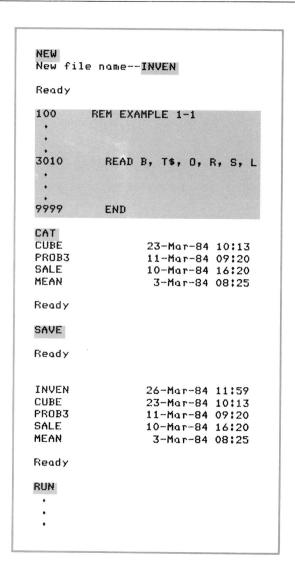

```
NEW
New file name--INVEN

Ready

100        REM EXAMPLE 1-1
  .
  .
  .
3010       READ B, T$, O, R, S, L
  .
  .
  .
9999       END

CAT
CUBE                       23-Mar-84 10:13
PROB3                      11-Mar-84 09:20
SALE                       10-Mar-84 16:20
MEAN                        3-Mar-84 08:25

Ready

SAVE

Ready


INVEN                      26-Mar-84 11:59
CUBE                       23-Mar-84 10:13
PROB3                      11-Mar-84 09:20
SALE                       10-Mar-84 16:20
MEAN                        3-Mar-84 08:25

Ready

RUN
  .
  .
  .
```

Upon checking a program *listing* (printout of the program), we discovered that the **READ** statement (3010) was incorrect. Upon logging on to the system, the correct procedure would be as follows:

1. Bring the original version of the program into memory using the **OLD** or **LOAD** command (as appropriate for your computer).
2. Enter whichever corrections are required. This may involve replacing current lines or adding new ones.
3. Save the corrected version back to auxiliary storage *before* doing anything else. Do not forget this step.

After the program has been corrected and saved, it may be run the same as if it had just been entered.

OTHER COMMANDS On many systems, if a command is given to save a program and another program is currently stored on disk under that same name, the old one is deleted. In other systems, the user is warned. Systems which warn the user usually have a **REPLACE** command which allows you to replace the old with the new.

Systems which ask for a file name when the **NEW** command is entered, usually have a **RENAME** or **NAME** command which allows you to change the name of the program currently in memory.

All systems provide some means for getting rid of programs on disk which are no longer desired. Depending upon the system, this might be done with the **UNSAVE**, **KILL**, or **REMOVE** command.

In all instances, you should check the manual from your computer manufacturer to see which of these are appropriate for your system.

Summary of Commands

Following is a summary (in alphabetic order) of the commands used in Chapters 1 and 2.

CAT	Lists the names of programs stored in the user's library.
LIST	Displays the program which is currently in the working area of memory.
NEW	Clears the work area of memory and prepares for the entry of a new program
OLD (or **LOAD**)	Makes a copy of a selected program stored in the library and places it in the memory work area.
RUN	Runs the program currently in the memory work area; if a program name is also specified, first loads the program from the library, then runs it.
SAVE	Stores the program currently in the memory work area in the library.
UNSAVE	(or equivalent) Deletes the named program from the library.

Summary of Statements

Following is a summary (in alphabetic order) of the Basic statements described in this chapter.

DATA	Allows data values (to be processed by the **READ**) to be included directly in a program.
END	Must be the last statement in the program (use the largest allowable line number in your system). Can also be used to terminate execution of the program.
GOSUB	Causes control of the program to be transferred to another statement in the program. Upon encountering a **RETURN** statement, control is returned to the statement following the **GOSUB**.

LET	Assignment statement causes the expression to the right of equal sign to be evaluated, then stores the result in the variable to the left. (The word **LET** may be omitted.)
PRINT	Prints values of designated variables or quoted descriptions to terminal.
READ	Reads consecutive values from the **DATA** statements into variables listed in the **READ** statement.
REM	Allows descriptive remarks to be included in the program. These are ignored by the Basic system.
RETURN	Returns control to the statement following the calling **GOSUB**. See the description of the **GOSUB**.
STOP	Halts execution of the program.

ANSWERS TO PRECEDING EXERCISES

2.1 All Basic program statement entries must have line numbers.

2.2 A descriptive remark is indicated by entering **REM** following the line number.

2.3 **73**—does not start with letter
SD—letter not followed by a digit (most microcomputer Basics allow two letters)
Q1298—too long
4C—first character not a letter

2.4 All Basic variables contain zero prior to execution. String variables are defined with "nothing"; that is, an entry with zero characters is assigned. This is commonly called a *null* string.

2.5 This exercise illustrates an important feature of the **DATA** statement: that is, fields are taken from the **DATA** statement to form the **DATA** pool without any reference to the "record" concept with which we are familiar. Values read into **A** and **B** are as follows.

Execution of READ	A	B
First	25	13
Second	281	16
Third	37	48
Fourth	122	53

2.6 The value for **N2** will begin in printing position 1.
The value for **N4** will begin in printing position 16.
The value for **N6** will begin in printing position 31.

2.7 a. 17   b. 23   c. 34

2.8 After returning from the Termination Routine, execution would continue to the "next" statement. In this case, the next statement is in what we know as the Initialization Routine (line 2010). The headings would be printed again and then the **RETURN** statement would be encountered. Since there is no place to which to return (execution did *not* get there via a **GOSUB**), an error will result. Features of the **GOSUB** and **RETURN** are described in the section that follows this exercise.

PROGRAMMING PROBLEMS

2.1 A **DATA** statement includes the following employee payroll information.

> Employee number
> Hours worked
> Pay rate
> Deductions

Write a program which will calculate the net pay as follows:

> Net pay = Hours × Rate − Deductions

Print each of the input quantities and the calculated net pay. Following is a **DATA** statement which represents a typical record.

```
9050    DATA 1427, "NANCY WILLIAMS", 45, 9.23, 67.01
```

2.2 An instructor keeps student examination information in the computer. Assume that there is one **DATA** statement for each student with the following information.

> Student name
> First hour exam
> Second hour exam
> Third hour exam
> Final exam

Write a program to calculate the total points earned as the sum of the three hour exam scores and twice the final exam score. Then calculate the average by dividing the sum by 5. Print the student name, total points, and average.
A sample **DATA** statement for this program is:

```
9010    DATA "K. ALLEN", 75, 82, 63, 86
```

2.3 A stock market investor keeps a record of all stocks which have been purchased and then resold. Assume that there is one **DATA** statement with the following information:

> Stock ID number
> Description
> Number of shares of stock
> Purchase price per share
> Sale price per share
> Total commission paid to broker

Write a program to calculate the profit (or loss). Print the stock ID number, description, number of shares, and the profit.

```
9050    DATA 4882, "JP DESIGNS", 200, 27.75, 31.38, 67.01
```

CHAPTER 3

Processing a Data Set

OBJECTIVES

This chapter expands on the principles introduced in Chapters 1 and 2 by providing the capability to process an entire file of data. **DATA** statements continue to be used. However, you should recognize that these processing principles apply equally whether the data file takes the form of **DATA** statements within the program or of a disk file exterior to the program. The important concepts which you will learn in this chapter are:

1. How to cause repeated execution of a module.
2. How to terminate repeated execution of a module upon detecting a trailer record at the end of the data file. (The concept of the trailer record is described in the Introduction—refer to Figure 9.)
3. The concept of accumulating quantities during repeated execution of a module, and of printing totals at the end of a report.

To these ends, you will learn about two additional Basic statements.

GOTO (unconditional transfer of control)
IF (conditional transfer of control)

Repetitive Processing

THE PROBLEM STATEMENT   The task of processing a one-record file might be okay for a first peek at Basic. But it leaves something to be desired for the bookstore manager of Example 1-1. To satisfy the manager's needs better, let us consider the following expansion of that example.

Example 3-1
The bookstore inventory file of Example 1-1 is to be included in the program as a series of **DATA** statements. The last data record is followed by a trailer record with a value of 9999 recorded for the Book Identification. The trailer record does not contain book data and should not be processed as a data record.

Obviously we are interested in programs which will process repeatedly, one record after the other. In fact, this concept was emphasized in the Introduction. More specifically, the set of flowcharts in the Introduction, Figure 6, illustrates the logic of processing the employee records in a payroll file. The program of Figure 2-1 of Chapter 2 to process one record involves a read–process–write sequence in the Processing Routine. The commonly used structured programming technique described in the Introduction is to alter this sequence to read the first record in the Initialization Routine; and then use a process–write–read sequence in the Process Routine. This makes it possible to "look ahead" in search of the trailer record used to mark the end of the data set. These principles are illustrated in Figure 3-1. We must remember that the trailer is *not* a data record; it merely signals the end of the data set. As in Figure 3-1, it may use a numeric field with a value of all 9's (or anything else which is appropriate). Or it might use a string field with some meaningful value such as EOF (standing for end of file).

Whatever is used, we have two needs:

1. The **GOSUB** which calls the Processing Routine must be repeatedly executed.
2. This repeated execution must be controlled such that execution of the **GOSUB** is terminated when the trailer record is detected.

Figure 3-1   (a) End of file. (b) Repeated processing logic.

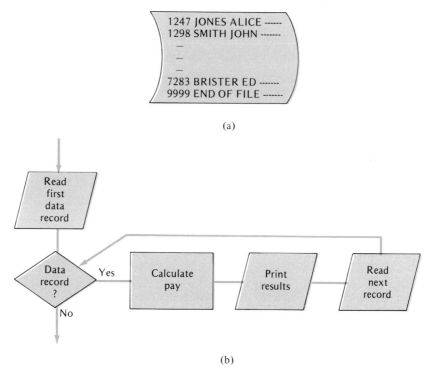

1247 JONES ALICE ------
1298 SMITH JOHN -------
—
—
—
7283 BRISTER ED -------
9999 END OF FILE -------

(a)

(b)

A SAMPLE PROGRAM— EXAMPLE 3-1 The program of Figure 3-2(a) is designed to process an entire data "file" (in the form of **DATA** statements). Here we see that the processing sequencing has been modified consistent with the technique illustrated by the flowchart of

Figure 3-2   (a) Processing a data file—Example 3-1.

```
100   REM   EXAMPLE 3-1
110   REM   PROGRAM TO UPDATE AN INVENTORY
120   REM   INPUT QUANTITIES AND NAMES ARE:
130   REM     B - BOOK NUMBER
140   REM     T$- BOOK TITLE
150   REM     O - OLD BALANCE
160   REM     R - COPIES RECEIVED
170   REM     S - COPIES SOLD
180   REM     L - COPIES LOST AND DESTROYED
190   REM   CALCULATED QUANTITIES AND NAMES ARE:
200   REM     N - NEW BALANCE
300                                    REM
1000 REM MAIN ROUTINE
1010      GOSUB 2010
1020        REM INITIALIZATION ROUTINE
1030      IF B=9999 THEN 1070
1040        GOSUB 3010
1050        GOTO 1030
1060          REM REPEATEDLY PROCESS UNTIL TRAILER DETECTED
1070      GOSUB 4010
1080        REM TERMINATION ROUTINE
1090      STOP
1100 REM END OF MAIN ROUTINE
1110                                    REM
2000 REM INITIALIZATION ROUTINE
2010      PRINT "BOOK", "BOOK", "OLD", "NEW"
2020      PRINT "NUMBER", "TITLE", "BALANCE", "BALANCE"
2030      PRINT
2040      READ B, T$, O, R, S, L
2050        REM READ FIRST RECORD
2060      RETURN
2070 REM END OF INITIALIZATION ROUTINE
2080                                    REM
3000 REM PROCESS ROUTINE
3010      LET N = O + R - S - L
3020      PRINT B, T$, O, N
3030      READ B, T$, O, R, S, L
3040      RETURN
3050 REM END OF PROCESS ROUTINE
3060                                    REM
4000 REM TERMINATION ROUTINE
4010      PRINT
4020      PRINT "PROCESSING COMPLETE"
4030      RETURN
4040 REM END OF TERMINATION ROUTINE
4050                                    REM
9000 REM        ** INPUT DATA **
9010      DATA 4451, "MODERN MATH", 453, 150, 313, 2
9020      DATA 4892, "IBM COBOL",   512,   0, 186, 4
9030      DATA 5118, "MICRO MENU",  518, 500, 160, 1
9040      DATA 6881, "PDP 11 BASIC",  0, 201,   0, 0
9050      DATA 7144, "MODERN DANCE",147, 180,  60, 1
9060      DATA 9999, "EOF",           0,   0,   0, 0
9999   END
```

(a)

Figure 3-2 (b) Output
for Example 3-1.

```
BOOK              BOOK              OLD              NEW
NUMBER            TITLE             BALANCE          BALANCE

4451              MODERN MATH       453              288
4892              IBM COBOL         512              322
5118              MICRO MENU        518              857
6881              PDP 11 BASIC      0                201
7144              MODERN DANCE      147              266

PROCESSING COMPLETE

                              (b)
```

Figure 3-1. That is, the first record is read in the Initialization Routine; then in the Process Routine, the sequence is calculate–print–read. Furthermore, we see that additional **DATA** statements have been added—the last one containing the trailer. We can see in Figure 3-2(b) that the output indeed consists of one line for each data "record" in the data set.

The segment of the program which is of primary interest is lines 1030 through 1050. Repeated execution of the **GOSUB** is cause by the **GOTO** statement at line 1050.

```
1050      GOTO 1030
```

This statement interrupts the normal sequential execution of statements and causes a branch to the statement which is specified. In that respect, it works the same as a **GOSUB**. However, the important difference is that there is no return associated with it. The **GOTO** is commonly referred to as an *unconditional branch* statement. As a rule, programs should be designed to minimize use of the **GOTO**. All too often, a program is thrown together with little preplanning. Then there is a major effort to "plug leaks" when the program does not perform properly. More often than not, this involves extensive use of the **GOTO** with a lot of corresponding jumping around. The end result is often a program that is a mess and is difficult to modify and maintain. In this book, the **GOTO** is used only within certain restrictive rules (described in the next chapter).

EXERCISE

3.1 What is the difference between the **GOSUB** and the **GOTO**?

CONTROLLING A PROCESSING LOOP Control of the loop created by the **GOTO** of line 1050 is achieved by the **IF** statement of line 1030. This statement is essentially a *conditional* **GOTO**. That is, execution will **GOTO** the specified statement only if a stated condition is true. We will study the **IF** in detail in Chapter 4; here we simply "use it because

Figure 3-3   Loop control—Example 3-1.

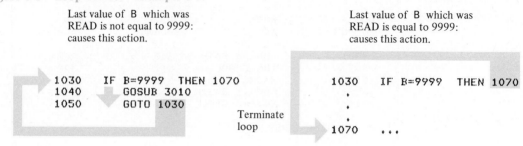

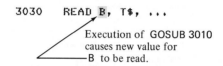

Execution of GOSUB 3010 causes new value for B to be read.

it works." Figure 3-3 illustrates how the **IF** works in this case. After the first record is read in the Initialization Routine, execution progresses to statement 1030. If the value read into **B** is not 9999, then nothing further happens at line 1030 and execution continues to the **GOSUB** at line 1040 (as shown, on the left, in Figure 3-3). After processing that record, the next one is read (line 3030) and control returned to the main program. We see that the last action *before* executing line 1030 is always to read the next record. Upon reading the trailer, **B** will equal 9999 and execution of the loop will be terminated as shown on the right in Figure 3-3.

EXERCISE

3.2 What will happen if the data set contains only the trailer record (no data records)?

Calculating Summary Totals

INCREMENTING A QUANTITY
The concept of a counter is commonly encountered in programming. For instance, it might be necessary to count the number of records processed, or to count the number of account balances exceeding the maximum allowable. The process of counting in Basic is illustrated by the simple program of Figure 3-4. The key to this operation is the **LET** statement at line 120:

```
120     C = C + 1
```

Among other things, this statement characterizes the difference between the equal sign as used in algebra and in Basic. In algebra, the equation

$$x = x + 1$$

Figure 3-4 A
counting loop.

```
100   PRINT "COUNTING SEQUENCE: 1-5"
110   IF C=5 THEN 150
120     C = C + 1
130     PRINT C
140     GOTO 110
150   PRINT "COUNTING SEQUENCE FINISHED"
160   END


RUNNH
COUNTING SEQUENCE: 1-5
  1
  2
  3
  4
  5
COUNTING SEQUENCE FINISHED
```

is never true, regardless of the value assigned to *x*; it is a contradiction. In Basic, the statement

$$C = C + 1,$$

is quite valid and very useful. Remember, the equal sign says, "Evaluate the expression on the right and assign that value to the variable on the left." Initially the value in C will be 0. Execution of the statement will cause the expression C + 1 to be evaluated as 0 + 1, or 1. Then the result, 1, will be stored back in C, replacing the previous value of 0. Control will be returned to statement 110 and, since the condition is not true, statement 120 will be executed again. This time 1 will be added to the value now stored in C(1), giving 2. This in turn will be stored back in C. Continuing, the value in C will reach 4. Upon executing the loop once more, C + 1 will be evaluated as 5, with the result being stored back into C, replacing the previous value of 4. The test at line 110 will be true, thus causing execution of the loop to be terminated. The overall result, as we see, is that C serves as a simple counter, or *accumulator,* being incremented by 1 each time through the loop.

THE CONCEPT OF
ACCUMULATING

The printed report of Figure 3-2(b) is certainly a convenient summary. However, it lacks one item which is commonly required in business data processing application: totals. For instance, the book store manager would probably be interested in the total number of books sold, lost, and so on. The concept of computing a total in a computer program is very similar to the way we would total a column of figures with a pocket calculator. For instance, in Figure 3-5, as each number is entered through the keyboard, it is added to the value in the calculator display. (It is *accumulated* in an *accumulator.*) Thus, when we are finished, the accumulator contains the final sum. Technically speaking, we are already familiar with the concept of accumulating from the counter of

Figure 3-5   The
concept of
accumulating.

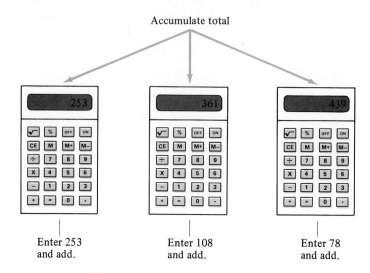

That is, the variable **C** accumulates a total being increased by 1
each time statement 120 is executed. This exact principle can be applied to
totaling quantities in the inventory program. For instance, assume that we
wish to total the number of copies lost or destroyed (**L**) using the variable **L1**
as an accumulator. Then each time a new record is read, we could accumulate values of **L** with the following statement.

```
L1 = L1 + L
```

Let us see how Example 3-1 can be expanded to incorporate this principle.

EXERCISE

3.3 The use of accumulators (such as **C** and **L1**) is based on a very important
assumption regarding the initial values of **C** and **L1**. What is it? Explain the
consequences if it were not true.

EXPANDING   Following is a redefinition of Example 3-1 which involves computing totals.
EXAMPLE 3-1

Example 3-2
In addition to the requirements of Example 3-1, totals are to be calculated
for the following quantities:

> Copies received
> Copies sold
> Copies lost or destroyed
> New balance of copies on hand

A counter is to be maintained which counts each record as it is read and
processed. The value of this counter should be printed together with the
details for each book. This then will serve as a line counter on the output
report. Print the calculated totals at the end of the report.

These additions to the problem do not change the overall logic of the program which we have been studying. In fact, the following modifications to the program are relatively minor.

1. The accumulation and the counter must be added to the Process module.
2. The counter variable must be added to the list of the **PRINT** statement.
3. Printing of the totals must be added to the Termination module.

These relatively simple modifications are shown shaded in the program of Figure 3-6. An extremely important point illustrated by this program is that we isolate the particular module (or modules) requiring modification in order to change the program. For a large program in "real life," such isolation is critical. A programmer does not want a change in one part of a program to cause problems in another, totally unrelated area. We might also notice the convenience of incrementing line numbers by 10. Here no changes were required; it was simply a matter of adding the required statements.

The result of running this program is shown in Figure 3-7. The summary lines at the end of the report are commonly referred to as exactly that— *summary lines*. The lines in the body of the report, of which there is one for each record processed, are called *detail lines*.

EXERCISE

3.4 What would be printed from the program of Figure 3-6 if the data records (lines 9010–9050) were omitted and only the trailer record (line 9060) were included?

ANSWERS TO PRECEDING EXERCISES

3.1 Both cause execution to proceed to a designated statement number. However, the **GOTO** causes an unconditional branch with no eventual return. The **GOSUB** is always used in conjunction with a **RETURN**, which causes execution to return to the statement following the calling **GOSUB**.

3.2 The program would execute properly (it would not crash). However, the printed results would appear rather strange. We would have the headings followed by the termination message. The reason is that the trailer record would be read in the Initialization Routine and the Processing Routine would never be executed.

3.3 Referring to the pocket calculator example of accumulating (Figure 3-5), the first thing we do when summing a set of numbers is to clear the accumulator. This sets the initial value to zero; otherwise we would begin with "garbage" in the accumulator and the results would be meaningless. The same thing applies to accumulators (such as C and L1) in the computer. Since Basic initializes all variables to zero before beginning execution, this is automatically taken care of for us. Later in this book, however, we will see examples in which "minor" totals are calculated and all such accumulators must be set to zero after each group of data records is processed.

3.4 The headings would be printed followed by the total lines (all values would be zero). No detail lines would be printed.

Figure 3-6
Accumulating
totals—Example 3-2.

```
100  REM   EXAMPLE 3-1
110  REM   PROGRAM TO UPDATE AN INVENTORY
120  REM   INPUT QUANTITIES AND NAMES ARE:
130  REM     B - BOOK NUMBER
140  REM     T$- BOOK TITLE
150  REM     O - OLD BALANCE
160  REM     R - COPIES RECEIVED
170  REM     S - COPIES SOLD
180  REM     L - COPIES LOST AND DESTROYED
190  REM   CALCULATED QUANTITIES AND NAMES ARE:
200  REM     N - NEW BALANCE
204  REM     C - LINE COUNT
206  REM     R1,S1,L1,N1 - ACCUMULATORS
210  REM                               REM
1000 REM MAIN ROUTINE
1010      GOSUB 2010
1020        REM INITIALIZATION ROUTINE
1030      IF B=9999 THEN 1070
1040        GOSUB 3010
1050        GOTO 1030
1060          REM REPEATEDLY PROCESS UNTIL TRAILER DETECTED
1070      GOSUB 4010
1080        REM TERMINATION ROUTINE
1090      STOP
1100 REM END OF MAIN ROUTINE
1110                                   REM
2000 REM INITIALIZATION ROUTINE
2010      PRINT "LINE","BOOK", "BOOK", "OLD", "NEW"
2020      PRINT "COUNT","NUMBER", "TITLE", "BALANCE", "BALANCE"
2030      PRINT
2040      READ B, T$, O, R, S, L
2050        REM READ FIRST RECORD
2060      RETURN
2070 REM END OF INITIALIZATION ROUTINE
2080                                   REM
3000 REM PROCESS ROUTINE
3010      LET N = O + R - S - L
3013      C = C + 1
3014      R1 = R1 + R
3015      S1 = S1 + S
3016      L1 = L1 + L
3017      N1 = N1 + N
3020      PRINT C, B, T$, O, N
3030      READ B, T$, O, R, S, L
3040      RETURN
3050 REM END OF PROCESS ROUTINE
3060                                   REM
4000 REM TERMINATION ROUTINE
4010      PRINT
4012      PRINT "TOTAL SUMMARY"
4013      PRINT
4014      PRINT "RECEIVED",R1
4015      PRINT "SOLD",S1
4016      PRINT "LOST, ETC.",L1
4017      PRINT "NEW BALANCE",N1
4018      PRINT
4020      PRINT "PROCESSING COMPLETE"
4030      RETURN
4040 REM END OF TERMINATION ROUTINE
4050                                   REM
9000 REM        ** INPUT DATA **
9010      DATA 4451, "MODERN MATH", 453, 150, 313, 2
9020      DATA 4892, "IBM COBOL",   512,   0, 186, 4
9030      DATA 5118, "MICRO MENU",  518, 500, 160, 1
9040      DATA 6881, "PDP 11 BASIC",  0, 201,   0, 0
9050      DATA 7144, "MODERN DANCE",147, 180,  60, 1
9060      DATA 9999, "EOF",          0,   0,   0, 0
9999      END
```

Figure 3-7   Sample output—Example 3-2.

```
LINE           BOOK           BOOK           OLD            NEW
COUNT          NUMBER         TITLE          BALANCE        BALANCE

1              4451           MODERN MATH    453            288
2              4892           IBM COBOL      512            322
3              5118           MICRO MENU     518            857
4              6881           PDP 11 BASIC   0              201
5              7144           MODERN DANCE   147            266

TOTAL SUMMARY

RECEIVED       1031
SOLD           719
LOST, ETC.     8
NEW BALANCE    1934

PROCESSING COMPLETE
```

PROGRAMMING PROBLEMS

3.1 The WLN Mercantile Company wishes to prepare a monthly report of all of its customers who exceeded their credit limit at any time during the month. The output report is to include:

- Appropriate descriptive headings.
- One detail line for each customer; the line is to include the customer number, the customer name, and the amount by which the credit limit was exceeded.
- A summary line with the number of customers processed for this report.

Following is a typical data set.

Customer Number	Name	Maximum Charge	Credit Limit
1258	A. BAKER	595.26	500
1992	J. CLAY	601.38	500
2801	N. DICKEY	997.23	950
3965	F. LONG	980.16	900
4489	K. JORDAN	710.32	600
9999	EOF	0	0

3.2 Net pay for each employee of the Yuba Consulting Company is to be calculated using the formula:

Net pay = Gross pay − Deductions − 20 × Number of dependents

Gross pay= Hours worked × Pay rate

The output report is to include:

- Appropriate descriptive headings.
- One detail line for each employee; the line is to include the employee number, gross pay, and net pay.
- Summary lines appropriately labeled which display the number of employees processed and the total gross amount paid out.

The following is a typical data set.

Employee Number	Hours Worked	Pay Rate	Deductions	Dependents
2083	36	8.23	25.73	2
2115	44	10.51	61.92	3
2218	40	6.25	59.23	0
2476	40	11.04	78.21	1
9999	0	0	0	0

3.3 The NMD Consulting Corporation pays certain expenses for each of its employees. Although there is no maximum, NMD has designated a "target" figure which each employee should attempt to avoid exceeding. A monthly expense report is desired which prints the following.

- A report title and appropriate headings.
- One detail line for each employee; the line is to include the employee name and total expenses.
- One summary line (appropriately labeled) with the average expenditure for all employees.
- One summary line (appropriately labeled) with the "target" amount.

In the following sample data set, the first record contains only *one* field: the target expense amount.

Target: 500

Employee Name	Travel	Lodging	Food	Misc.
A. SMITH	125.37	283.00	128.25	65.02
R. JONES	80.20	310.20	142.85	107.63
C. WONG	0.00	0.00	0.00	0.00
D. LARA	212.80	85.65	63.71	49.25
F. COMPTON	92.75	265.24	122.12	20.00
R. DAMON	83.79	65.80	48.51	12.50
EOF	0	0	0	0

3.4 One of the important statistics maintained by McDaniel Airlines is the load factor for each flight. The load factor is computed as:

Load factor = (Passengers/Capacity) × 100

For instance, an aircraft with a 150-passenger capacity carrying 120 passengers would have a load factor of:

LF = (120/150) × 10 = 80

A load factor report is required which gives the following information.

- Descriptive headings, including the date.
- One detail line for each flight; the line is to include the flight number, passenger capacity, passengers carried, and load factor.
- Summary lines (appropriately labeled) with the number of flights processed and the average load factor of all flights.

In the following sample data set, the first record contains only *one* field: the current date.

Date: NOV 21

Flight Number	Capacity	Passengers
27	125	125
06	108	51
82	95	91
63	108	106
99	0	0

3.5 The WIN Marketing Company desires a computerized mailing system. From various files, it will prepare address labels which are used for mailing promotional literature. Each label is six lines in height (can hold six lines). Thus, for each record, a total of six lines (including blanks) must be printed. The output requirements are:

- One header label with the job description.
- For each data record one label is to be printed as follows:

    Name
    Address
    City and Zip

- The last label must include a summary line with the number of labels printed.

In the following sample data set, the first record contains only *one* field: the job description.

Job Description: WINDSURFER SURVEY

Name	Address	City	Zip
AL JONES	125 B STREET	LONG PINE	91234
NANCY WILLIAMS	254 LAS VEGAS	SHORT PINE	91162
CARLTON FISK	1252 32ND AVE	CONCORD	91150
JOAN BUDNE	983 HOMDALE	SWEETWATER	91233
EOF	0	0	0

CHAPTER 4

Conditional Operations

OBJECTIVES

The focus of this chapter is on the principle of performing needed operations on a conditional basis. For instance, a bonus is to be paid *only if* sales exceed the quota. From a structured programming point of view, this involves the third of three structures: selection. From this chapter, you will learn about the following.

1. The general form of the **IF** statement, which serves, in effect, as a conditional transfer statement.
2. The concept of relational operators and relational expressions (such expressions may be either true or false) which form the basis for conditional operations.
3. Comparison of string quantities.
4. Implementation of the selection construct using the simple form of the **IF** statement. This involves the principle of the block **IF-THEN** and **IF-THEN-ELSE** forms.
5. Use of logical operators (**AND** and **OR**) in forming **IF** test conditions.
6. Rules regarding use of the **GOTO** statement.

Basic Form of the IF Statement

THE SELECTION CONCEPT The emphasis in the first three chapters has been on the mechanics of Basic and writing relatively simple programs. From a structured programming viewpoint, we have used the two structures, sequence and looping (see the Introduction Figure 8). Each program has handled every record (except the trailer) in exactly the same way as every other record. However, most programs require that certain operations be performed *only if* certain conditions exist. For instance:

- A bonus is to be paid *only if* a salesperson's total sales exceed the quota.
- An output line is to be printed *only if* the updated inventory level falls below the reorder level.

A more complex requirement might be:

- If a salesperson's total sales fall below the quota, then add $200 to the gross pay. Otherwise add 10 percent of the total sales.

Here we are obviously dealing with a selection-type construct (refer to the Introduction, Figure 8). In flowchart form, these two sales examples would be illustrated as shown in Figure 4-1. The form in Figure 4-1(b) is a true selection construct (carry out *either* of two actions depending upon a condition); the form of Figure 4-1(a) is actually a special case. Examples in this book make extensive use of both forms.

Figure 4-1   (a) A single selection. (b) Alternate selections.

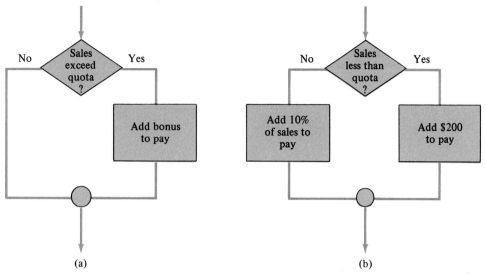

(a)

(b)

In a selection process, the operations to be carried out may involve a single statement or a series of statements, or execution of a separate module. In structured programming, the respective forms of Figures 4-1(a) and (b) appear as shown in Figure 4-2. Some languages include features which correspond almost exactly to these forms. In this book, the two forms are simulated using the simple **IF** and **GOTO** statements.

THE IF STATEMENT   The basis for performing conditional operations is the **IF** statement which was introduced in Chapter 3 to force repeated execution of the Process Routine. In American National Standard Minimal Basic, the **IF** has the relatively res-

Figure 4-2   (a) The IF-THEN form. (b) The IF-THEN-ELSE form.

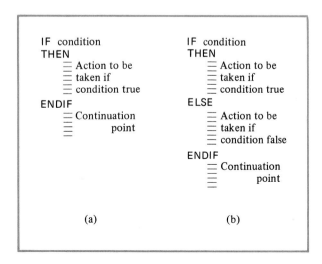

```
IF  condition
THEN
    ≡ Action to be
    ≡ taken if
    ≡ condition true
ENDIF
    ≡ Continuation
    ≡        point
```

(a)

```
IF  condition
THEN
    ≡ Action to be
    ≡ taken if
    ≡ condition true
ELSE
    ≡ Action to be
    ≡ taken if
    ≡ condition false
ENDIF
    ≡ Continuation
    ≡        point
```

(b)

tricted form as used in Chapter 3. That is, it serves as a conditional **GOTO**. Although most versions of Basic include a more versatile form of the **IF**, most examples in this book will use the simple form. This will require a bit more programming effort but the resulting programs will work on any Basic system. The form which we encountered in Chapter 3 is:

IF (*particular condition true*) **THEN** (*go to a statement number*)

Technically the general form of the **IF** statement is:

IF <*relational expression*> **THEN** <*statement number*>

RELATIONAL OPERATORS AND EXPRESSIONS The part of the **IF** statement which forms the test basis is commonly called the *relational expression.* In general, a relational expression involves two arithmetic quantities (often each is a single variable or constant) and a *relational operator.* The general form is:

<arithmetic expression> <relational operator> <arithmetic expression>

Two examples of relational expressions are shown in Figure 4-3. The first example states that "B is equal to 9999." It is important to recognize that the equal sign is used differently here than in the **LET** statement. (The **LET** statement would say "place a value of 9999 in the variable **B**.") Obviously, if **B** contains a value of, for instance, 1876, then this relational expression will be false. Only if **B** contains 9999, will it be true. This is illustrated by the two cases shown in Figure 4-4(a).

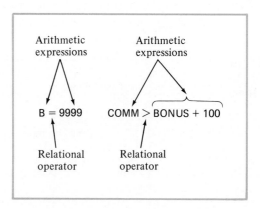

Figure 4-3 Relational expressions.

The second states that "**COMM** is greater than **BONUS**+100" (the symbol > is a mathematical symbol meaning "greater than"). Obviously this can be either true or false. We see this in the two samples of Figure 4-4(b). In evaluating a relational expression, the computer performs any necessary

Figure 4-4
Relational
expressions.

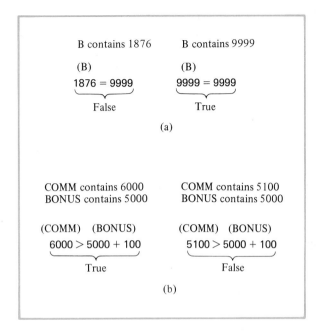

calculations, then makes the designated comparisons. The expression is determined to be either true or false.

Relational operators available to the Basic programmer are the following.

| | | | Result if H has a value of 50 | |
Symbol	Meaning	Examples	Evaluation of Expression	Value
>	Greater than	H> 0	50 > 0	True
=	Equal to	H= −1	50 = −1	False
<	Less than	H< 100	50 < 100	True
>=	Greater than or equal to	H>= 50	50 >= 50	True
<=	Less than or equal to	H <= 25.3	50 <= 25.3	False
<>	Not equal to	2*H–10<> 90	2*50 − 10 <> 90	False

It is important to recognize that the relational symbols are valid only in the form shown. That is, >=, <=, and <> are valid but =>, =<, and >< are *not* valid.

COMPARING STRING QUANTITIES All of the examples to this point involve the comparison of numeric quantities. However, some of the programming problems at the end of Module 3 require testing for an EOF trailer record. Needless to say, string quantities can be tested in the **IF** statement just as readily as can numeric quantities. For instance, the **IF** statement of Figure 3-2 could as easily have been:

```
1030      IF T$ = "EOF" THEN 1070
```

The concept of equality is rather obvious. That is, the above condition is true (T$ = "EOF") only if **T$** contains the value EOF. Any minor variation will not do; for example, if **T$** contains EFO, EO, or EOFA, the condition is false. This is no different than with numbers: for instance, 12567 is not equal to 12576.

   In determining whether one string quantity is "less than" or "greater than" another, a simple alphabetic ordering is used. In other words, the letter A is the "smallest" letter and Z the "largest". Thus JOHNSON is "smaller" than SMITH (even though JOHNSON has more letters). As a rule, most of our comparison of string quantities will be limited to whether or not two quantities are equal. The following examples illustrate the comparing of string quantities.

Expression	Value in B$	Value in C$	Value of Expression
B$ = "EOF"	EOF		True
B$ = "EOF"	JONES		False
B$ > C$	SMITH	LEE	True
B$ > C$	BROWN	LEE	False
B$ > C$	LEE	LEE	False

EXERCISE

4.1 Consider the following IF statement:

   IF 3.2*T7>=16 THEN 290

   a. Identify the relational expression.
   b. What will occur when
        T7 = –10?
        T7 = 5?
        T7 = 20?

USING THE IF FOR CONDITIONAL OPERATIONS To illustrate using the **IF** for selection, let us consider the following example.

Example 4-1
Within an inventory control program, the updated inventory level **L** stock balance **B** for the inventory item number **N** has just been calculated. If **L** is less than the reorder level **R**, then print an error message.

Figure 4-5 (a) Conditional execution of a statement. (b) True condition. (c) False condition.

```
300     IF L>=R THEN 360
310         REM PRINT MESSAGE
320         PRINT
330         PRINT 'Stock number',N
340         PRINT 'Stock level',L
350         PRINT 'Reorder level',R
360     (next statement)
```

Condition true:
  L equals or exceeds R
  for instance, L = 600; R = 500

Condition false:
  L less than R
  for instance, L = 400; R = 500

```
300     IF L>=R THEN 360
310         REM PRINT MESSAGE
320         PRINT
330         PRINT 'Stock number',N
340         PRINT 'Stock level',L
350         PRINT 'Reorder level',R
360     (next statement)
```
(b)

```
300     IF L>=R THEN 360
310         REM PRINT MESSAGE
320         PRINT
330         PRINT 'Stock number',N
340         PRINT 'Stock level',L
350         PRINT 'Reorder level',R
330     (next statement)
```
(c)

Without a doubt, the sequence in Figure 4-5(a) is the simplest way of handling this. In (b) we see how each of the two conditions is handled. On the left, if **L** is 600 and **R** is 500, then the inventory level is satisfactory and the message is not printed. In the case on the right, the condition is false (meaning that the level does not equal or exceed the reorder level) so execution "falls through" and the message is printed.

One confusing aspect of handling the test in this way relates to the manner in which the code is written. That is, the example statement says:

"Print if **L** is less than **R**"

The **IF** statement test says:

"Do not print (jump over the print)
if **L** is equal to or greater than **R**."

Sometimes this "reverse thinking" is confusing and leads to errors. Figure 4-6 shows an alternate to this which is somewhat more consistent with the English statement of the problem. Although it may appear a bit clumsy, it provides good documentation, especially when the action also involves an **ELSE** option. Following are important features of this form.

1. The beginning and ending of the **IF** block are clearly marked by "block markers," the **THEN** and **ENDIF** remark lines (303 and 340).
2. The first statement following each of the block markers is assigned the next line number following the block marker line number. There will never be a reason to insert lines between the block marker and the line specified in the transfer (in line 300 or 302).

**Figure 4-6   The block
IF form.**

To the statement following
the THEN block marker.

To the statement following
the ENDIF block marker.

```
300        IF  L<R  THEN    304
301           REM ELSE
302               GOTO    341
303 REM    THEN
304           PRINT
310           PRINT "Stock number",N
320           PRINT "Stock level",L
330           PRINT "Reorder level",R
340 REM    ENDIF
341        ... (next statement)
```

For a simple **IF-THEN** situation, either of the two forms (Figure 4-5 or Figure 4-6) can be used. If the form of Figure 4-5 is clear, then use it. However, in either form, be certain to indent as shown in these examples in order clearly to mark the beginning and end of the statements to be executed on a conditional basis.

More on the IF

**ADVANCED IF
CONCEPTS**

Many Basics have more sophisticated forms of the **IF**, which makes programming life easier. This section describes three such forms found in many versions of Basic. If yours has them, then by all means use them.

The first allows the inclusion of an executable statement following the key word **THEN**. Figure 4-7 shows how an error message may be printed with this form.

**Figure 4-7
Advanced IF form.**

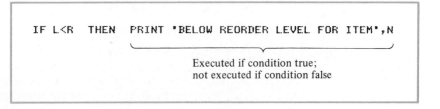

The second involves an **IF-THEN-ELSE** which has the form

IF <relational expression> **THEN** <statement number> **ELSE** <statement number>

In other words, the transfer to one statement or the other will occur depending upon the outcome of the test. Then the form of the block **IF** in Figure 4-6 can be simplified as shown in Figure 4-8.

Figure 4-8   Using the
IF-THEN-ELSE form.

```
300          IF L<R THEN 302 ELSE 341
301 REM   THEN
302              PRINT
310              PRINT "Stock number",N
320              PRINT "Stock level",L
330              PRINT "Reorder level",R
340 REM   ENDIF
341              ... (next statement)
```

The third advanced feature relates to the **REM** statement rather than the **IF**. In many timesharing systems, a **GOTO** must *not* specify a **REM** statement. For instance, in Figure 4-6 it would be illegal for statement 302 to say **GOTO 340**. However, in many Basics this is permissible. If this is the case with your system, then always **GOTO** a **REM** which is clearly marked as a point to which transfer is controlled. The sequence of Figure 4-6 would then take the form of Figure 4-9.

Figure 4-9
Branching to REM
statements.

```
300          IF L<R THEN    303
301              REM ELSE
302                  GOTO    350
303 REM   THEN
310              PRINT
320              PRINT "Stock number",N
330              PRINT "Stock level",L
340              PRINT "Reorder level",R
350 REM   ENDIF
360              ... (next statement)
```

EXERCISES

In the following exercises, use whatever advanced **IF** features your system happens to have.

4.2 The NP Bank deducts a service charge of $5 for any account in which the new balance **B** falls below $200. Write a sequence which will decrease **B** by 5 if **B** is less than 200.

4.3 Expand Exercise 4.2 to also print the message "ACCOUNT BELOW MINIMUM" and increment the counter **C** by 1.

THE BLOCK Examples thus far have illustrated the **IF-THEN** form of Figures 4-1(a) and
IF-THEN-ELSE 4-2(a). Let us now consider an example which illustrates the full selection
FORM structure (**IF-THEN-ELSE**) shown in Figures 4-1(b) and 4-2(b).

Example 4-2

Each salesperson record in a file includes the following:

Salesperson name
Total sales

If the total sales (S) are less than $20,000, then the salesperson's commission (C) is calculated as 8 percent of the total sales. If the sales reach $20,000, the commission is 10 percent of the total sales. Maintain a count of how many employees fall in each category. Write a program segment to perform this operation.

Actually the **IF-THEN-ELSE** block sequence shown in Figure 4-10 is a logical extension of the **IF-THEN** form of Figure 4-6. In this case, we see that *either* of the two blocks will be executed. Also, the general form provides excellent documentation and, if used consistently, minimizes the chance of inadvertent programming errors.

Figure 4-10   The IF-THEN-ELSE block form.

```
500        IF S<20000 THEN 504
501              REM ELSE
502                    GOTO 531
503 REM THEN
504        C = 0.08*S      Executed if S
510        C1 = C1 + 1     less than 20000
520        GOTO 551
530 REM ELSE
531        C = 0.1*S       Executed if S
540        C2 = C2 + 1     not less than 20000
550 REM ENDIF
551        ... (next statement)
```

EXERCISE

4.4 What would occur in the sequence of Figure 4-10 if the **GOTO** at line 520 were accidentally left out?

AN IF WITHIN AN IF The generality of this form of the block **IF** simulation is clearly illustrated by the following expansion of Example 4-2.

Example 4-3

The salespeople of Example 4-2 are identified by a special code field **C$** which contains "M" for management people. For each manager-level salesperson, perform the operations as stated in Example 4-2. For all others, set the commission **C** to 500.

From an overall point of view, this problem is a typical **IF-THEN-ELSE** form. That is, if the person is a manager, then take one action; otherwise, take another. In our stepwise refinement of the problem, we see that the conditional action to be taken *also* includes a further action to be taken on a conditional basis. This **IF** within an **IF** action is illustrated by the flowchart of Figure 4-11(a). The segment of code to perform the desired operation is shown in Figure 4-11(b). Note the use of indentation, which serves as documentation to the programmer regarding the relationships between various segments of the program. To clarify the logic, the two major blocks are shaded. The first of the two major blocks is identical to the version of Figure 4-10, except that the line numbers are changed appropriately.

Figure 4-11   An   IF   within   an   IF—Example 4-3. (a) Flowchart. (b) Program segment.

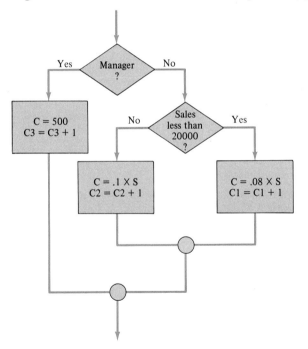

```
700        IF C$="M" THEN 704
701             REM ELSE
702                  GOTO 761
703 REM THEN
704             IF S<20000 THEN 708
705                  REM ELSE
706                       GOTO 731
707 REM        THEN
708                  C = 0.08*S
710                  C1 = C1 + 1
720                  GOTO 751
730 REM        ELSE
731                  C = 0.1*S
740                  C2 = C2 + 1
750 REM        ENDIF
751             GOTO 781
760 REM ELSE
761             C = 500
770             C3 = C3 + 1
780 REM ENDIF
781        ... (next statement)
```

Advanced Program Logic

The example used in this section deals with multiple selection criteria, which are commonly encountered in programming. The solution uses two features not found in all versions of Basic: the **IF-THEN-ELSE** statement, and the **AND** and **OR** operators.

MULTIPLE CONDITIONS Frequently a problem will require that several tests be made on a data field to determine whether or not a particular action is to be taken. For instance, let us consider the following example.

Example 4-4

Each record in an employee file includes the following.

> Employee number
> Employee name
> Accumulated sick leave (days)
> Age
> Seniority (years)

Calculate a special sick leave credit and print the number and name of each employee who meets the following requirements:

> Accumulated sick leave equal to or greater than 120
> AND
> Age greater than 65 or Seniority greater than 30

Great care must be used in dealing with problems of this type since it is very easy to become confused. For instance, how would we interpret the following when doing the evaluating?

1. (Sick leave condition and Age condition or Seniority condition)

Is this to be interpreted as

2. (Sick leave condition and Age condition) or Seniority condition

or as

3. Sick leave condition and (Age condition or Seniority condition)

Clearly the example statement suggests form 3 (that is, Age and Seniority conditions grouped together). We see that an individual must satisfy the Sick leave criterion, and also one of the other two. In form 2, it is possible to qualify by meeting only the Seniority condition. For instance, if Sick leave = 50 (not qualifying), Age = 50 (not qualifying), and Seniority = 31 (qualifying), then the person qualifies by form 2. The ambiguity of form 1 is resolved in form 3. You should always double check what is required before attempting to program it.

LOGICAL
OPERATORS
By now we are familiar with the relational operators $<$, $>$, $=$, and so on, which we use to form relational expressions. In addition to these, many versions of Basic also include the *logical operators* **AND** and **OR**. Logical operators allow us to build complex test conditions for use in the **IF** statement. In general, we have

<relational expression> <logical operator> <relational expression>

For example, the following are all valid forms which can be used as the test condition in an **IF** statement.

```
W<20 OR H>40

F1>3 AND F2>5

A>18 AND A<65
```

Overall the **AND** and **OR** can be interpreted much the same as in ordinary English. That is, the overall expression

test condition 1 **AND** test condition 2

is true only if both test conditions 1 and 2 are true. Otherwise it is false. Similarly,

test condition 1 **OR** test condition 2

is true if either or both of the two individual conditions is true. Example 4-4 takes this one step further in that it involves three test conditions. We see the Basic form in line 3100 of Figure 4-12.

Whenever a complex test form consisting of **AND**s and **OR**s is evaluated, the **AND**s are done first and then the **OR**s. (This is analogous to evaluating an arithmetic expression where multiplications are done before additions.) Much confusion can be avoided, however, by using parentheses since operations within parentheses are performed first. Overall this serves as good documentation and avoids confusion. Thus statement 3100 of Figure 4-12 will be evaluated as indicated by the numbered descriptions in Figure 4-13.

EXERCISES

4.5 Would the test condition of statement 3100 be evaluated correctly if the parentheses around the **OR** grouping were removed? Explain.

4.6 An earlier example tests to determine if **A** is between 18 and 65 by using the following.

```
A>18 AND A<65
```

Since **A** is being tested in both cases, could this be written as follows? Explain.

```
A>18 AND <65
```

Figure 4-12   Multiple test conditions—Example 4-4.

```
3000 REM PROCESS ROUTINE
3010 REM    VARIABLES TESTED
3020 REM      L   SICK LEAVE
3030 REM      A   AGE
3040 REM      S   SENIORITY
     .
     .
     .
3100       IF L>=120 AND (A>65 OR S>30) THEN 3111 ELSE 3201
3110 REM THEN
3111           LET C = ...
     .          .
     .          .
     .          .
3190           PRINT E, E$, C
3200 REM ENDIF
3201       ... (next statement)
     .
     .
     .
3300       READ E, E$, L, A, S
3310       RETURN
```

**Figure 4-13
Evaluating multiple
test conditions.**

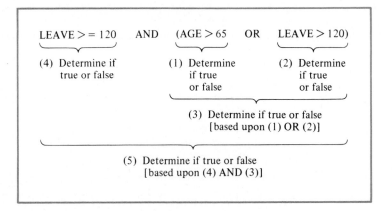

PROGRAMMING   One of the goals of structured programming is to eliminate "casual" use of the
TECHNIQUES   GOTO statement. Since the Basic language was not designed as a structured language, there must be certain restraints on using the GOTO. Its use in
forming Basic block-IFs is clearly spelled out in preceding examples. In
addition, the following rules should be followed.

1. Every module should have a single entry point (at the beginning of the
   module) and a single exit (at the end of the module). In other words,
   there should not be two different RETURN statements in a module.

2. Use of the **GOTO** should be limited to internal use within a module. Then the problem of the program logic "jumping all over the place" is minimized.

3. Under certain conditional operations, a **GOTO** within a module may branch to the exit from the module (the **RETURN**).

4. As a general rule, a **GOTO** should branch only to a line with a greater line number.

5. If your system allows transfer of control to an **REM** statement, then *always* use the line number of a descriptive **REM** in any transfer statement.

If structured techniques which employ only the three basic structures (sequence, loop, and selection) are used in designing a program, then it should be relatively easy to work within the foregoing rules.

EXERCISE

4.7 The concept of reading the first record in the Initialize routine and subsequent records at the end of the Process routine is one way of implementing structured techniques in Basic. Another approach is illustrated in Figure 4-14, which is a modified version of Figure 3-2(a), Example 3-1. Note the following regarding this program.

1. The **READ** has been eliminated from the Initialize routine.
2. The **READ** statement in the Process routine has been moved from the end to the beginning of that routine.
3. An **IF** statement following the **READ** tests to determine whether the trailer has been detected.

Will output of this program be any different from that of the program in Figure 3-2? Is this program consistent with the previously defined four rules for structuring programs? Explain your answer.

ANSWERS TO PRECEDING EXERCISES

4.1 a. The relational expression is **3.2∗T7>=16**.

b. **T7**= −10; condition false; continue to next statement.
   T7=5; condition true; **GOTO** statement 290.
   T7=20; condition true; **GOTO** statement 290.

4.2
```
100        IF B<200 THEN 104
101            REM ELSE
102                GOTO 111
103 REM THEN
104                B = B - 5.00
110 REM ENDIF
111        ...(next statement)
```

or

```
100        IF B >=200 THEN 120
110            B = B - 5.00
120        ...(next statement)
```

Figure 4-14   **Program segments for Exercise 4-7.**

```
        .
        .
        .
1030        IF B=9999 THEN 1070
1040        GOSUB 3010
        .
        .
        .
2000 REM INITIALIZATION ROUTINE
2010        PRINT "LINE", "BOOK", "BOOK", "OLD", "NEW"
2020        PRINT "NUMBER", "TITLE", "NUMBER", "BALANCE", "BALANCE"
2030        PRINT
2050 REM END OF INITIALIZATION ROUTINE
2060 REM
3000 REM PROCESSING ROUTINE
3010        READ B, T$, O, R, S, L
3020        IF B=9999 THEN 3070
3030        N = O + R - S - L
3040        C = C + 1
3050        PRINT C, B, T$, O, N
3060        READ B, T$, O, R, S, L
3070        RETURN
3080 REM END OF PROCESSING ROUTINE
        .
        .
        .
```

```
4.3 100        IF B<200 THEN 104
    101            REM ELSE
    102                GOTO 131
    103 REM THEN
    104            B = B - 5.00
    110            PRINT "ACCOUNT BELOW MINIMUM"
    120            C = C + 1
    130 REM ENDIF
    131        ...(next statement)
```

or

```
    100        IF B<=200 THEN 141
    110            B = B - 5.00
    120            PRINT "ACCOUNT BELOW MINIMUM"
    130            C = C + 1
    140 REM ENDIF
    141        ...(next statement)
```

4.4 On the false condition (**S** not less than 20000), execution would properly transfer to statement 531. On a true condition (**S** less than 20000), execution would properly transfer to statement 504. However, without line 520, execution would continue to statement 531. Thus **C** would always be calculated as if the false condition had occurred. In this case, both the **C1** and **C2** counters would be incremented.

4.5 No. Since **AND**s are handled before **OR**s, removal of the parentheses would cause the condition to be evaluated as if it were

```
(L>=120 AND A>65) OR S>30
```

4.6 The form

```
A>18 AND <65
```

is not valid since <65 (to the right of **AND**) is not a relational expression. Remember, the form is

<relational expression> <logical operator> <relational expression>

4.7 The output of the two programs would be identical. Yes, the program meets the structured requirements. That is, the **GOTO** (line 3020) branches to the exit point of the module (rule 3).

PROGRAMMING PROBLEMS

4.1 Each record in an input file contains three fields **A**, **B**, and **C**. Write a program to find the largest value for each set of **A**, **B**, and **C** and place it in the variable **L**. Print the input quantities and **L**. The file will be terminated with a trailer value of 9999 for **A**; no data value will be 9999.

4.2 Write a program for the data set of Problem 4.1 which will rearrange the values for each set of **A**, **B**, and **C** so that **A** contains the smallest value, **B** the next, and **C** the largest. In this problem, it will be necessary to interchange values between variables which will require a temporary storage variable. For instance, **A** and **B** would be interchanged by the following.

```
100     T = A
110     A = B
120     B = T
```

4.3 This program is designed to perform a check of customer charge accounts to determine all customers who have exceeded their allowable charge limit. Each record in the data file includes the following information.

      Account number
      Customer name
      Balance at beginning of month
      Total charges during month
      Total credits during month
      Credit limit

A trailer record with 9999 for the account number is included in the file. Write a program to calculate the new balance (add charges to beginning balance and subtract credits) and compare the new balance with the credit limit. For only those accounts which exceed the credit limit, print the following.

> Account number
> Customer name
> New balance
> Credit limit

4.4 This problem is to compute gross pay of employees and company totals. Each record in the input file includes the following data.

> Employee number
> Hourly pay rate
> Hours worked: Monday
>   Tuesday
>   Wednesday
>   Thursday
>   Friday

The file will be followed by a trailer record with 9999 for the employee number. For each employee, calculate regular hours, overtime hours (anything over 40 hours per week), and gross pay. Pay at the rate of 1½ times the hourly rate for all overtime hours. Accumulate regular hours, overtime hours, and gross pay for all employees. Output for each employee must include appropriate headings and the following.

> Employee number
> Regular hours
> Overtime hours
> Hourly rate
> Gross pay

After processing the last record, print a summary line for accumulated values of regular hours, overtime hours, and gross pay.

4.5 Modify Problem 4.4 to calculate overtime hours as all hours worked in excess of nine hours in any given day or 40 in the entire week; use whichever criterion yields the maximum overtime. For instance, if an employee worked 12, 8, 8, 8, and 8 hours, the regular hours would be 40 and overtime hours four (based on 44 hours for the week). However, one who worked 12, 8, 8, 8, and 6 hours would be credited with 39 regular hours and three overtime hours (based on 12 hours for Monday).

4.6 Each record of a college class file includes the following.

> Actual enrollment
> Course name (maximum of 14 letters)
> Instructor name (maximum of 12 letters)
> Course number
> Section number
> Maximum permissible enrollment
> Minimum permissible enrollment

A trailer record will be included which has a value of 9999 for the course number. A report is to be printed with one line for each class which includes the course number, section number, course name, instructor name, actual enrollment, and the word:

OVER if Actual enrollment > Maximum permissible
UNDER if Actual enrollment < Minimum permissible
Blank otherwise ok

4.7 Each record in a salesperson file includes the following information (the trailer record contains EOF for the Salesperson name).

Salesperson name
Units sold
Unit commission
Base pay
Bonus point
Bonus

Write a program to calculate the commission (units sold × unit commission) and determine the gross pay for each salesperson as follows:

$$\text{Gross pay} = \begin{cases} \text{Base pay} & \text{if commission less than base pay} \\ \text{Commission} & \text{if commission between base pay and bonus point} \\ \text{Commission} + \text{Bonus} & \text{if commission greater than bonus point} \end{cases}$$

As output, print the salesperson name, commission, and gross pay.

4.8 A credit card company assesses a monthly service charge of 1 ½ percent on the first $500. of the balance due and 1 percent on the balance due above $500. The input record for each customer includes the balance due as follows:

Customer number
Customer name
Balance due (dollars and cents)

Write a program to calculate the service charge; print all input quantities, service charges, and the total amount (balance due plus service charge). Use appropriate headings.

4.9 Using a file of registered voters as a source, write a program that will produce a listing of the names of Democrats who are married and have an annual income of at least $15,000. The registered-voter records contain the following data.

Name
Street address
City, state, Zip code
Annual income (dollars)
Party of registration: R = Republican
                        D = Democratic
                        I = Independent
Marital status: 1 = Married
                 2 = Not married

CHAPTER 5

Using Data Files

OBJECTIVES

A central focus of business data processing is the handling and manipulation of data files. This important concept is the subject of Chapter 5. Of necessity, many of the descriptions in this chapter are general in nature and do not apply specifically to a given version of Basic or a particular computer. This is attributable to the fact that particulars of file-handling methods vary considerably from computer to computer. However, the general characteristics of file handling described in this chapter are typical of those implemented in most versions of Basic. Topics about which you will learn in this chapter include the following.

1. The nature of sequential files and file processing.
2. Making files ready for use within the program with the **OPEN** statement.
3. The I/O channel concept which makes it possible to relate a file external to a program to the program.
4. Performance of file input and output operations.
5. Termination of the use of a file.

Basic Concepts of Files

INTRODUCTION   Without a doubt, the single most "nonstandard" item in all of Basic relates to file handling. This is partly due to the fact that handling of data files on disk is tied closely to the operating system of the computer being used. There is no such thing as an operating system "standard." One thing that all systems have in common, however, is that information is stored on disk in the form of files and that each file has a name for identification purposes. Many systems limit the name to six characters, but others do not. For instance, the "typical" catalog listing of Figure 2-9 shows that particular user as having four program files (**CUBE**, **PROB3**, **SALE**, and **MEAN**). In any timesharing system, a wide variety of files will be stored. For instance, a given user might have Basic program files, data files, command files, and so on. To simplify the distinction between different types of files, some systems allow the complete *filename* to include an extension which is separated from the name by a period or a slash. For instance, **MEAN.BAS** might be used to indicate a Basic program stored as a file and **MEAN.DAT** as the data file to be used with the program. The rules for selecting filenames are defined by the operating system of each computer rather than the Basic system itself. You must get this information from your installation.

Even though methods of file handling vary from system to system, certain *functions* must be performed on all systems. In most systems, the programmer is responsible for all of them.

1. Files to be used by the program must be "made ready" for use. This involves designating within the program the names of the files (which are *external* to the program) that are to be used.
2. The programmer must be able to read data from an existing file and write information to a new file.
3. When file processing is complete, any "loose ends" relating to the files must be cleaned up.

These three capabilities are illustrated in this book through an example. In all probability, the exact form of the file processing statements will be different than those of your system. Any such differences will be primarily in syntax and not in basic principle relating to the three functions described.

THE NATURE OF SEQUENTIAL FILES

A *sequential file* is one in which information must be processed in the order in which it is stored in the file. In other words, prior to processing the 20th record, the 19 preceding it must be read. As a general rule, sequential files are processed by beginning with the first record and proceeding, record by record, until the entire file has been processed. The end of a sequential file is usually marked by some type of indicator or special record to mark the end of the file. However, all examples in this book will continue to use the trailer record concept to mark the end of the data.

In contrast to sequential files, many versions of Basic also provide *random files*. A random file allows access to records in whatever order they are needed. For instance, the 20th record could be the first (or only) record processed in a given run.

A FILE PROCESSING EXAMPLE

Many example programs in the remainder of this book will use input data files and will write the results to output files. Such output files can then be printed on a separate printer. To illustrate file processing, let us consider the following minor variation of Example 3-1.

Example 5-1

The inventory control program of Example 3-1 is to be modified to process data which is stored in an input file named **INVDAT**. Each record of this file contains the book title, old inventory balance, copies received, copies sold, and copies lost. Following the last data record is the trailer with EOF in place of the book title. A new file named **INVOUT** is to be created and all calculated results written to this file.

A complete program to perform these operations using input and output files is shown in Figure 5-1.

Figure 5-1   A program to process input and output files.

```
100   REM   EXAMPLE 5-1
110   REM   PROGRAM TO UPDATE AN INVENTORY
120   REM   INPUT QUANTITIES AND NAMES ARE:
130   REM     B - BOOK NUMBER
140   REM     T$- BOOK TITLE
150   REM     O - OLD BALANCE
160   REM     R - COPIES RECEIVED
170   REM     S - COPIES SOLD
180   REM     L - COPIES LOST AND DESTROYED
190   REM   CALCULATED QUANTITIES AND NAMES ARE:
200   REM     N - NEW BALANCE
210                                         REM
1000 REM MAIN ROUTINE
1010       GOSUB 2010
1020         REM INITIALIZATION ROUTINE
1030       IF B=9999 THEN 1070
1040         GOSUB 3010
1050         GOTO 1030
1060           REM REPEATEDLY PROCESS UNTIL TRAILER DETECTED
1070       GOSUB 4010
1080         REM TERMINATION ROUTINE
1090       STOP
1100 REM END OF MAIN ROUTINE
1110                                         REM
2000 REM INITIALIZATION ROUTINE
2004       OPEN 'INVDAT' FOR INPUT AS FILE #1
2005       OPEN 'INVOUT' FOR OUTPUT AS FILE #2
2006         REM OPEN FILES
2008       PRINT 'INVENTORY PROCESSING BEGUN'
2010       PRINT #2, 'BOOK', 'BOOK', 'OLD', 'NEW'
2020       PRINT #2, 'NUMBER', 'TITLE', 'BALANCE', 'BALANCE'
2030       PRINT #2
2040       INPUT #1, B, T$, O, R, S, L
2050         REM READ FIRST RECORD
2060       RETURN
2070 REM END OF INITIALIZATION ROUTINE
2080                                         REM
3000 REM PROCESS ROUTINE
3010       LET N = O + R - S - L
3020       PRINT #2, B, T$, O, N
3030       INPUT #1, B, T$, O, R, S, L
3040       RETURN
3050 REM END OF PROCESS ROUTINE
3060                                         REM
4000 REM TERMINATION ROUTINE
4010       PRINT #2
4020       PRINT #2, 'PROCESSING COMPLETE'
4023       CLOSE #1
4024       CLOSE #2
4025         REM CLOSE FILES
4027       PRINT 'INVENTORY PROCESSING COMPLETE'
4030       RETURN
4040 REM END OF TERMINATION ROUTINE
4050                                         REM
9000 REM        ** INPUT DATA **
9010       DATA 4451, 'MODERN MATH', 453, 150, 313, 2
9020       DATA 4892, 'IBM COBOL',   512,   0, 186, 4
9030       DATA 5118, 'MICRO MENU',  518, 500, 160, 1
9040       DATA 6881, 'PDP 11 BASIC', 0, 201,   0, 0
9050       DATA 7144, 'MODERN DANCE',147, 180,  60, 1
9060       DATA 9999, 'EOF',           0,   0,   0, 0
9999   END
```

Display a message at the terminal that processing has begun. → (line 2008)

Display a message at the terminal that processing has gone to successful completion. → (line 4027)

Preparing a File for Use

Since files are stored separately and are completely independent of the program, each program must designate the files to be used. This action is called *opening* the file. Commonly encountered versions of the open statement are:

OPEN
FILE
DEFINE FILE

Examples in this book all use **OPEN**. In most systems, the open statement names the file to be processed, designates operations to be performed, and opens a "communication channel" between the program and the file. Each file to be processed in a program must be specified in an open statement. The **OPEN**s from the program of Figure 5-1 are illustrated here in Figure 5-2. In these examples, we see the data filenames which are *external* to the program (that is, they are meaningful to the operating system and not the program) being related to a channel number which is internal to the program. Thus the selected file can be referred to within the program by the internal channel number which has been defined in the **OPEN**.

Figure 5-2   The OPEN statement.

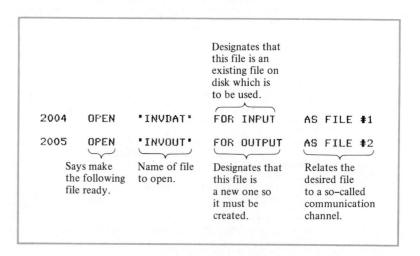

When an existing file is to be opened, the system must be told that the program will be working with an existing file. The system then searches its directory for the named file and, upon finding it, makes it ready for use. However, if there is no such file, the open operation will fail and an error will be generated. Line 2004 of Figure 5-2 designates the input data file **INVDAT** as the input file in this example.

With the "programming tools" which we have considered thus far, an open failure will automatically cause termination of the program. Thus the user should take care to ensure that the filename is spelled properly.

Most timesharing computer systems include a high-speed printer for printing program results (output). Although it is possible to set up a system to allow printing directly to the printer, that is not usually done. The reason simply relates to efficiency: the printer must serve many users. As a result, most programs create a new file (an *output* file), then write all program output to that file. Other capabilities are normally provided for automatically sending completed output files to the printer for fast and efficient printing.

The open statement of line 2005 in Figure 5-1 (and 5-2) uses the option **FOR OUTPUT**. When this statement is executed, the new filename (**INVOUT** in this case) is entered into the system directory and space is reserved for the file. At this point, the file will be empty, since nothing has been written to it. If there is already a file with this name, the existing file will be deleted and the new one created as if the old one had never existed. It is important to realize that no warning is given. A careless programmer can easily lose a file in this way.

Closing a File

All files which are opened in a program should be closed before terminating execution of the program. On some systems, this is done automatically so the programmer need not be concerned with the close function. With many others, if an output file is left open at the end of a program, then part of the output might be lost. Each open statement must specify the external file name, the channel number, and normally **INPUT** or **OUTPUT**. On the other hand, most systems which require an explicit closing operation, require only that the associated channel number be specified. Thus the close statements in lines 4023 and 4025 of Figure 5-1 contain much less detail than the corresponding opens in lines 2004 and 2005.

File Input and Output

The program from which this example was taken (Figure 3-2) includes the following **READ** statement.

```
3030      READ B, T$, O, R, S, L
```

Each time this statement is executed, the next "record" will be read from the data pool. The sequential file read statement works in essentially the same way. Each time the read is executed, the next record will be read from the data file. The commonly encountered Basic keywords used to read from a sequential file are:

READ
INPUT
GET

However, in order for the system to know which file (a program may have one or more input files open) is indicated, the corresponding channel number must be specified. When writing to a file, exactly the same is required. Thus the keyword designating the input or output is followed by the channel number, and then the list of variables. A detailed explanation of the **INPUT** is shown in Figure 5-3.

Figure 5-3   Using the channel number for I/O operations.

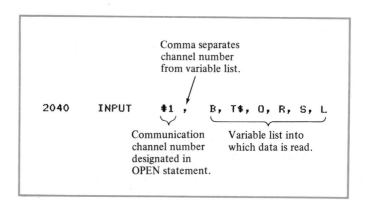

READING FROM AN EXISTING FILE Needless to say, whenever we must process data from an input file, we must know exactly what data is stored. For instance, the problem definition for Example 5-1 states exactly what fields are included in the file. Then the input list must correspond to the data read. This is identical to the concept of processing from the **DATA** statements in previous modules. Each time the **INPUT** statement is executed, the next record is accessed. If the input process is repeated (with no end-of-file test), an error condition will occur when an attempt is made to read beyond the last record.

PRINTING TO A NEW FILE Like the input statement, the keywords for file output (and the exact statement format) vary from system to system. Commonly encountered keywords for sequential file output are:

WRITE
PRINT
PUT

Following is the **PRINT** statement from the program of Figure 5-1.

```
3020    PRINT #2, B, T$, O, N
```

In general form, the **PRINT** is identical to the **INPUT** in that the list is preceded by the channel number to which the output file has been associated. Each time the **PRINT** statement is executed, a new line will be written to the output file.

Some systems provide wide flexibility in performing file output; others are more restrictive. In some, the output is written to a so-called "teletypewriter" file which takes on an appearance similar to that of the **DATA** statement but without the keyword **DATA**. In others, it is written to the file exactly as if it had been written directly to the terminal. In such systems, any output list which is allowable with the **PRINT** statement can be used with the **PRINT #** form of the statement. For instance,

```
800    PRINT "LENGTH:", L, "WIDTH:", W
```

will cause the output to be displayed on the terminal. The form

```
810    PRINT #3, "LENGTH:", L, "WIDTH:", W
```

will cause the same line of output to be written to the file associated with channel 3.

EXERCISE

5.1 Following is the skeleton of a program which a student prepared.

```
100   REM MAIN PROGRAM
110        GOSUB 1000
120        IF A=0 THEN 150
130          GOSUB 2010
140          GOTO 120
150        GOSUB 3010
160        STOP
1000 REM INITIAL ROUTINE
1010       OPEN "TESTDA" FOR INPUT AS FILE #2
1020       OPEN "TESTOU" FOR OUTPUT AS FILE #3
1030       INPUT #2, A,B
1040       RETURN
2000 REM PROCESSING ROUTINE
2010       C = 2*A + 2*B
2020       D = A*B
2030       PRINT #2, A,B,C,D
2040       INPUT #2, A,B
2050       RETURN
3000 REM TERMINAL ROUTINE
3010       CLOSE #2
3020       CLOSE #3
3030       RETURN
9999    END
```

The results of running the program were very strange—the file **TESTOU** did not contain anything. What is wrong with the program?

ANSWER TO PRECEDING EXERCISE

5.1 The output file is opened on channel 3; the **PRINT** statement prints to channel 2.

PROGRAMMING PROBLEMS

Additional file processing programming problems can be selected from Chapter 4.

5.1 An automobile rental agency charges for its car rentals on the following basis:

$14.95 per day plus
$0.14 per mile plus
a variable insurance charge

Each record in the file **AUTOS** includes the following fields.

discount code
    1–10% discount on per day charge
    2–12% discount on per day and mileage charges
    other—no discount
number of days rented
total mileage
insurance charge

Write a program to process this file and compute the charge for each rental. Each detail line must include the input data and the charge. At the end of the report, print this total, the number of rentals processed, and the number of discounts of each type. The file will be ended by a trailer record with zero for the number of days.

5.2 A teacher maintains the data file **EXAM** with each record containing the following information.

Student name
Exam 1 score
Exam 2 score
Final exam score

Write a program to calculate the average score for each student using the formula:

Average = (Exam 1 + Exam 2 + 2 × Final exam)/4

Students are allowed to have the result of either Exam 1 or Exam 2 ignored if the score is less than 50. If there is such a case, then delete the score from the calculation and divide by 3. To simplify the program, assume that no student will have more than one score less than 50.

Output for each student must include the student name and average. Also calculate the average scores for each of the three exams and print them at the end of the report. A trailer record will be included with EOF in place of the student name.

CHAPTER 6

Report Generation

POSITIONING FIELDS ON THE OUTPUT LINE
Use of the Semicolon
The **TAB** Function

EDIT MASKS
The Concept of the Edit Mask
Simple Form of the **PRINT-USING**
Edit Images for String Fields

EDITING A COMPLETE LINE
Format Planning
A Program Segment

MORE ON THE **PRINT-USING**
Inserting Commas in Numeric Quantities
Floating Dollar Sign
The Asterisk Fill

FUNCTIONS
The Concept of the Function
The **DATE$** and **TIME$** Functions
Breaking a String Into Parts
The **LEN** Function

CONCATENATION OF STRINGS
Editing a Social Security Number

A TYPICAL REPORT
Problem Statement
Program Planning—Example 6-2
A Program—Example 6-2

PRINTER PAGE CONTROL
Planning for Output
Program Planning—Example 6-3
A Program—Example 6-3

OBJECTIVES

The primary focus to this point has been on learning the basics of programming; now it is time to concentrate on a bit more detail. From this chapter, you will learn the essentials of putting your program output together in a good, easy-to-read form. Broad topics in this chapter include the following.

1. Line formatting, which means arranging output on a line according to defined requirements, is discussed. This includes using edit masks to define the output appearance of numeric fields, which allows us to insert such things as extra punctuation and dollar signs in our numeric output. The key to these capabilities is the **PRINT-USING** statement.
2. The use of functions in a program is illustrated. Those described in this chapter include:

DATE$ TAB
LEN   TIME$
LEFT$
MID$
RIGHT$

The latter three allow us to break strings into parts for needed string manipulations.
3. The practical aspects of printing a readable business report is illustrated with two examples. Controlling output in progressing from page to page is included in an example.

Positioning Fields on the Output Line

USE OF THE SEMICOLON   Up to this point, not very much attention has been given to details of formatting program output. Whenever data is printed using the **PRINT** statement, the variables in the list have been separated by commas. This has caused each data field to be printed beginning with the next "tab" position on the printed line. It is possible to override the automatic tabbing operation by separating the variables in the list by semicolons. An example **PRINT** statement and its corresponding output are shown in Figure 6-1. Because of the manner in which printing works, the semicolon provides us with an interesting (and useful) capability. That is, a semicolon after the last field will cause the cursor (or printing element) to maintain its current position for the next **PRINT**. Thus the following **PRINT** statements produce exactly the same output as that of Figure 6-1.

```
600    PRINT A;              700    PRINT A;B;
610    PRINT B;C             710    PRINT C
```

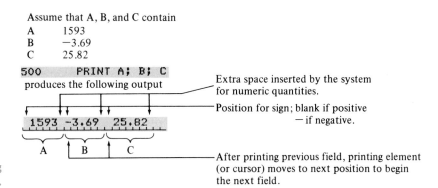

Figure 6-1   Printing using the semicolon.

THE TAB FUNCTION

Positioning of output is improved by combining use of the semicolon with the **TAB** function. The typical terminal has 80 printing positions or columns (some have 132). The **TAB** function can be used to specify the column at which printing is to begin. For instance, the programmer could use the **TAB** to cause a summary line to begin in column 30. However, to use the **TAB**, the programmer must know how the columns are numbered. In some Basic systems, the first column is numbered 0 (followed by 1 and so on). In others, the first column is numbered 1. Whichever technique is used, the **TAB** designates the column in which printing is to begin. Two sets of examples illustrate this in Figure 6-2.

Figure 6-2   Using the TAB function. (a) First column numbered 0. (b) First column numbered 1.

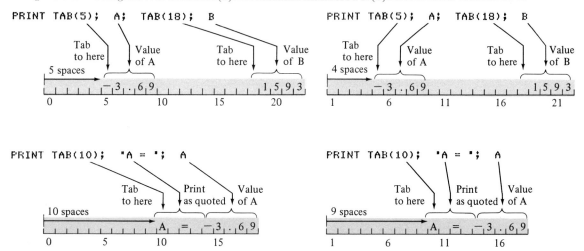

Note: Some systems do not require the semi–colon following the TAB.

(a)   (b)

EXERCISE

6.1 The following variables in a program have the values indicated.

$$X = -381 \qquad Y = 49.768 \qquad Z = 1.934$$

Show how they will be printed by each of the following **PRINT** statements. Take into account whether your system numbers the first column 0 or 1.

a. 100   PRINT X;Y;Z
b. 200   PRINT TAB(6);X;TAB(14)Z
c. 300   PRINT "X IS: ";X;TAB(15);"Z IS: ";Z

Edit Masks

THE CONCEPT OF THE EDIT MASK Although the semicolon and **TAB** function are useful in letting us position output data, they do leave much to be desired. Perhaps the most obvious shortcoming that we have experienced has been our inability to control decimal positioning and alignment in a column of numbers. For example, if a program is to print dollar-and-cents amounts, the following column of numbers on the right would be far better than that on the left.

```
257.33          257.33
16.87            16.87
482.6           482.60
31               31.00
1.732             1.73
```

Our output has been that shown on the left; let us now consider how to get that shown on the right. To begin with, whenever we are writing a program, we will know (or had better find out) the nature of the data. For instance, a program to calculate gross pay for employees will be dealing in the hundreds, or perhaps thousands, of dollars for each employee—certainly not millions. Thus usually we will have a good idea of the general size of the results we expect from a program. With this information, we can then plan the *format* of our output in order to obtain an appealing, easy-to-read end result. Let us assume, for example, that we wish to print a dollar-and-cent quantity which will range from zero to 999.99 (refer to the preceding examples). What we really need is a means to describe the exact form in which the number is to be printed out. In programming, such a device is commonly referred to as an *edit mask* or a *format image*. For instance, the format image in which we are interested would appear as shown in Figure 6-3. To produce this form in an output line, we would have to use a string field mask which the system can utilize as a "model" in deciding just how to arrange things. In forming the mask, the pound sign (#) is used to indicate a position into which an output digit must be placed. Within the mask, the decimal point must be placed exactly where we want it printed within the output field. Thus the edit mask for our dollar-and-cents amount would appear as shown in Figure 6-4.

Figure 6-3   Format image for output field.

Figure 6-4   A simple edit mask.

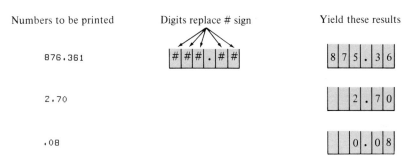

SIMPLE FORM OF THE PRINT-USING   Special formatting of output via edit masks is done with the **PRINT-USING** statement. In essence, this statement says: "**PRINT** the indicated quantities **USING** a designated image." Let us assume that the variable **A** contains the dollar-and-cent amount in which we are interested. Then statement 600 of Figure 6-5 would print it in the way to which we have become accustomed in Basic. However, the **PRINT-USING** statement of line 700 directs the system to "use" the image following the keyword **USING** in determining output format. The output of this statement would be exactly as shown in Figure 6-4.

Figure 6-5   The PRINT-USING statement.

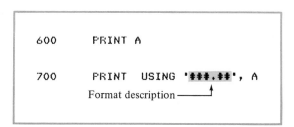

If needed, two or more fields can be printed with a **PRINT-USING** merely by appropriately expanding the mask as needed. This is illustrated in Figure 6-6.

The following commentary relates to the **PRINT-USING**.

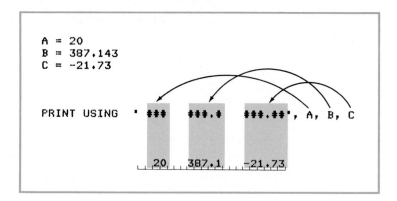

Figure 6-6   Printing several fields.

1. Pound signs (#) to the left of the decimal for which there are no digits are replaced with blanks. For instance, the amount 23.78 would be edited into the image ####.## as ƀƀ23.78.
2. If the image includes a pound sign to the left of the decimal point, then a zero will be placed there whenever the output field is less than 1.0. For example, .23 would be edited into the image of item 1 above as ƀƀƀ0.23.
3. If the variable value to be printed contains more digits to the right of the decimal than the space provided, the system automatically rounds off. For instance, 123.673, 123.675, and 123.679 would be edited into the mask of item 1 as 123.67, 123.68, and 123.68 respectively.
4. If the variable value to be printed is larger than provided for by the edit mask, then an error results. Most systems will print the actual value but ignore the edit mask.
5. There must be one numeric mask for each variable in the list. Spaces within the overall mask are included in the output line as illustrated in Figure 6-6. In other words, the mask is truly an image of the output line.

EDIT IMAGES FOR STRING FIELDS Although string fields do not present the same type of problem that numeric fields do, edit images are essential for overall line formatting. To illustrate editing of string fields, let us assume that we have a description field **D$** which will never be more than nine positions. Although exact forms vary from one version of Basic to another, most have the following in common.

1. One position must be reserved in the edit mask for each character in the string field to be printed.
2. If the string field to be printed is shorter than the edit mask, then it will be positioned to the left (*left-aligned*) within the mask area and the right-most positions filled with spaces.
3. If the string field to be printed is longer than the edit mask, then the right-most characters in excess of the edit mask length will be discarded.

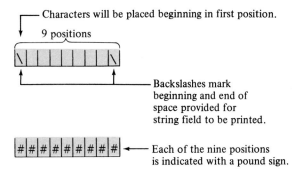

Characters will be placed beginning in first position.

9 positions

Backslashes mark beginning and end of space provided for string field to be printed.

Each of the nine positions is indicated with a pound sign.

Examples

String data to be printed	Printed results
TEXTBOOKS	TEXTBOOKS
TEXT-BOOK	TEXT-BOOK
TEXT BOOK	TEXT BOOK
BOOK	BOOK
SEVERAL BOOKS	SEVERAL B

Figure 6-7 A string field edit mask.

The two most common methods for indicating string fields are shown in Figure 6-7. The first uses the backslash character to mark the beginning position and the ending position of the field. The other technique uses the pound sign in exactly the same way it is used with numeric fields. For both cases, the results of editing will be as shown.

EXERCISE

6.2 What will be printed by the statement

```
500     PRINT USING "#####.#", C
```

for the following values of C (use ƀ to indicate a blank position)?

12345.6
12345.
682.11
12.9
0.68

Editing a Complete Line

FORMAT PLANNING The real power and flexibility of the **PRINT-USING** derive from its ability to designate a wide variety of formats for numerous fields on a line. To illustrate this concept, let us consider the following example.

Example 6-1

In an employee payroll processing system, a detail report is required for each employee. Design the heading and detail lines for the following fields.

Employee number (assume always 4 digits—treat as string)
Employee name (maximum of 16 positions)
Regular pay (maximum of 999.99)
Overtime pay (maximum of 999.99)
Total pay (maximum of 1999.98)

In an actual programming environment, one of the important tasks is laying out how the results are to be printed. This is often referred to as *format planning* and is a painstaking job regardless of which programming language is being used. It involves such tasks as laying out column headings which are descriptive and are aligned above the columns, determining spacing between various fields, and defining edit images to be used for output quantities. To accomplish this with a minimum of effort requires that some type of a layout form be used such as that shown in Figure 6-8(a). Here we see that the spacing has been coordinated between fields of both the heading lines and the detail line (actual data which is processed) to give a neat, balanced form.

A PROGRAM SEGMENT In the **PRINT-USING** forms of Figures 6-5 and 6-6, the edit mask is included within the print statement. In addition to this form, most versions of Basic allow the mask to be specified separately. The designation of a string variable or of a special edit mask statement containing the mask are two commonly encountered forms, that is,

PRINT USING *<string variable>*, *<output list>*

or

PRINT USING *<line number>*, *<output list>*

Both of these forms are illustrated in the program segments of Figure 6-9 (page 106). Examples in this book use the first form (string variable). You

Figure 6-8   Example 6-1. (a) Layout form for printed output (b) Sample output.

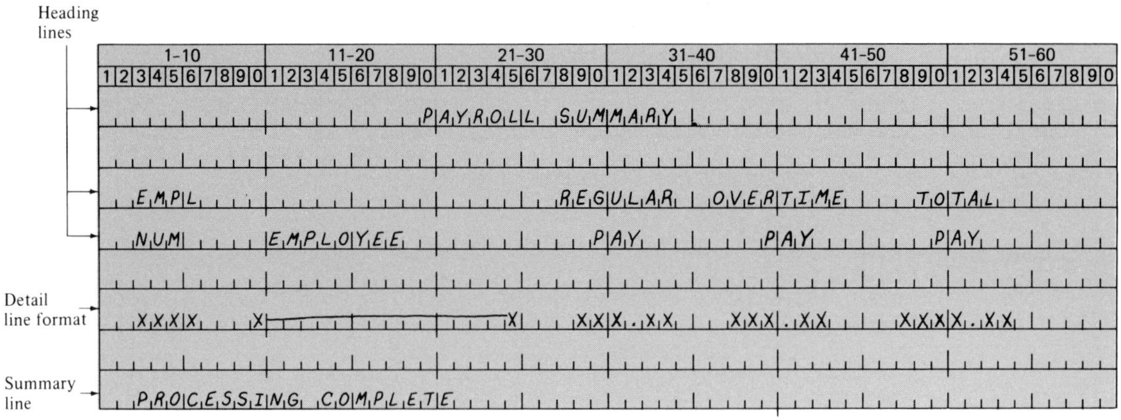

(a)

```
                   PAYROLL  SUMMARY

       EMPL.                  REGULAR  OVERTIME    TOTAL
       NUM      EMPLOYEE        PAY      PAY        PAY

       0113     ALFRED  JONES   378.53   82.01    460.54
       0162     NANCY  MACK     412.61    0.00    412.61
       0261     WILLIAM PIERCE  308.08  105.16    413.24
       0423     NEIL  COLE      488.12    0.00    488.12

       PROCESSING  COMPLETE
```

(b)

should check to see which form your system uses, and if it is different, keep the difference in mind when studying other examples in this book.

In Figure 6-9(a), we see the exact line image for the detail line defined in the string variable **D$**. The **PRINT** statement of line 3530 then specifies this mark with:

USING D$

Correspondingly, in Figure 6-9(b), the system knows that line 2040 contains an edit mask because of the colon (:). The **PRINT** statement of line 3530 specifies this mask through the following portion of the statement.

USING 2040

The manner in which both of these statements function is illustrated by Figure 6-10.

Figure 6-9   Two forms of the PRINT-USING.

```
2000 REM DEFINE OUTPUT FORMATS
2010      H1$ = "                        PAYROLL  SUMMARY"
2020      H2$ = "   EMPL                      REGULAR  OVERTIME    TOTAL"
2030      H3$ = "   NUM      EMPLOYEE           PAY      PAY       PAY"
2040      D$  = "  \  \   \                 \   ###.##   ###.##   ####.##"
2050      S$  = "  PROCESSING COMPLETE"
2060 REM PRINT REPORT HEADINGS
2070      PRINT USING H1$
2080      PRINT
2090      PRINT USING H2$
2100      PRINT USING H3$
2110      PRINT
  .
  .
  .
3530      PRINT USING D$, N$,E$,P1,P2,P9
  .
  .
  .
4030      PRINT USING S$
```

(a)

```
2000 REM DEFINE OUTPUT FORMATS
2010      :                        PAYROLL  SUMMARY
2020      :   EMPL                      REGULAR  OVERTIME    TOTAL
2030      :   NUM      EMPLOYEE           PAY      PAY       PAY
2040      :   ####   ################   ###.##   ###.##   ####.##
2050      :   PROCESSING COMPLETE
2060 REM PRINT REPORT HEADINGS
2070      PRINT USING 2010
2080      PRINT
2090      PRINT USING 2020
2100      PRINT USING 2030
2110      PRINT
  .
  .
  .
3530      PRINT USING 2040, N$,E$,P1,P2,P9
  .
  .
  .
4030      PRINT USING 2050
```

(b)

Figure 6-10   Printing under control of an edit mask.

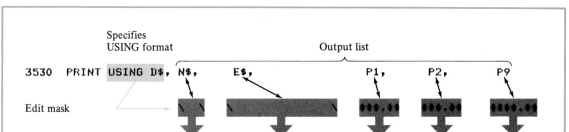

The **PRINT-USING** statement of line 3530 uses this same approach: that is, the edit mask for the entire line is defined as a separate field (**D$**). Figure 6-10 illustrates how Basic handles this statement. When the **PRINT-USING** is executed, an image of the mask is used and fields in the output list are matched with individual edit images within the designated string. It is important to realize that the string field containing the edit image (**D$** in this case) or the statement 2040 mask form is *not* destroyed by the **PRINT** statement. Thus it is not necessary to execute statement 2040 each time the **PRINT-USING** is executed.

Referring again to Figure 6-9, the headings are printed by the corresponding statements of lines 2070, 2090, and 2100. Needless to say, these **PRINT** statements (and the corresponding statements 2010–2030) could have been replaced by Figure 6-11. As a general rule, this form is somewhat clumsier and errors in alignment are more easily made than when laying them all out as with statements 2010–2050 of Figure 6-9.

Figure 6-11   Alternate forms to print headings

```
2070    PRINT TAB(19);"PAYROLL SUMMARY"
2090    PRINT "   EMPL  ;TAB(27);:"REGULAR   OVERTIME    TOTAL"
2100    PRINT "   NUM      EMPLOYEE";TAB(29);;"PAY";TAB(49);:"PAY"
```

EXERCISE

6.3 The following statements appear in a program.

```
200    L$ = "#####ØØ####.####ØØ\ØØØØØØØØØØ\ØØØ##"
400    PRINT USING L$, A, B, C$, D
```

Note: The character Ø is included only to indicate spacing.

Assuming the following values for the list variables, sketch the output line as it would be printed (use the Ø to indicate a blank position).

A = 37
B = 256.8338
C$ = EXAMPLE D
D = 2

More on the PRINT-USING

Reports generated in a business data processing environment typically require considerable manipulation of numeric quantities. For example, commas are inserted for large values or dollar signs may be required. The **PRINT-USING** provides for these needs.

INSERTING COMMAS IN NUMERIC QUANTITIES For numeric quantities which are 1000 or greater, it is convenient to insert commas to improve readability. That is, 13865 and 5681372 are normally written as 13,865 and 5,681,372 respectively. Many versions of Basic provide for the insertion of commas every 3 digits to the left of the decimal point (if any). For this, the programmer need insert but *one* comma to the left of the decimal point in the edit image. Figure 6-12 illustrates this concept; remember, only one comma in each individual mask is required to trigger the automatic insertion of commas as needed by the number. However, notice that for numbers which reach one million or more, the final output will include *two* commas even though the mask only contains one. Thus it is necessary to include an extra # character to accommodate it.

Figure 6-12
Inserting commas in numeric fields.

EXERCISE

6.4 This question relates to including a dollar sign with a numeric quantity (the topic of the next section). One way of achieving this is illustrated by the following.

```
PRINT "$";

PRINT USING "###.##",A
```

Show how the printed output would look with values for **A** of 123.45, 28.91, and 1.67. What is wrong with it?

FLOATING DOLLAR SIGN Some versions of Basic include a special provision for editing numeric fields to include a floating dollar sign (Exercise 6.4). This is achieved by preceding the edit mask with *two* dollar signs ($$). The result will be a single dollar sign preceding the first significant digit of the field (see Figure 6-13). We should note that one of the dollar signs will be replaced with a digit and the other is printed. For instance, in the first example, the pound sign to the left of the comma and one of the dollar signs serve as digit positions.

Figure 6-13
Including a dollar sign

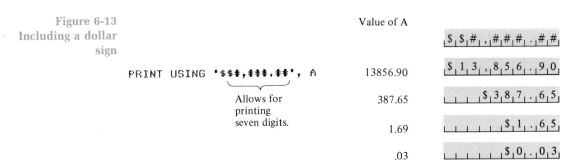

THE ASTERISK FILL When printing checks, it is common practice to replace leading zeros with asterisks to prevent overzealous people from typing in a few extra digits. This is called *asterisk check protection* and is done in Basic by using two consecutive asterisks in the edit mask as illustrated in Figure 6-14. Notice that one *or* both of the asterisk characters will be replaced by digits if the field is large enough.

Figure 6-14 The asterisk fill.

Value of A

```
PRINT USING "**#,###.##",A      12345.69
```

Allows for printing five digits.

6580.30

25.87

6.00

EXERCISES

6.5 Using the edit mask

***,###.##

how would each of the following be printed?

62534.21
1249.6
0.01698
7891507

6.6 Repeat Problem 6.5 for the following edit mask.

$$####,###.##

Functions

THE CONCEPT OF THE FUNCTION In programming, there exist many operations which are general in nature and commonly performed. These include such basic operations as calculating a square root or taking the absolute value of a number. Since Basic includes no specific arithmetic operators beyond +, −, *, /, and ** (^), these quantities must be obtained by programming means. Fortunately for the user, many of the common operations are "preprogrammed" and available as *functions*. For instance, the following statement 200 calculates the square root of **X** and places the value in **Y**.

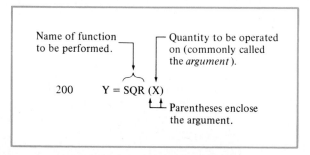

Name of function to be performed.

Quantity to be operated on (commonly called the *argument*).

200   Y = SQR (X)

Parentheses enclose the argument.

During execution of the program, the computer will:

1. Obtain the value for the argument (**X** in this case).
2. Give this value to a special routine named **SQR** (included as part of the Basic system), which will calculate the square root of **X**.
3. Assign the result to **Y** by virtue of the **LET** statement.

Basic includes a wide variety of different types of functions. We shall use several of them here in order to enhance our reports.

THE DATE$ AND TIME$ FUNCTIONS Heading lines which are printed at the top of the computer-generated page tell which report is printed. In addition to the name of the report, there is also other information that should be printed. For instance, most reports include a date, which may be the date the report was run, or even some past or future date. A budget status report, for example, might be printed on June 5 for all transactions through June 1. In addition to the date, it is sometimes convenient to know the time of day the report was run. Was the run made at the start of the day or at the end after the day's activities were recorded? For this need, many versions of Basic include two functions: **DATE$** to give a date and **TIME$** to give the time. Their use is illustrated in Figure 6-15. There are many different versions of this function. Some do not include a dollar sign on the name (for instance, **DATE**) and others use an argument. Also, some give both the date and time when asked for the date. If your system has one or both of these functions, then use them. The dating of program output is a common and useful practice.

Figure 6-15 The DATE$ and TIME$ functions.

```
200      PRINT "SUMMARY REPORT DATED "; DATE$
300      PRINT "UPDATE COMPLETED AT "; TIME$; DATE$
```

(a)

```
SUMMARY REPORT DATED 21-FEB-84
UPDATE COMPLETED AT 13:29    21-FEB-84
```

(b)

BREAKING A STRING INTO PARTS Programmers in business data processing commonly deal with Social Security numbers. A program might include the string variable **S$** for this purpose. When the number is read into the computer and stored, it commonly consists of simply the 9 digits without punctuation. A number such as 532242005 is adequate for internal operations in the computer but leaves something to be desired for printed reports. As we know, Social Security numbers are grouped by the first 3, the next 2, and the last 4 digits. In other words, the preceding number would be 532–24–2005. Basic provides three functions to break strings into "substrings"; **LEFT$**, **MID$**, and **RIGHT$**. These are illustrated in Figure 6-16. Unfortunately the **RIGHT$** function does not work the

Figure 6-16   Substring functions.

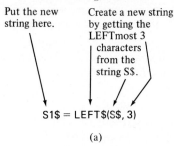

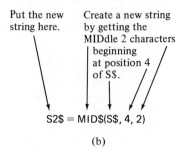

(a)   (b)

Obtaining the right portion is commonly done in two different ways depending on the version of Basic. Systems which allow the forms on the right provide the programmer with greater versatility.

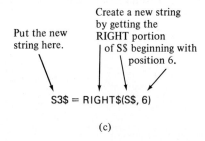

(c)

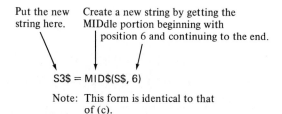

Note: This form is identical to that
         of (c).

or

Put the new   Create a new string
string here.   by getting the
                         RIGHTmost 4 characters
                                               from S$.

S3$ = RIGHT$(S$, 4)

(d)

same way in all versions of Basic. In the example of the **RIGHT$** function in Figure 6-16(c), it is important to note the difference between the **LEFT$** and **RIGHT$** functions. The **LEFT$** says "how many" characters; the **RIGHT$** says from "a given point on." Examples in this book use the **RIGHT$** as illustrated in Figure 6-16(c).

By use of these functions, the previous value of **S$** (532242005) will be printed as shown by both of the statements that follow.

```
532-24-2005

PRINT S1$; "-"; S2$; "-"; S3$

PRINT LEFT$(S$,3); "-"; MID$(S$,4,2); "-"; RIGHT$(S$,6)
```

Note that the function may be used directly in the **PRINT** statement itself yielding exactly the same output as the **S1$**, **S2$**, **S3$** form.

THE LEN FUNCTION Sometimes we will be working with a string quantity whose length we wish to confirm. For instance, if a Social Security number is read from a file, we may need to check it to be certain that its length is 9. This is done with the **LEN** function, which returns the length of a string field. Its use is illustrated by the following two examples.

```
500      Y=LEN(S$)

600      IF LEN(S$) <> 9 THEN 604 ELSE 631
```

In statement 500, the length (number of characters) in **S$** will be placed in the numeric variable **Y**. For instance, if **S$** contains a valid Social Security number, then **Y** will be given a value of 9. Statement 600 illustrates using the length function as part of an **IF**.

EXERCISE

6.7 If the value stored in **A$** is ABC123456, then what will be in **B$** after each of the following statements?
a. `B$ = LEFT$(A$,2)`
b. `B$ = MID$(A$,1,2)`
c. `B$ = MID$(A$,3,5)`
d. `B$ = RIGHT$(A$,7)`
e. `B$ = RIGHT$(A$,9)`
f. `B$ = MID$(A$,9,1)`
g. `B$ = RIGHT$(A$,12)`

Concatenation of Strings

EDITING A SOCIAL SECURITY NUMBER A very common operation when working with string fields is to combine two or more to form another. This is called *concatenation* and is done with a **LET** statement and the operator +. For instance, in a preceding section, the Social Security number was broken into three parts **S1$**, **S2$**, and **S3$**, and then printed with inserted hyphens. Let us assume that we have a program in which the Social Security number is printed in a number of different places. In such a case, it would be convenient to build a copy of it which includes the hyphens. This is easily done by either of the following statements:

```
S9$ = S1$ + "-" + S2$ + "-" + S3$
S9$ = LEFT$(S$,3) + "-" + MID$(S$,4,2) + "-" + RIGHT$(S$,6)
```

Of course, the first example assumes that **S1$**, **S2$**, and **S3$** have been previously extracted from **S$**. Thus if **S$** contained 532242005 (length of 9), the statement: `PRINT S9$`

would print: `532-24-2005`

Note that the string components have been "tacked on" to one another in the order indicated by the **LET**. Of course, the length of the result (**S9$** in this case) is the sum of the lengths of the components (11).

A Typical Report

PROBLEM STATEMENT In the preceding sections of this module, we have studied a variety of techniques for use in generating reports. Let us now consider an expansion of the inventory example which incorporates most of these methods.

Example 6-2

Each record in a bookstore inventory file includes the following information.

Field	Maximum Length or Value
Stock number	69999 (99999 used for trailer)
Book title	27 characters
Author	11 characters
Unit cost	39.99 (maximum value)
Reorder level	4 digits
Beginning on hand	4 digits
Quantity sold	3 digits
Quantity received	3 digits
Quantity on order	3 digits
Type code	1 character
	H—hardcover
	P—paperback

The purpose of this report is to summarize information on books which have dropped below designated stock levels as follows:

(Updated copies on hand + Quantity on order) < Reorder level

In addition to printing detailed information for each of these books, it will be necessary to calculate totals. The bookstore manager wishes to know the total number of copies on hand and the total inventory value (number of copies times unit cost) for each of the two categories: hardcover and paperback. A monthly report summary is to be printed with the following output:

1. A report heading with the date.
2. Appropriate column headings describing output quantities.
3. For each input record falling below the reorder level, one detail line containing:

   Book stock number
   Author
   Title
   Updated number of copies on hand
   Inventory value (copies on hand × book price)
   HARD or PAPER to identify book as hardcover or paperback

4. One summary line for each type of book (hard and paper) with the total number of copies and total inventory value.

The output format is defined in Figure 6-17, which includes both a print chart and a sample output.

Figure 6-17   (a) Print specifications for Example 6-2. (b) Sample output for Example 6-2.

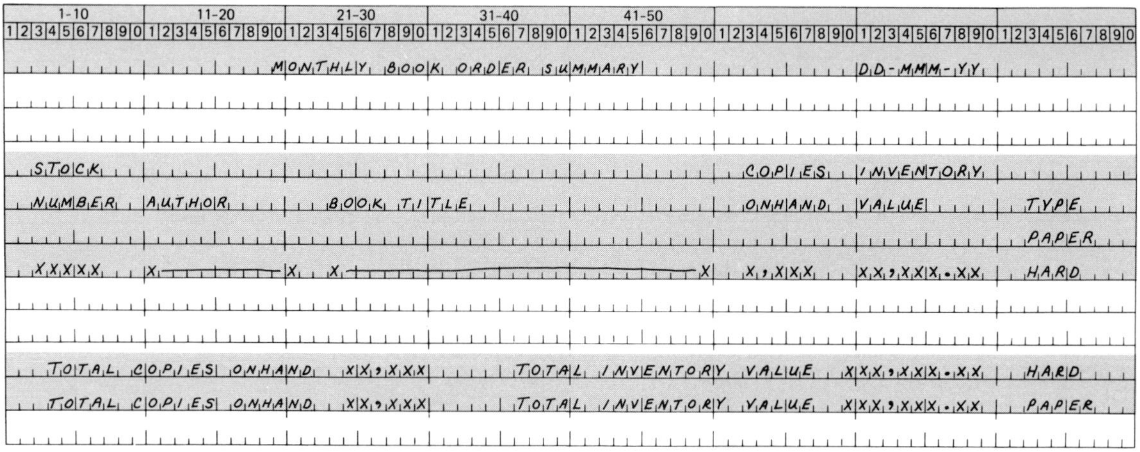

(a)

```
                    MONTHLY BOOK ORDER SUMMARY


        STOCK                                          COPIES      INVENTORY
        NUMBER  AUTHOR       BOOK TITLE                ONHAND      VALUE           TYPE

        11573   HARCOURT     PUBLISHERS HANDBOOK          352      5,244.80        HARD
        21446   ALLAN        CELESTIAL NAVIGATION         125        812.50        PAPER
        23891   PRICE        THE QUANDARY OF 162        1,053     10,519.47        HARD
        44812   MC DANIEL    THE EFFECT OF THE INEVITABLE CURRENT  1,201  10,748.95  HARD
        47736   BYRD         LIFE IN THE POLAR REGIONS     85        335.75        PAPER


                 TOTAL COPIES ONHAND    2,706    TOTAL INVENTORY VALUE   26,513.22   HARD
                 TOTAL COPIES ONHAND      210    TOTAL INVENTORY VALUE    1,148.25   PAPER
```

(b)

PROGRAM
PLANNING—
EXAMPLE 6-2

Modularization of this problem will be taken one step further than that of previous examples. That is, in addition to the three basic modules—initialization, process, and termination—we shall include two others. They will be a separate routine for printing headings and a routine to process records that fall below the reorder level. These are illustrated by the hierarchy chart of Figure 6-18. We can think of this chart as comprising two levels: The first or *A* level consists of initialization, process, and termination. The second of *B* level consists of those modules called by the first level—Heading and Process Record. As we shall see in the example which follows, this carefully planned modularization is relatively easy to modify when the needs of the problem are expanded. Furthermore, a program consisting of several pages and including modules called by other modules which are in turn called by still other modules can become very cumbersome. However, if the modules have been identified and placed systematically using hierarchy charts, this problem can be reduced significantly. Referring to Figure 6-18, modules called by *A*-level modules are identified as *B*-level modules, and so on. As we shall see, these module identifications are reflected in the program.

The logic of this problem is illustrated by the set of flowcharts in Figure 6-19. We see that the updated inventory balance is calculated for each book

Figure 6-18
Hierarchy chart for
Example 6-2.

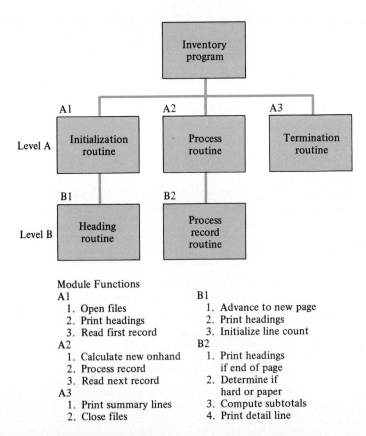

Module Functions

A1	B1
1. Open files	1. Advance to new page
2. Print headings	2. Print headings
3. Read first record	3. Initialize line count
A2	B2
1. Calculate new onhand	1. Print headings
2. Process record	if end of page
3. Read next record	2. Determine if
A3	hard or paper
1. Print summary lines	3. Compute subtotals
2. Close files	4. Print detail line

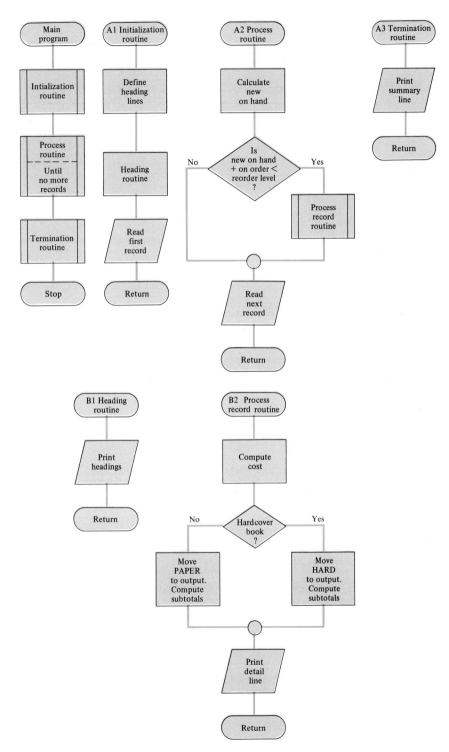

Figure 6-19
Flowcharts for
Example 6-2.

record read. However, that record is processed only if the reorder criterion is met. In the process record routine, separate calculations are performed, depending upon whether the book is hardcover or paperback.

A PROGRAM— The program of Figure 6-20 corresponds exactly to the flowcharts in Figure
EXAMPLE 6-2 6-19. Note that the main program is included first, followed by the first-level routines, which are, in turn, followed by the second-level routines. The following exercises bring out some other important features of this program.

Figure 6-20   A program—Example 6-2.

```
100 REM EXAMPLE 6-2
110 REM    BOOK ORDER SUMMARY REPORT
120 REM    THIS PROGRAM PRINTS A STATUS SUMMARY REPORT FOR ALL BOOKS FOR WHICH THE
130 REM    NEW BALANCE PLUS ON-ORDER QUANTITY FALLS BELOW THE REORDER LEVEL.
140 REM    INPUT QUANTITIES ARE:
150 REM       S$    STOCK NUMBER
160 REM       B$    BOOK TITLE
170 REM       A$    AUTHOR
180 REM       C     COST
190 REM       L     REORDER LEVEL
200 REM       O     OLD INVENTORY BALANCE
210 REM       S     SOLD
220 REM       R     RECEIVED
230 REM       R1    ON ORDER
240 REM       T$    TYPE
250 REM    CALCULATED QUANTITIES ARE:
260 REM       N     NEW BALANCE
270 REM       V     INVENTORY VALUE
280 REM    ACCUMULATED TOTALS
290 REM       B1    INVENTORY BALANCE (HARD COVER)
300 REM       V1    INVENTORY VALUE (HARD COVER)
310 REM       B2    INVENTORY BALANCE (PAPERBACK)
320 REM       V2    INVENTORY VALUE (HARD COVER)
330                                     REM
1000 REM MAIN PROGRAM
1010 REM
1020       GOSUB  2010
1030          REM INITIALIZATION ROUTINE
1040       IF S$="99999" THEN 1050
1041          GOSUB  3010
1042          GOTO 1040
1043             REM PROCESS ROUTINE UNTIL NO MORE DATA
1050       GOSUB  4010
1060          REM TERMINATION ROUTINE
1070       STOP
1080          REM END PROGRAM
1090                                     REM
2000 REM **A1**    INITIALIZATION ROUTINE
2010       H1$="                    MONTHLY BOOK ORDER SUMMARY                     \           \"
2020       H2$=" STOCK                                                  COPIES   INVENTORY"
2030       H3$=" NUMBER   AUTHOR         BOOK TITLE                     ONHAND   VALUE       TYPE"
2040       D$ ="   \   \    \                                    \    #,###   ##,###.##   \   \"
2050       T1$="    TOTAL COPIES ONHAND   ##,###      TOTAL INVENTORY VALUE   ###,###.##"
2060          REM   DEFINE OUTPUT LINE FORMATS
2061                                     REM
2070       OPEN "INVEN" FOR INPUT AS FILE #1
2080       GOSUB 6010
2090          REM PERFORM HEADING ROUTINE
2100       INPUT #1, N$,B$,A$,C,L,O,S,R,R1,T$
2110       RETURN
2120 REM END OF INITIALIZATION ROUTINE
2130                                     REM
```

Figure 6-20 (Continued)

```
3000 REM **A2**  PROCESS ROUTINE
3010      N = 0 + R - S
3020      IF N + R1 >= L THEN 3130
3021         GOSUB 7010
3022           REM  PROCESS RECORD ROUTINE IF COMPUTED VALUE IS BELOW REORDER LEVEL
3130      INPUT #1, N$,B$,A$,C,L,O,S,R,R1,T$
3140      RETURN
3150 REM END OF PROCESS ROUTINE
3160                                      REM
4000 REM **A3**   TERMINATION ROUTINE
4010      PRINT
4015      PRINT
4020      T$ = 'HARD'
4030      PRINT  USING T1$, B1,V1,T$
4040      T$ = 'PAPER'
4050      PRINT  USING T1$, B2,V2,T$
4051        REM  PRINT TOTAL LINES FOR HARD COPY & PAPERBACK
4060      CLOSE #1
4070      RETURN
4080 REM END OF TERMINATION ROUTINE
4081                                      REM
6000 REM **B1**   HEADING ROUTINE
6010      PRINT  USING H1$,  DATE$
6020      PRINT
6025      PRINT
6030      PRINT  USING H2$
6040      PRINT  USING H3$
6050      PRINT
6060      RETURN
6070 REM END OF HEADING ROUTINE
6071                                      REM
7000 REM **B2**   PROCESS RECORD ROUTINE
7010      V = N * C
7020      IF T$ = 'H' THEN 7022 ELSE 7061
7021 REM    THEN
7022           T$ = 'HARD'
7030           B1 = B1 + N
7040           V1 = V1 + V
7050           GOTO 7100
7060 REM    ELSE
7061           T$ = 'PAPER'
7070           B2 = B2 + N
7080           V2 = V2 + V
7090 REM    ENDIF
7100      PRINT  USING D$, N$,A$,B$,N,V,T$
7110      RETURN
7120 REM END OF PROCESS RECORD ROUTINE
7130                                      REM
9999    END
```

EXERCISES

6.8 At lines 4020 and 4040 in the termination routine and 7022 and 7061 in the process record routine, the variable T$ is changed from its one-character type code (from input) to HARD or PAPER. Explain why this is done.

6.9 What changes would be needed if the required total values were to include *all* books in the file and not simply those which were below the reorder level?

Printer Page Control

PLANNING
FOR OUTPUT
Let us consider an expansion of Example 6-2 where, upon filling one page with output, the continuous-form computer paper is repositioned to the top of a new page and the headings are printed again. For this, we must determine

how many detail lines can be printed on each page. In Example 6-2, heading lines are printed at the top of the page, detail lines in the body of the page, and a summary line at the bottom of the page. Counting lines in the printer spacing chart of Figure 6-17, we see that the heading requires six lines (including blanks) and the summary requires four lines (including blanks). In addition, we will leave a one-inch margin at the top and the bottom of the page. By using a continuous form with an 11-inch page and printing at six lines per inch, we would have room for 44 detail lines.

Example 6-3

Modify Example 6-2 to print 44 detail lines on each page. Print headings at the top of each new page. Print the summary after all records have been processed.

PROGRAM PLANNING— EXAMPLE 6-3 The overall logic of this example is virtually identical to that of Example 6-2 (Figure 6-19). In the flowcharts of the heading and process record routines of Figure 6-21, the relatively minor additions to make the needed change are shaded. The use of a line counter is nothing new to us; we used it in earlier examples. However, in this example, with each new page the counter must be *initialized* back to zero in order to start the line count over. This operation is to be done in the heading routine. In the process record routine, prior to printing each line the counter will be compared with 44 for full-page determination.

A PROGRAM— EXAMPLE 6-3 Careful planning when designing a program can make a world of difference in programming and later modification. We see in the flowcharts (Figures 6-19 and 6-21) that the changes are relatively minor. The Heading and Process Record routines are shown in Figure 6-22 with appropriate additions for the required change. Only *five* more statements (shaded in Figure 6-22) are required to make this somewhat complicated modification. Line 6012, which is repeated here,

```
6012    PRINT CHR$(12);
```

causes a special code represented by **CHR$(12)** to be transmitted to the printer. This code causes a *form-feed* action to take place which positions the printer to the top of a new page. In some systems, the keyword **PAGE** can be used in place of **CHR$(12)**.

Figure 6-21
Flowcharts for
Example 6-3.

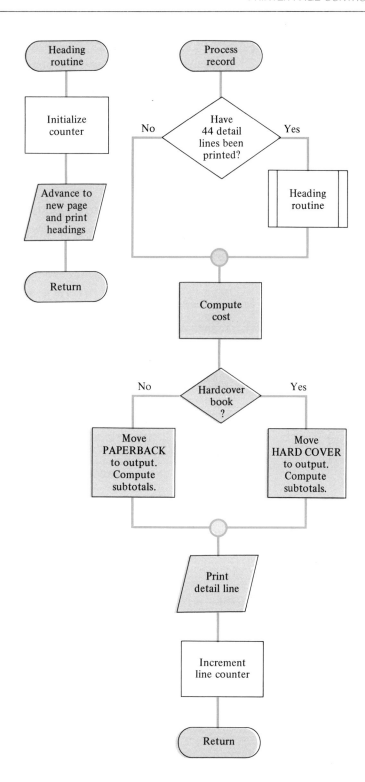

Figure 6-22   Program
modifications for
Example 6-3.

```
6000 REM **B1**    HEADING ROUTINE
6010      L1 = 0
6011         REM INITIALIZE THE LINE COUNTER, L1
6012      PRINT  CHR$(12);
6013         REM ADVANCE TO NEW PAGE
6015      PRINT  USING H1$,  DATE
6020      PRINT
6025      PRINT
6030      PRINT  USING H2$
6040      PRINT  USING H3$
6050      PRINT
6060      RETURN
6070 REM END OF HEADING ROUTINE
6071                                       REM
7000 REM **B2**    PROCESS RECORD ROUTINE
7010      IF L1<44 THEN 7015
7011         GOSUB 6010
7012            REM NEW PAGE IF CURRENT PAGE FULL
7015      V = N * C
7020      IF T$ = "H" THEN 7022 ELSE 7061
7021 REM    THEN
7022            T$ = "HARD"
7030            B1 = B1 + N
7040            V1 = V1 + V
7050            GOTO 7100
7060 REM    ELSE
7061            T$ = "PAPER"
7070            B2 = B2 + N
7080            V2 = V2 + V
7090 REM    ENDIF
7100      PRINT  USING D$, N$,A$,B$,N,V,T$
7105      L1 = L1 + 1
7106         REM  INCREMENT LINE COUNTER L1
7110      RETURN
7120 REM END OF PROCESS RECORD ROUTINE
7130                                       REM
9999    END
```

EXERCISE

6.10 The importance of modularizing by function is well illustrated in progressing from Example 6-2 to 6-3. For instance, in Figure 6-20 the printing of the heading lines could have been done in the Initialization routine merely by changing line numbers 6010 through 6050 to 2102 through 2106. Had this been done, what changes would have been required in progressing from Example 6-2 to 6-3?

ANSWERS TO PRECEDING EXERCISES

6.1

(a)
```
 - 3. 8. 1     4. 9 . 7. 6. 8     1 . 9. 3. 4
0          5          10          15          20
```

(b)
```
               - 3. 8. 1           1 . 9. 3. 4
0          5          10          15
```

(c)
```
 X. I. S. :   - 3. 8. 1       Z. I. S. :    1 . 9. 3. 4
0          5          10          15          20          25
```

6.2 12345.6, 12345.0, ␢␢682.1, ␢␢12.9, ␢␢␢␢0.7

6.3 ␢␢37␢␢256.834␢␢␢EXAMPLE␢D␢␢␢␢␢␢␢2

6.4 The output for the three cases would be:

```
$123.45
$␢28.91
$␢␢1.67
```

As a rule, it is desirable to have the $ immediately to the left of the first digit rather than "dangling" in front as in the second and third examples. This is commonly referred to as a *floating dollar sign*.

6.5
```
*62,534.21
**1,249.60
******0.02
```
number too large for mask

6.6
```
␢␢␢$62,534.21
␢␢␢␢␢␢␢$1,249.60
␢␢␢$0.02
$7,891,507.00
```

6.7 a. AB
    b. AB—note: produces same result as (a).
    c. C1234
    d. 456—note: some versions will produce C123456.
    e. 6—note: some versions will produce ABC123456.
    f. 6—note: produces same result as (e).
    g. Null—**A$** consists of only nine characters. *Note:* On some systems, this will produce an error condition.

6.8 The variable **T$** is changed to HARD or PAPER in order to print the required book type in both the detail line and the summary lines. For example, the **PRINT** statement of line 7100 includes **T$** in its list. This corresponds to the last mask field definition in line 2040.

6.9 It would be necessary to do the subtotal computation in the process routine (beginning at line 3000) rather than the process record routine (beginning at line 7000). For this, also refer to the flowcharts of Figure 6-19. However, it would still be necessary to use a selection process to maintain separate subtotals.

6.10 If the heading routine were not written as a separate module, the lines of code (currently 6010 through 6050) would have to be duplicated in the process record routine as well as the heading routine.

PROGRAMMING PROBLEMS

6.1 Referring to Problem 4.3, assume that the input quantities have the following restrictions:

> Account number—always 4 digits (treat as a string)
> Customer name—maximum of 20 positions
> New balance—never to exceed 9999.99
> Credit limit—never to exceed 9999.99

Expand the requirements of Problem 4.3. Main headings and column headings should appear as follows:

```
               OVER-LIMIT REPORT        31-FEB-84
              CUSTOMER ACCOUNT SYSTEM

     CUST                              NEW      CREDIT
     NUM      NAME                   BALANCE    LIMIT
```

Numeric quantities in the detail line should be edited to include the comma and decimal point as appropriate.

6.2 For Problem 4.8, assume that the input quantities have the following restrictions:

> Account number—6 digits
> Customer name—maximum of 20 positions
> Balance due—less than 8,000

6.3 Expand Programming Problem 4.9 to include two lines of appropriate main headings (include the system date) and one or more lines of column headings. (See the example of Problem 6.1.) Edit all numeric quantities as is appropriate considering their size.

6.4 For the purpose of issuing checks, a company maintains a file with the following information for each check to be written.

> Payee—maximum of 20 positions
> Amount—not to exceed $5,000

Since checks are printed on preprinted forms, only the variable information must be printed. Write a program which will print the following for each payee:

Print Line	Field	Beginning Print Position
First	Check number	46
Second	Current date	41
Fifth	Payee	6
	Amount	40

CHAPTER 7

Group Totals

OBJECTIVES

From Chapter 6 you got an idea of what the notion of report generation means. This chapter takes that concept one step further with group total concepts. In a nutshell, group totals arise from the fact that in many batch processing operations, records in a data file may be arranged by groups. For instance, sales may be grouped by division for a marketing company. In this chapter, you will learn how to extend the principles from Chapter 6 for the purpose of producing subtotals and totals in a report. This chapter does not include any new Basic language rules; the focus is on applying those tools about which you learned in previous chapters.

Page Totals

PROBLEM DEFINITION The production of printed reports which are attractive in appearance and easy to read is one of the business programmer's main jobs. Many of these reports require totals, and even subtotals, for groups of records. Examples 6-2 and 6-3 approximate the type of "real-life" programming which is required in the business world. Let us consider a modification of this example to include printing subtotals as well as totals.

Example 7-1
The output report for Example 6-3 is to be modified as follows:

1. At the bottom of each page, print a summary line which includes:

   number of books on hand (for that page)
   inventory value of those books

2. It will not be necessary to distinguish between hardcover and paperback books in accumulating totals.

The report summary line at the end of the report will consist of the grand totals for all books included in this report (no distinction between hardcover and paperback).

Because of the modular design of this program, this expansion is every bit as simple as the expansion in going from Example 6-2 to 6-3.

USING ACCUMULATORS The most important facet of this example relates to the use of accumulators. Our first exposure to accumulators was in Example 3-2, in which a line counter and book totals were maintained. In Example 6-3, the accumulator **L1** accumulated a count of the lines for each page (and was set to zero at each page). These examples illustrate the fact that an accumulator is always associated with a specific data group. In Example 3-2, the data group consisted of the entire file, while in Example 6-3, the data group consisted of data (a count of lines printed) on one page. Accumulators must always be initialized to zero at the beginning of the data group with which they are associated, and their contents must be printed at the conclusion of the data group with which they are associated. This is exactly like using a pocket or desk calculator to add columns of figures. For instance, we clear the calculator, add in the numbers, and record the result. If we have several columns or "groups," we repeat the process for each group as illustrated in Figure 7-1.

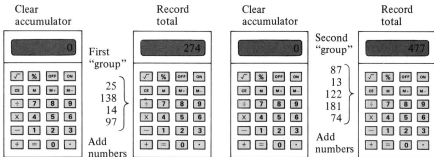

Figure 7-1
Accumulating totals.

An examination of Example 7-1 reveals that two data groups ("current page" and "entire file") are required. Accumulator requirements and characteristics are summarized in Table 7-1.

Table 7-1
Accumulators
for Example 7-1

Accumula-tor Name	Accumulates	Initialized at	Incremented by
L1	Number of lines printed on current page	Beginning of each page	1 each time a detail line is written
B1	Total of updated onhand on current page	Beginning of pro-gram and end of each page	Updated onhand from each de-tail record which is printed
V1	Total of inventory value on this page	Beginning of pro-gram and end of each page	Inventory value for each detail record which is printed
B9	Total of updated onhand for all records printed	Beginning of program	B1 at the end of each page
V9	Total of inventory value for all records printed	Beginning of program	V1 at the end of each page

It should be noted that the "entire file" data group can be considered to be made up of all the "current page" data groups. For this reason, only the lower level (current page) accumulators are incremented from the detail record. The higher level (entire file) accumulators are incremented from the page totals rather than from the detail records. Each grand total is thus a sum of page totals rather than a sum of detail amounts. This "sum of sums" concept is more efficient for the computer and is considered a better technique in cases where the final total must balance to a predetermined total.

With these concepts in mind, the Process Current Record routine involves:

```
Process Current Record
    If full page, then
        print page totals
        add page totals to grand totals
        initialize page totals and line count to zero
        skip to new page and print headings.
    Compute inventory value for this record.
    Add detail values (inventory on hand and value) to page totals.
    Save appropriate message (PAPER or HARD).
    Print detail line.
    Increment line counter.
```

Before proceeding further, attempt to answer the following question. It involves a common type of error which most beginners encounter.

EXERCISE

7.1 With the exception of the page total operations, the above steps are as described by the Process Record Routine flowchart of Figure 6-21. What would be the error of including the page total operations as part of the Heading Routine?

PROGRAM PLANNING   The preceding English description of the process record routine is reflected directly in the flowchart of Figure 7-2. Boxes which represent an expansion of this problem over that of Example 6-3 are unshaded. The corresponding hierarchy chart is shown in Figure 7-3 in which we see three *levels* of modules. We should note here that the heading routine is defined as a second-level module (*B*-level). However, it is also called from another *B*-level module (process record) so its level number is enclosed in parentheses to indicate that it was first used elsewhere. The same is true of the page total routine.

Figure 7-2   Flowchart for Example 7-1.

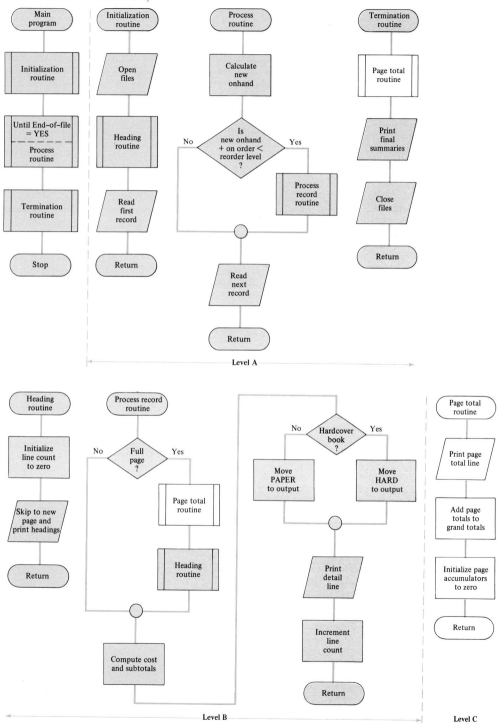

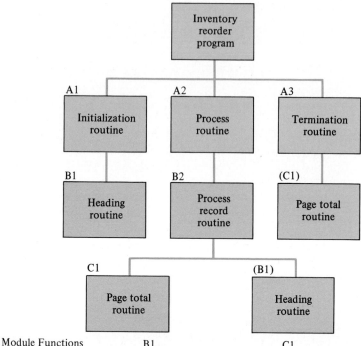

Module Functions

A1
1. Open files
2. Print headings (B1)
3. Read first record

A2
1. Calculate new onhand
2. Process record (B2)
3. Read next record

A3
1. Print page summary (C1)
2. Print total summary
3. Close files

B1
1. Advance to new page
2. Print headings
3. Initialize line count

B2
1. If end of page then
   print page totals (C1)
   print headings (B1)
2. Determine if hardcover
   or paperback
3. Compute page subtotals
4. Print detail line

C1
1. Print page
   summary line
2. Add page totals
   to grand totals
3. Initialize page
   accumulators
   to zero.

Figure 7-3
Hierarchy chart for
Example 7-1.

EXERCISE

7.2 In the process record routine of Figure 7-2, the first action taken is to determine whether a full page has been printed. Would the result be any different if this check were made immediately before the print detail line box? What if it were made immediately after the increment line count box? If different, explain.

A PROGRAM—
EXAMPLE 7-1

Once a program has been carefully designed and the logic thoroughly checked, actual coding is relatively easy. The program of Figure 7-4 corresponds exactly to the flowchart of Figure 7-2. Again, if we compare this program with that of Example 6-3, we see relatively minor changes in the code. Some of the changes reflect the nondistinction between hardcover and paperback when accumulating. However, the more important changes reflect handling page totals. These additions to the program are shaded in Figure 7-4. They correspond to the shaded boxes in Figure 7-3. Further consideration of this program is left to Exercises 7-3 and 7-4.

One of the beauties of modularizing is the isolation of various functions into relatively independent modules. This greatly simplifies the tasks of programming, debugging, and modification.

EXERCISES

7.3 In entering the program of Figure 7-4, the programmer accidentally left out line 7100 (the **RETURN** statement). Describe what will happen when the program is run.

7.4 The importance of setting accumulators to zero for each group is stressed in the discussion of Table 7-1. The page total accumulators (**B1** and **V1**) are initialized in the page total routine (lines 9060 and 9070). Thus these accumulators will not be initialized by the program prior to starting the *first* group. Perhaps they should also be set to zero in the initialization routine. Comment on this.

Group Total Principles

In everyday life, the computer's impact is most frequently felt as the producer of some sort of individualized document. Whether it is a bill from a department store, an automobile registration notification, or a student grade report, the general nature of the document is the same: a compilation of data about one particular person or thing. How does the computer do it? How can it select, from the data for thousands of customers or students, the required data to print one bill or one grade report? The answer lies in two basic principles of computer programming: *control groups* and *group total logic*.

Figure 7-4   Program solution—Example 7-1.

```
100 REM EXAMPLE 7-1
110 REM     BOOK ORDER SUMMARY REPORT
120 REM     THIS PROGRAM PRINTS A STATUS SUMMARY REPORT FOR ALL BOOKS FOR WHICH THE
130 REM     NEW BALANCE PLUS ON-ORDER QUANTITY FALLS BELOW THE REORDER LEVEL.
140 REM     INPUT QUANTITIES ARE:
150 REM       S$   STOCK NUMBER
160 REM       B$   BOOK TITLE
170 REM       A$   AUTHOR
180 REM       C    COST
190 REM       L    REORDER LEVEL
200 REM       O    OLD INVENTORY BALANCE
210 REM       S    SOLD
220 REM       R    RECEIVED
230 REM       R1   ON ORDER
240 REM       T$   TYPE
250 REM     CALCULATED QUANTITIES ARE:
260 REM       N    NEW BALANCE
270 REM       V    INVENTORY VALUE
280 REM     ACCUMULATED INVENTORY TOTALS
290 REM       L1   LINE COUNTER
300 REM       B1   BALANCE (FOR PAGE TOTALS)
310 REM       V1   VALUE (FOR PAGE TOTALS)
320 REM       B9   BALANCE (FOR GRAND TOTALS)
330 REM       V9   VALUE (FOR GRAND TOTALS)
340                                     REM
1000 REM MAIN PROGRAM
1010 REM
1020        GOSUB  2010
1030           REM INITIALIZATION ROUTINE
1040        IF S$="99999" THEN 1050
1041           GOSUB  3010
1042           GOTO 1040
1043           REM PROCESS ROUTINE UNTIL NO MORE DATA
1050        GOSUB  4010
1060           REM TERMINATION ROUTINE
1070        STOP
1080           REM END PROGRAM
1090                                     REM
2000 REM **A1**    INITIALIZATION ROUTINE
2010        H1$="                    MONTHLY BOOK ORDER SUMMARY              \    \"
2020        H2$=" STOCK                                       COPIES   INVENTORY"
2030        H3$=" NUMBER   AUTHOR        BOOK TITLE           ONHAND   VALUE      TYPE"
2040        D$ =" \    \    \          \    \                \  #,### ##,###.##  \    \"
2050        T1$="    TOTAL COPIES ONHAND ##,###      TOTAL INVENTORY VALUE  ###,###.##"
2055        G$ ="GRAND TOTALS    COPIES ONHAND ###,###    INVENTORY VALUE   ###,###.##"
2070        OPEN "INVEN" FOR INPUT AS FILE#1
2080        GOSUB 6010
2090           REM PERFORM HEADING ROUTINE
2100        INPUT #1, N$,B$,A$,C,L,O,S,R,R1,T$
2110        RETURN
2120 REM END OF INITIALIZATION ROUTINE
2130                                     REM
2160           REM  DEFINE OUTPUT LINE FORMATS
2161                                     REM
3000 REM **A2**  PROCESS ROUTINE
3010        N = O + R - S
3020        IF N + R1 >= L THEN 3130
3021           GOSUB 7010
3022           REM  PROCESS RECORD ROUTINE IF COMPUTED VALUE IS BELOW REORDER LEVEL
3130        INPUT #1, N$,B$,A$,C,L,O,S,R,R1,T$
3140        RETURN
3150 REM END OF PROCESS ROUTINE
3160                                     REM
```

Figure 7-4 (Continued)

```
4000 REM **A3**    TERMINATION ROUTINE
4010      GOSUB 9010
4011         REM PAGE TOTALS
4020      PRINT
4025      PRINT
4030      PRINT USING G$, B9,V9
4031         REM PRINT GRAND TOTALS
4040      CLOSE #1
4050      RETURN
4060 REM END OF TERMINATION ROUTINE
4061                                    REM
6000 REM **B1**    HEADING ROUTINE
6010      L1 = 0
6011         REM INITIALIZE THE LINE COUNTER, L1
6012      PRINT  CHR$(12);
6013         REM ADVANCE TO NEW PAGE
6015      PRINT  USING H1$,  DATE$
6020      PRINT
6025      PRINT
6030      PRINT  USING H2$
6040      PRINT  USING H3$
6050      PRINT
6060      RETURN
6070 REM END OF HEADING ROUTINE
6071                                    REM
7000 REM **B2**    PROCESS RECORD ROUTINE
7010      IF L1<44 THEN 7020
7011         GOSUB 9010
7012            REM PAGE TOTAL ROUTINE
7013         GOSUB 6010
7014            REM NEW PAGE IF CURRENT PAGE FULL
7020      V = N * C
7030      B1 = B1 + N
7040      V1 = V1 + V
7050      IF T$ = "H" THEN 7052 ELSE 7071
7051 REM    THEN
7052            T$ = "HARD"
7060            GOTO 7081
7070 REM    ELSE
7071            T$ = "PAPER"
7080 REM    ENDIF
7081      PRINT  USING D$, N$,A$,B$,N,V,T$
7090      L1 = L1 + 1
7091         REM  INCREMENT LINE COUNTER L1
7100      RETURN
7110 REM END OF PROCESS RECORD ROUTINE
7120                                    REM
9000 REM PAGE TOTAL ROUTINE
9010      PRINT
9020      PRINT  USING T1$, B1,V1
9030      PRINT
9031         REM  PRINT PAGE TOTAL LINE
9040      B9 = B9 + B1
9050      V9 = V9 + V1
9051         REM  ADD PAGE TOTALS TO GRAND TOTALS
9060      B1 = 0
9070      V1 = 0
9071         REM  ZERO PAGE ACCUMULATORS
9080      RETURN
9090 REM END OF PAGE TOTAL ROUTINE
9091                                    REM
9999      END
```

CONTROL GROUPS The concept of control groups is illustrated in Figure 7-5, which shows a portion of a file of college class cards. The file contains one card for each class which each student is taking. In Figure 7-5(a), the records are randomly arranged; they are in no particular sequence, and the records for each student are scattered throughout the file. With the records in this arrangement, it would be necessary to go through the entire file each time one student's grade report was to be printed. An improvement is shown in Figure 7-5(b) where the records have been grouped by student number, so that all of the records for each student are together. A closer look at Figure 7-5(b) will show that the records have been put into *sequence* according to the student number, starting with the lowest number and ending with the highest. In this example, the student number is the *control field;* a group of records with the same control field is called a *control group.*

A control group, then, is a group of records which have an identical control field, and the control field is the field in the record which contains the identifier of the control group. This concept is basic to any type of processing which produces an output record from a group of input records. For example, when the telephone company prepares the phone bills each month, it starts out with a file containing a record of each call made and each payment received. This file initially is in no usable sequence. However, when the file is sorted on telephone number, all of the records for each telephone number are brought together, so that one bill can be prepared for each customer. A file of records can always be grouped into control groups by sorting the file on the proper control fields. There are many standardized programs available to perform these tasks.

Figure 7-5   (a) File in random sequence. (b) File in sequence by student number.

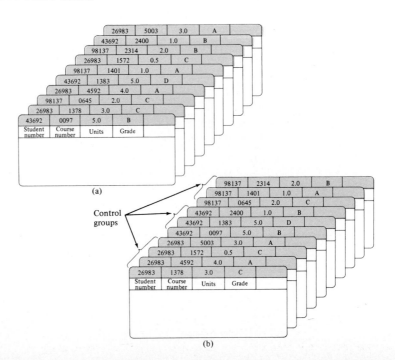

EXERCISES

7.5 Fill in the blanks: In order to arrange the records in a file by control _____ it is necessary to sort them on the proper control _____ .

7.6 A department store maintains a file of records of all sales made during the previous month. Each record contains information about one sale, including the customer number, the salesperson number, the inventory number for the item which was sold, the date of sale, and the amount of sale. Name the field in the record which would be most likely to be the control field for each of the following reports.

   a. Sales volume report for each salesperson
   b. Sales listing by day
   c. Total quantity of each item sold during the month
   d. Customer billing

GROUP TOTAL LOGIC In Chapter 6, we studied the concept of computing totals for the updated inventory and the inventory value. Page totals were printed at the end of each page and grand totals were printed at the end of the report. In data processing, these page totals are a simple form of what is commonly referred to as *group totals*. That is, they represent the totals for a particular group of records (the group which is printed on the page). Of course, the records which compose a page group have no logical relationship such as that of the control group in Figure 7-5(b). However, the needs are similar: that is, the computer must read all of the records for the first control group, print the total for that group, read all of the records for the second control group, print the total for that group, and so on. This type of operation is known as a *group total operation,* and the logic to implement it is known as *group total logic.*

What, exactly, is involved in group total logic? When we look at an illustration such as Figure 7-5(b), the processing of control groups seems quite simple, because we can see the entire file; the end of one group and the beginning of the next are obvious. But the situation is more difficult for the computer. To illustrate why, give several blank cards to a friend, with the request to write the number "1" on some of them and the number "2" on the rest. Have your friend place the cards in sequence (all of the 1's, followed by all of the 2's), and then show you the cards one at a time, each time asking, "Is this the last card with the number 1 on it?." From this activity, you will quickly see that you have absolutely no way of telling when you are looking at the last record in the group. Only when we see the first card with a 2 do we know that we have seen all of the 1 cards. The basic technique which we use involves remembering the number on the card just read, reading the next card, and then comparing the two numbers.

Group total logic involves effectively the same principles; expanding them as appropriate yields the following.

1. Read the next record.
2. Compare the control field on the record just read with the previous control field which is being "saved."

3. If the control fields are equal then:
    • Process the detail record.
4. If the control fields are different then:
    • Perform the group total operations.
    • Save the control field of this record.
    • Continue processing with the record which triggered the group total operation.

The overall concept of group total logic is illustrated by the flowchart segment of Figure 7-6. The process of saving the control field is accomplished merely by defining another variable and storing the desired field in it using the **LET** statement. Use of such a *save variable* is illustrated and described in Figure 7-7.

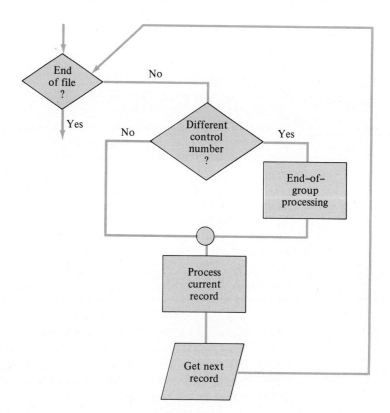

Figure 7-6   Group total logic.

Figure 7-7   Detecting the end of a control group.

(a)

0138
0138
0097
0097
0097
0097

Input Record

0097

MOVE

0097

Save variable

The first record is read and its control field (0097) is moved to the save variable.

(b)

0138
0138
0097
0097
0097

0097

Input record

0097

COMPARISON: EQUAL

0097

Save variable

The second record is read and its control field is compared to the first stored in the save variable. (Records which have already been read are shaded.) Since the fields are equal, the control change has not yet occurred so detail processing should continue.

(c)

0138
0138

0097
0097
0097
0097

Input record

0138

COMPARISON: UNEQUAL

0097

Save variable

After repeated detail processing, the first record of the next control group is read and its control field is compared to that in the save variable. Since they are different, the computer has encountered the end of the previous group (0097) and must perform group total operations for that group.

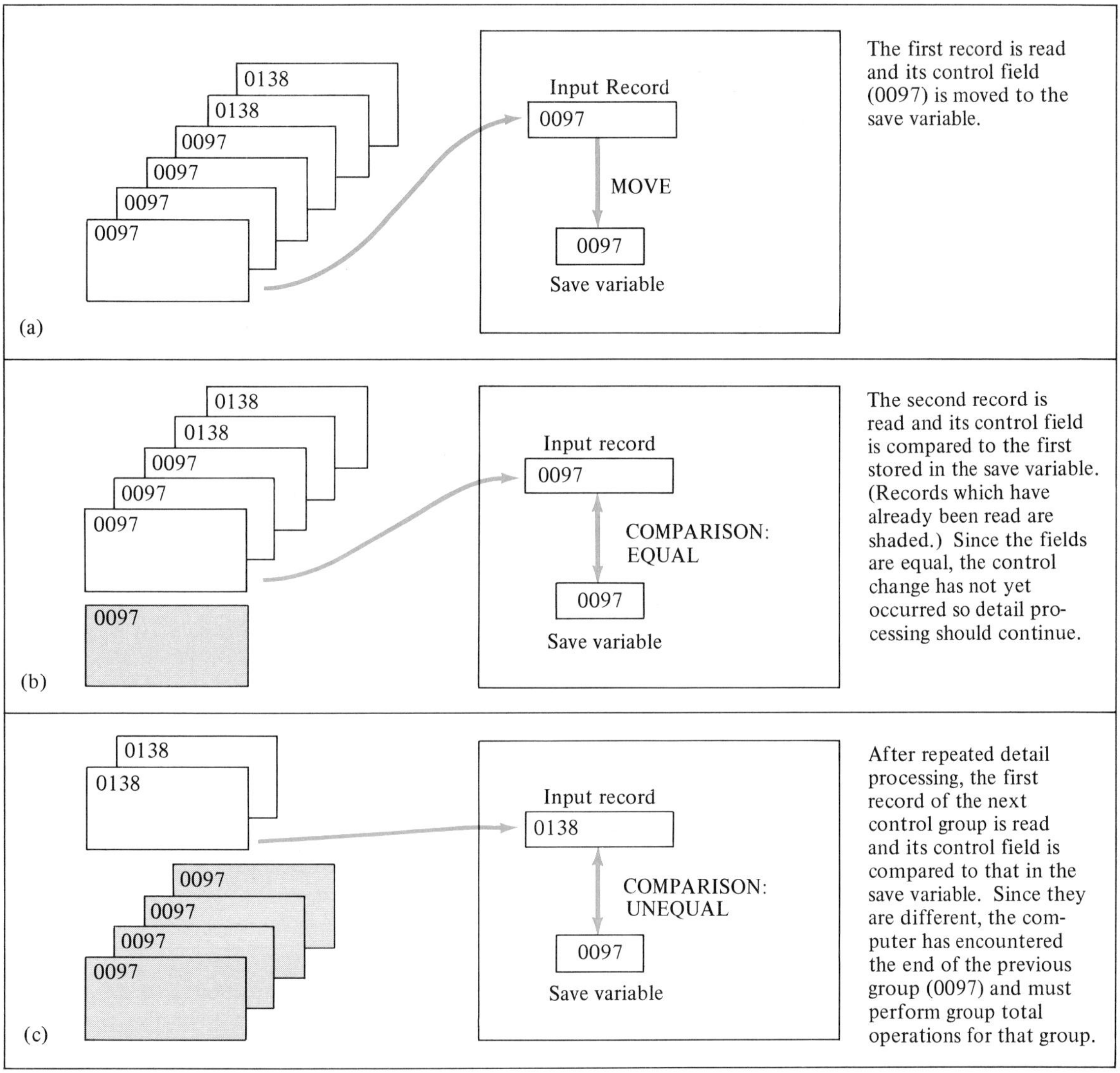

EXERCISES

7.7 Before a program can be written using group total logic, how must the records of the input file be arranged?

7.8 As we have learned in the preceding section, the end of a control group is indicated by a change in the control group number. What other condition indicates the end of a control group?

A GROUP TOTAL EXAMPLE

Example 7-2

Write a program to produce an "Employee Hours Worked" listing. The input file consists of time-worked records, each of which includes the number of hours an employee worked on a particular job. Each input record contains the following information.

Field	Size
Employee number	5 digits
Job number	4 digits
Hours worked	9.9 (maximum value)

Records in the input file are in ascending sequence by employee number.

For each employee record, one line of output is to be printed consisting of the employee number, job number, and number of hours worked from each input record. After the last line for each employee, print the total number of hours worked by that employee. At the end of the report, print the total number of employees and the average number of hours worked per employee.

This problem statement gives us the input data format and also the necessary information to develop the print layout chart shown in Figure 7-8(a). [Figure 7-8(b) includes a sample output to provide an idea of just what the report will look like.] Notice the following points about the chart.

1. There are three types of printed lines:
   - Detail line (one from each time-worked record)
   - Group Total line (total hours worked for one employee)
   - Final Total line (total for the entire file)
2. The chart contains enough lines to show the line spacing between each type of line (detail to detail, detail to group total, group total to detail, and group total to final total).
3. The group total (total hours worked for each employee) has been identified with an asterisk to make the listing easier to read.
4. To keep the example as simple as possible, page and column headings have been omitted.

The overall logic of this solution is virtually identical to that of Example 6-3, which is flowcharted in Figure 6-21. The important difference lies in the means for finding the control break; that is, encountering a different control field value as opposed to obtaining a full page of output. A partial set of flowcharts for this problem is shown in Figure 7-9. The module A2-PROCESS here performs effectively the same function as the module PROCESS-

Figure 7-8 (a) Print
layout chart—
Example 7-2.
(b) Sample output—
Example 7-2.

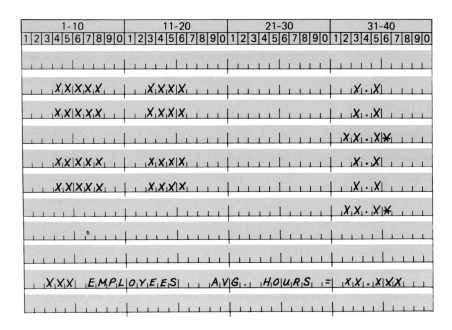

(a)

```
    12345        6789         3.5
    12345        4321         8.6
    12345        1357         4.0
                             16.1*
    23456        1234         3.8
                              3.8*
    34567        8901         4.9
    34567        6543         5.7
    34567        1234         6.9
                             17.5*
    45678        7654         3.2
    45678        1234         8.6
    45678        2345         3.2
                             15.0*
    56789        1234         4.8
    56789        2345         9.0
                             13.8*
    67890        1234         9.9
                              9.9*


    6 EMPLOYEES    AVG. HOURS = 12.683
```

(b)

Figure 7-9   Group totals—Example 7-2.

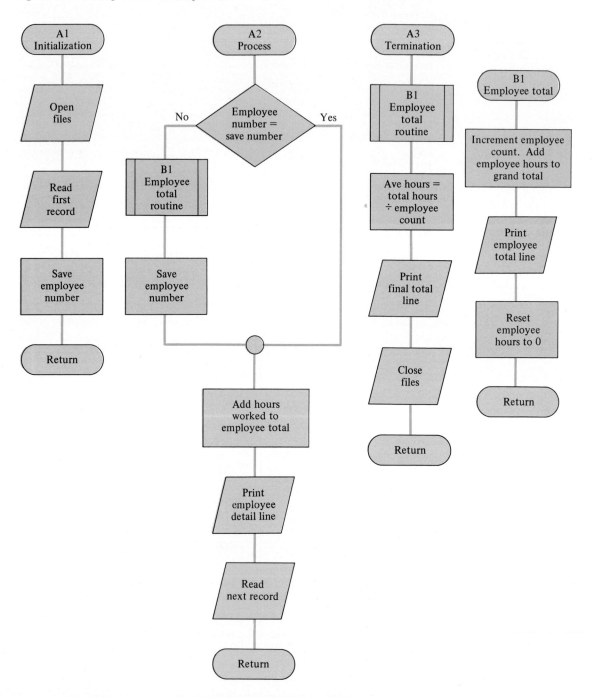

Figure 7-10   Group totals—Example 7-2.

```
100   REM EXAMPLE 7-2     HOURS WORKED SUMMARY PROGRAM
110   REM    PROGRAM VARIABLES ARE:
120   REM      INPUT QUANTITIES
130   REM         E$        EMPLOYEE NUMBER
140   REM         J$        JOB IDENTIFICATION NUMBER
150   REM         H         HOURS WORKED
160   REM      ACCUMULATORS
170   REM         C         NUMBER OF EMPLOYEES PROCESSED
180   REM         H1        HOURS WORKED BY EMPLOYEE
190   REM         H9        TOTAL HOURS FOR ALL EMPLOYEES
200   REM      OTHER VARIABLES
210   REM         E1$       SAVE VARIABLE FOR EMPLOYEE NUM.
220   REM         A         AVERAGE HOURS WORKED
230                                                 REM
1000 REM MAIN PROGRAM
1010      GOSUB  2010
1011         REM INITIALIZATION ROUTINE
1020      IF E$="99999" THEN 1030
1021         GOSUB  3010
1022         GOTO 1020
1023            REM PROCESS ROUTINE UNTIL NO MORE DATA
1030      GOSUB  4010
1040      STOP
1041         REM END PROGRAM
1042                                                 REM
1996 REM    ****************************************************
1997 REM    *      A-LEVEL ROUTINES
1998 REM    ****************************************************
1999                                                 REM
2000 REM **A1**   INITIALIZATION ROUTINE
2010      D$ = '   \    \        \   \              #.#'
2020      T$ = '                                 ##.##'
2030      G$ = '   ### EMPLOYEES   AVG. HOURS = ##.##'
2031         REM   FORMAT FOR OUTPUT LINES
2040      OPEN "EMPLOY" FOR INPUT AS FILE #1
2041         REM   OPEN FILE
2050      INPUT #1, E$,J$,H
2060      E1$ = E$
2070      RETURN
2080 REM END OF INITIALIZATION ROUTINE
2081                                                 REM
3000 REM **A2**   PROCESS ROUTINE
3010      IF E$=E1$ THEN 3040
3020         GOSUB 6010
3021            REM  EMPLOYEE TOTAL ROUTINE IF NEW NUMBER
3030         E1$ = E$
3031            REM  SAVE NEW NUMBER
3040      H1 = H1 + H
3050      PRINT  USING D$,E$,J$,H
3060      INPUT #1, E$,J$,H
3070      RETURN
3080 REM END OF PROCESS ROUTINE
3081                                                 REM
4000 REM **A3**   TERMINATION ROUTINE
4010      GOSUB  6010
4011         REM EMPLOYEE TOTAL ROUTINE (LAST EMPLOYEE)
4020      A = H9/C
4021         REM   CALCULATE AVERAGE HOURS WORKED
4030      PRINT
4040      PRINT
4050      PRINT  USING G$,C,A
4051         REM PRINT TOTAL LINE
4060      CLOSE #1
4070      RETURN
4080 REM END OF TERMINATION ROUTINE
4081                                                 REM
5996 REM    ****************************************************
5997 REM    *      B-LEVEL ROUTINES
5998 REM    ****************************************************
5999                                                 REM
6000 REM **B1**   EMPLOYEE TOTAL ROUTINE
6010      C = C + 1
6020      H9 = H9 + H1
6021         REM   INCREMENT EMPLOYEE COUNT AND ACCUMULATE HOURS
6030      PRINT  USING T$,H1
6040      H1 = 0
6050      RETURN
6060 REM END OF EMPLOYEE TOTAL ROUTINE
6061                                                 REM
9999      END
```

RECORD in Figure 6-21. Actually the logic of Figure 7-9 is somewhat simpler than that of the corresponding Figure 6-21 because of fewer detailed functions to be performed.

A SAMPLE PROGRAM— EXAMPLE 7-2 The program of Figure 7-10 corresponds exactly to the flowchart in Figure 7-9. The variable **E1$** is used as a "save variable" to hold the current group employee number. The level break occurs when the newly read number (in E$) differs from the saved value. We see this test in statements 3010 through 3040, which are repeated here.

```
3010        IF E$=E1$ THEN 3040
3020            GOSUB 6010
3021                REM  EMPLOYEE TOTAL ROUTINE IF NEW NUMBER
3030            E1$ = E$
3031                REM  SAVE NEW NUMBER
3040        H1 = H1 + H
```

If the numbers differ, then the employee total routine is executed and the new number is saved in the variable **E1$**.

EXERCISE

7.9 The employee total routine (line 6000) is executed from the process routine (at line 3020) whenever a level break occurs. It is also executed from the termination routine (at line 4010). What would happen if line 4010 were omitted?

Page Control

A VARIABLE SPACING EXAMPLE The purpose of Example 7-2 was to demonstrate a technique for developing the necessary program logic for group totals; in order to keep the example simple, headings were omitted. Normally, however, page and column headings are required, and often the exact interline spacing is specified. Example 7-3 illustrates these points.

Example 7-3

This problem is the same as Example 7-2. In addition, report and column headings are required. The report heading line is to include the words TIME WORKED LISTING and a page number; column headings are to be appropriate. There are to be two blank lines between the column heading and the first detail line, one blank line between each employee total line and the following detail line, and two blank lines between the last employee total line and the final total line. A print layout chart and sample output for this example appear in Figure 7-11.

Figure 7-11 (a) Print layout chart—Example 7-3. (b) Sample output—Example 7-3.

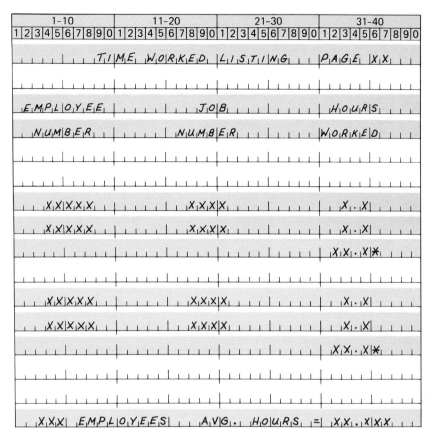

(a)

```
            TIME WORKED LISTING    PAGE 12

         EMPLOYEE          JOB         HOURS
          NUMBER          NUMBER       WORKED


          15733           9115          6.0
          15733           9115          8.0
          15733           9115          3.5
          15733           3085          4.5
          15733           3085          8.0
          15733           3085          5.5
                                       35.5*


          15869           9115          5.5
          15869           3085          6.5
                                       12.0*
```

(b)

As we can see, the specifications for the vertical spacing of the printed output are extremely detailed. Specifications of this nature result from experience on the part of the systems analyst as to what is required to produce printed output which is both attractive and easy to read. As a result, such specifications are commonly encountered by the working programmer.

In this case, care must be taken in managing the line counter. That is, in all previous examples the line counter was incremented by 1 for each detail line printed. Now, however, the incrementing will depend upon what type of line is to be printed.

In determining the number of lines to be printed on a page, let us use the following.

11-inch paper at 6 lines/inch = 66 lines/page

Top margin: 1 inch = 6 lines
Bottom margin: 1 inch = 6 lines
Heading lines (including blanks) = 6 lines

Body of report = 66 – 6 –6 – 6 = 48 lines/page

In using top and bottom margins, the general rule is never to print in the top margin. To accomplish this, the computer operator will set up the printer in such a way that the "first print line" will be the first line of the heading area. This means that a **PRINT** statement with **CHR$(12)** will position the paper for printing at the first line of the heading area. The rules regarding the bottom margin are slightly more flexible. The general rule is that a detail line may never be printed in the bottom margin. However, a group total line may be printed in the bottom margin, because it is considered better to print the group total with its associated detail lines rather than on a page all by itself. For practical purposes, then, we may say that we do not have to be concerned about whether or not a page is full when printing a group total line, but we must make sure that a detail line is not printed in the bottom margin. This means that the placement of the full-page test in the overall logic is important. This, together with the overall program logic, is illustrated in the flowchart of Figure 7-12.

A SAMPLE PROGRAM— EXAMPLE 7-3 Once again we see a relatively easy modification to an existing program. Following are additional features which are required.

1. A heading routine will be required which will be executed from both the process record routine and the initialization routine. (This requirement is identical to that of Example 7-1—see Figures 7-2 and 7-3.)
2. A line counter will be required. It will be incremented by 1 for each detail line and by 2 for each employee summary line (see Figure 7-11).

Figure 7-12   Variable line spacing—Example 7-3.

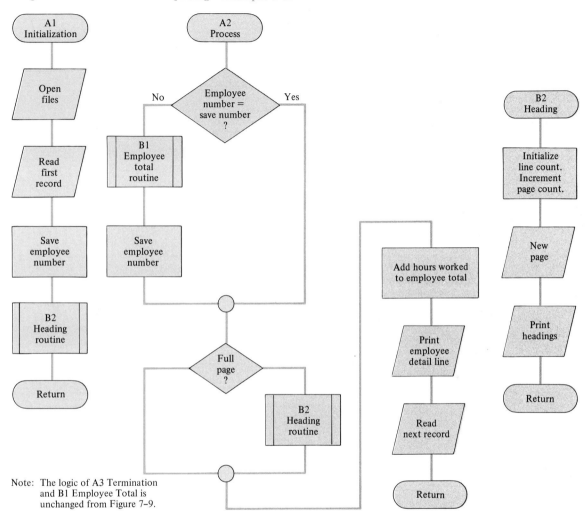

3. A page counter will be needed which will be incremented by 1 for each page of output.

These modifications are included in the program of Figure 7-13. Extension of this program over that of Example 7-2 involves the insertion of a relatively few lines (shaded in Figure 7-13) and the addition of a heading module. Relative to the discussion of page control in the preceding section, note the placement of the full-page test (line 3040).

Figure 7-13   Variable line spacing—Example 7-3.

```
100   REM EXAMPLE 7-3      HOURS WORKED SUMMARY PROGRAM
110   REM    PROGRAM VARIABLES ARE:
120   REM      INPUT QUANTITIES
130   REM         E$        EMPLOYEE NUMBER
140   REM         J$        JOB IDENTIFICATION NUMBER
150   REM         H         HOURS WORKED
160   REM      ACCUMULATORS
165   REM         L         LINE COUNTER
166   REM         P         PAGE COUNTER
170   REM         C         NUMBER OF EMPLOYEES PROCESSED
180   REM         H1        HOURS WORKED BY EMPLOYEE
190   REM         H9        TOTAL HOURS FOR ALL EMPLOYEES
200   REM      OTHER VARIABLES
210   REM         E1$       SAVE VARIABLE FOR EMPLOYEE NUM.
220   REM         A         AVERAGE HOURS WORKED
230                                                 REM
1000  REM MAIN PROGRAM
1010       GOSUB   2010
1011          REM INITIALIZATION ROUTINE
1020       IF E$="99999" THEN 1030
1021          GOSUB   3010
1022          GOTO 1020
1023            REM PROCESS ROUTINE UNTIL NO MORE DATA
1030       GOSUB   4010
1040       STOP
1041          REM END PROGRAM
1042                                                 REM
1996  REM    ************************************************
1997  REM    *      A-LEVEL ROUTINES
1998  REM    ************************************************
1999  REM                                           REM
2000  REM **A1**    INITIALIZATION ROUTINE
2004       H1$= "             TIME WORKED LISTING    PAGE ##"
2005       H2$= " EMPLOYEE         JOB              HOURS"
2006       H3$= "  NUMBER         NUMBER           WORKED"
2010       D$ = "   \     \           \    \        #.#"
2020       T$ = "                               ##.#X"
2030       G$ = "  ### EMPLOYEES    AVG. HOURS = ##.##"
2031          REM  FORMAT FOR OUTPUT LINES
2040       OPEN "EMPLOY" FOR INPUT AS FILE #1
2041          REM  OPEN FILE
2045       GOSUB 8010
2046          REM  HEADING ROUTINE
2050       INPUT #1, E$,J$,H
2060       E1$ = E$
2070       RETURN
2080  REM END OF INITIALIZATION ROUTINE
2081                                                 REM
```

Figure 7-13 (Continued)

```
3000 REM **A2**    PROCESS ROUTINE
3010      IF E$=E1$ THEN 3040
3020         GOSUB 6010
3021            REM  EMPLOYEE TOTAL ROUTINE IF NEW NUMBER
3030            E1$ = E$
3031            REM   SAVE NEW NUMBER
3040      IF L <= 48 THEN   2045
3041         GOSUB 8010
3042            REM HEADING ROUTINE
3045      H1 = H1 + H
3050      PRINT  USING D$, E$,J$,H
3055      L = L + 1
3060      INPUT #1, E$,J$,H
3070      RETURN
3080 REM END OF PROCESS ROUTINE
3081                                             REM
4000 REM **A3**    TERMINATION ROUTINE
4010      GOSUB  6010
4011         REM EMPLOYEE TOTAL ROUTINE (LAST EMPLOYEE)
4020      A = H9/C
4021         REM  CALCULATE AVERAGE HOURS WORKED
4030      PRINT
4040      PRINT
4050      PRINT  USING G$, C,A
4051         REM PRINT TOTAL LINE
4060      CLOSE #1
4070      RETURN
4080 REM END OF TERMINATION ROUTINE
4081                                             REM
5996 REM    **********************************************
5997 REM    *     B-LEVEL ROUTINES
5998 REM    **********************************************
5999                                             REM
6000 REM **B1**    EMPLOYEE TOTAL ROUTINE
6010      C = C + 1
6020      H9 = H9 + H1
6021         REM  INCREMENT EMPLOYEE COUNT AND ACCUMULATE HOURS
6030      PRINT  USING T$, H1
6034      PRINT
6036      L = L + 2
6040      H1 = 0
6050      RETURN
6060 REM END OF EMPLOYEE TOTAL ROUTINE
6061                                             REM
8000 REM **B2**    HEADING ROUTINE
8010      L = 0
8020      P = P + 1
8021         REM  INITIALIZE LINE COUNT AND INCREMENT PAGE COUNT
8030      PRINT CHR$(12);
8031         REM  ADVANCE TO NEW PAGE
8040      PRINT  USING H1$,P
8050      PRINT
8060      PRINT  USING H2$
8070      PRINT  USING H3$
8080      PRINT
8090      PRINT
8100      RETURN
8110 REM END OF HEADING ROUTINE
8111                                             REM
9999    END
```

EXERCISE

7.10 A programmer concludes that the best way to handle page control is to

Print a detail line, then
count it, then
test for full page.

To this end, the programmer changes the order of certain statements as follows:

```
3045      H1 = H1 + H
3050      PRINT USING...
3055      L = L + 1
3056      IF L<=48 THEN 3060
3057          GOSUB 8010
3058              REM HEADING ROUTINE
3060      INPUT 1, E$, J$,H
```

Will the printed report be the same as or different from that of the original program? Explain your answer.

ANSWERS TO PRECEDING EXERCISES

7.1 This sequence necessarily would involve printing the page summary line for the records processed on this page and then skipping to the next page for the headings. This would be adequate for the Process Record Routine. However, the Heading Routine is also performed from the Initialization Routine so that a page summary would be printed before record processing had even begun.

7.2 If the full-page check were performed immediately before printing, the results would be incorrect. This error would occur because the values for the current record would be added to the subtotal and included in the current page totals. However, the current record would be printed on the next page.
The results would be identical to those of Figure 7-2 if the full-page check were made after incrementing the line count.

7.3 If the **RETURN** at line 7100 were omitted, the computer would "see" the process record routine beginning at line 7000 and continuing through to the **RETURN** at line 9080. Each time a record was processed, the page total routine would also be processed. Thus the page totals would contain only the current values since they would be set to zero after each record.

7.4 All numeric variables are set to zero by the computer system prior to beginning execution of the program. Thus it is not necessary to initialize them in the initialization routine. However, this is not true of most other languages. Variables commonly contain "garbage" which is simply the leftovers from whatever was using the computer before.

7.5 Group, field

7.6 a. Salesperson number
     b. Date of sale
     c. Item inventory number
     d. Customer number

7.7 They must be in sequence by the control field.

7.8 The end of the file. This exercise introduces a very important concept—the fact that the end-of-file condition signals the end of the last group as well as the end of the file. This is analogous to the fact that midnight signals the end of the hour which began at 11:00 P.M., as well as the end of the day which began the preceding midnight. As a result, the termination routine will be required to print the summary for the last group as well as the grand total summary. This is identical to the method used in Example 7–1 involving page summaries.

7.9 There will be no total line printed for the last employee and the last employee will not be included in the report summary.

7.10 Overall the output form will be identical except for the one condition when a level break occurs immediately after the last line has been printed on a page. Since the form feed is performed right after printing the detail line, the employee total will be printed at the top of the next page. With the logic of Figure 7-12, it will be printed in the bottom margin of the preceding page.

PROGRAMMING PROBLEMS

7.1 Each record in a student information file contains the following.

Field	Size or Maximum Value
Student number	7 digits
Name	23 positions
Major code	999
Grade-point average	4.00

The records in this file have been sorted into sequence by major field code (code which indicates the student's major). Write a program which will print a listing for each major field code, showing the student's name, major field code, and grade-point average. Start each major field code on a new page. At the top of each page, print the heading LISTING BY MAJOR FIELD and appropriate column headings. Leave one blank line before and after the column heading line and print 43 single-spaced detail lines on each page. At the end of each major field listing, print a line saying

nnn STUDENTS IN MAJOR FIELD *mmm*

(*nnn* is the number of students and *mmm* is the major field code just completed.)

7.2 A monthly sales listing is to be prepared from a sales file which represents sales for the month. The records are in sequence by item number. For each input record, print the item number, customer number, quantity sold, unit price, and sales amount. At the end of each item number, print a line which says TOTAL FOR ITEM # *nnnn* followed by the sum of the quantity sold column and the sum of the sales amount column. Print an asterisk (*) to the right of each total to make it stand out. Print appropriate page and column headings at the top of each page.

Single-space all printed lines. Do *not* start each new item number on a new page. A total of 54 lines is available on each page for all printing (headings, detail, and total). The format for the input record is as follows:

Field	Size or Maximum Value
Record ID code	2 digits
Customer number	4 digits
Date of sale	6 digits (month, day, year)
Item number	4 digits
Quantity sold	2,000
Price of one item (dollars and cents)	49.99
Salesperson ID number	2 digits

7.3 For each sale, an appliance store records the following information into a record.

Field	Size or Maximum Value
Salesperson number	3 digits
Customer number	7 characters
Date of sale	6 digits (month, day, year)
Amount of sale	19,999.99

At the end of the month, the files are sorted into sequence on salesperson number, which means that all of the cards for salesperson 001 will be grouped together, followed by the cards for salesperson 002, and so on. Write a program that will print a report for each salesperson. The summary for each salesperson must begin on a new page. Appropriate headings are to include the salesperson number. Detail line output must include:

> Customer number
> Date of sale
> Amount of sale

For each salesperson, a total sales summary line must be printed. If total sales are at least $75,000, then include the words:

> MEMBER OF THE —BIG 75— CLUB

At the end of the listing, print the words THE MONTHLY SELLING STAR IS and the number of the salesperson with the highest total sales (assume that no two sales totals are equal).

7.4 Gas meters that serve the customers of a natural gas company are read in thousands of cubic feet. On each billing, the initial and the final monthly readings are included; the amount consumed is the difference between these two quantities. However, the charge is based on the number of therms consumed, which is a measure of the heat-producing capabilities of gas. (Some gases are "richer" than others—that is, they produce more heat per cubic foot.) Thus the meter reading difference is multiplied by a thermal factor to give the number of therms. The input data file includes a single master information record followed by customer records, one for each customer. Contents of these records include:

Master Record

Field	Typical Values
Thermal factor	1.077
Flat rate	1.22
Basic cost per therm	0.073

Customer Record

Field	Typical Values
Account number	128709
Initial meter reading	3597
Final meter reading	3698

Typical values that are shown for flat rate and basic cost per therm represent $1.22 and $0.073 (7.3 cents) respectively. Being ecologically inclined, the company bases the actual charge on a sliding scale—the more gas used, the higher the per-therm price, as follows:

Number of Units (Therms) Consumed	Price Factor
Less than 50	1.00
51 to 150	1.10
151 to 300	1.15
More than 300	1.18

As an example calculation, let us assume the following.

Meter reading (difference)	=	200
Flat rate	=	1.50
Basic cost per therm	=	0.08
Thermal factor	=	1.1

Therms consumed = 200 × 1.1 = 220

Flat rate	=	1.50
First 50 therms: 50 × 1.00 × 0.08	=	4.00
Next 100 therms: 100 × 1.10 × 0.08	=	8.80
Last 70 therms: 70 × 1.15 × 0.08	=	6.44

Total charge $20.74

Write a program to calculate each customer's charges and print:

Account number
Initial meter reading
Final meter reading
Thermal factor
Number of therms consumed
Total charge

Print 22 detail lines per page. Include page numbering at the top of each page and page totals for the total therms and charges at the bottom. Print grand totals for therms and charges.

CHAPTER 8

Interaction with the Computer

INTERACTIVE DATA INPUT
Transactional and Batch Processing
A Simple Interactive Program

USE OF IMMEDIATE MODE
Statements in Immediate Mode
Interrupting Execution

OBJECTIVES

This chapter covers two primary topics. The first relates to the interactive form of the **INPUT** statement. With it, you can enter data into a program from the terminal. The second relates to interacting with the computer while it is running your program. This tool will allow you to stop execution of your program temporarily and to inquire into its status. This involves executing Basic statements immediately upon entering them into the computer.

Interactive Data Input

TRANSACTIONAL AND BATCH PROCESSING All of the examples we have studied to this point are typical business data processing *batch processing* applications. In a batch processing environment, data is accumulated over a period of time, and then processed in batches. For instance, in the hours-worked examples of Chapter 7, the hours-worked records for each employee were accumulated during the week and then processed at the end of the week. In the early days of data processing, business operations were almost exclusively batch. The typical business computer included magnetic-tape units for data storage and a punched card reader for getting data into the computer. The hours-worked example would have been handled by punching all time information into cards, and then loading the cards into the computer at the end of the week to run paychecks.

Actually many applications (such as payroll) are well suited to batch processing. But inventory control is in a different category. If a company runs an inventory program once per week (indicating how much of each item is in stock), the report could be badly obsolete by the end of the week. What is needed is a system whereby data can be entered into the computer immediately upon its receipt. When an order is shipped for 500 copies of the book *Life in the Polar Regions,* the inventory figure in the computer is immediately reduced by 500. In this way, the computerized information is up to date rather than several days, or perhaps a month, old. Processing of this type is commonly referred to as *transactional processing.* It is available to users through data files which are *online* and always available. Such processing is now very widely used. Most minicomputers, having been designed for interactive use, are well suited to transactional processing.

An extensive treatment of interactive file manipulation is beyond the scope of this book. The interactive capabilities described in this chapter, however, are an important segment of learning to program.

A SIMPLE INTERACTIVE PROGRAM Let us assume, as is so often the case, that our bookstore manager of Chapter 1 has "seen the light" and wishes to use computerized data processing to maintain store records. Through a series of work sessions, a set of computerized data files is designed for handling the store needs. The overall system will require a set of programs to allow for placing data entered from the keyboard into the files, for updating file information, for generating needed reports from data in the files, and so on. We have drawn the assignment of writing the *data entry program:* this will allow someone to enter information into the system for new books. Since the program is to be modularized, we will be working on only a portion of it. The concept of interactive processing is illustrated by this example.

Example 8-1

Prepare a program which will accept the following data from the keyboard.

> Book identification number
> Book title
> Beginning inventory balance

As each record is entered, it will be edited and saved in a file by a module beginning at line 7000. (We are not responsible for this module; another programmer will write it.) A count of how many records have been entered and a tally of the total number of books must be maintained and printed when data entry is complete. Processing is to be terminated by entering a book ID number of 9999.

The program of Figure 8-1 illustrates two important points: the interactive **INPUT** statement (shaded in the program) and the value of modularizing a program.

This **INPUT** statement, repeated here

```
3060     INPUT N,T$,B
```

has the same form as the **INPUT #**. The difference between the two is that the **INPUT #** gets data from a file but the **INPUT** causes the computer to stop and await data from the keyboard. Whenever an **INPUT** statement of this type is encountered, the computer displays a question mark (?) prompt and awaits input from the keyboard. Figure 8-2 is a typical interactive session with this program. Upon entering each set of values in response to the prompt, we must depress the RETURN key so that the computer will know that we have completed that entry. As each new book record is entered (shaded in Figure 8-2), it is processed in lines 3010–3040 of the program. Notice that the book title must be included within quotes only when the title itself includes a comma. (The reason for this is the subject of an exercise at the end of this section.) Upon entering the trailer value, execution of the process routine is terminated and the totals for the session are printed by the termination routine.

Figure 8-1   Interactive computing—Example 8-1.

```
100 REM EXAMPLE 8-1
110 REM BOOK INVENTORY DATA ENTRY PROGRAM
120 REM INPUT QUANTITIES AND NAMES ARE:
130 REM    N - BOOK NUMBER
140 REM    T$- TITLE
150 REM    B - BEGINNING BALANCE
160 REM CALCULATED QUANTITIES AND NAMES ARE:
170 REM    C - LINE COUNT
180 REM    B1- ACCUMULATOR FOR B
190                                             REM
1000 REM MAIN PROGRAM
1010       GOSUB 2010
1011          REM INITIALIZE
1020       IF N = 9999 THEN 1030
1021          GOSUB 3010
1022          GOTO 1020
1023             REM REPEATEDLY PROCESS UNTIL NO MORE DATA
1030       GOSUB 4010
1031          REM PERFORM TERMINATION OPERATIONS
1040       STOP
1041          REM TERMINATE PROCESSING
1142 REM END OF MAIN PROGRAM
1143                                            REM
2000 REM INITIALIZATION ROUTINE
2010       PRINT "THIS DATA ENTRY PROGRAM ALLOWS YOU TO ENTER NEW RECORDS"
2020       PRINT "INTO THE ONLINE BOOK INVENTORY SYSTEM."
2030       PRINT "FOR EACH BOOK, THE FOLLOWING FIELDS MUST BE ENTERED:"
2040       PRINT "    BOOK NUMBER"
2050       PRINT "    TITLE"
2060       PRINT "    BEGINNING BALANCE"
2070       PRINT "FIELDS MUST BE SEPARATED BY A COMMA WHEN ENTERED."
2080       PRINT "ENTER 9999 FOR THE BOOK NUMBER TO TERMINATE."
2090       PRINT
2100       PRINT
2110          REM PRINT DIRECTIONS TO DATA ENTRY PERSON
2120       PRINT "NEXT RECORD";
2130       INPUT N,T$,B
2140          REM READ FIRST DATA RECORD
2150       RETURN
2160 REM END OF INITIALIZATION ROUTINE
2170                                            REM
3000 REM PROCESSING ROUTINE
3010       GOSUB 7010
3020          REM EDIT INPUT DATA AND WRITE TO FILE
3030       C = C + 1
3040       B1 = B1 + B
3050       PRINT "NEXT RECORD";
3060       INPUT N,T$,B
3070       RETURN
3080 REM END OF PROCESSING ROUTINE
3090                                            REM
4000 REM TERMINATION ROUTINE
4010       PRINT
4020       PRINT
4030       PRINT "NUMBER OF RECORDS PROCESSED =";C
4040       PRINT "TOTAL NUMBER OF BOOKS =";B1
4050       RETURN
4060 REM END OF TERMINATION ROUTINE
4070                                            REM
7000 REM DUMMY EDIT AND FILE WRITE ROUTINE
7010 REM NOTE: THIS ROUTINE IS TO BE PREPARED BY A. SMITH
7020       RETURN
7030 REM END OF DUMMY EDIT AND FILE WRITE ROUTINE
9999    END
```

```
THIS DATA ENTRY PROGRAM ALLOWS YOU TO ENTER NEW RECORDS
INTO THE ONLINE BOOK INVENTORY SYSTEM.
FOR EACH BOOK, THE FOLLOWING FIELDS MUST BE ENTERED:
     BOOK NUMBER
     TITLE
     BEGINNING BALANCE
FIELDS MUST BE SEPARATED BY A COMMA WHEN ENTERED.
ENTER 9999 FOR THE BOOK NUMBER TO TERMINATE.


NEXT RECORD? 4451, 'BEG BASIC', 453
NEXT RECORD? 4892, 'ECONOMICS', 512
NEXT RECORD? 5118, 'COBOL, THE ELEMENTS', 82
NEXT RECORD? 6881, 'THE IBM PC',   0
NEXT RECORD? 7144, 'BASIC PLUS', 147
NEXT RECORD? 9999, 'EOF' ,0


NUMBER OF RECORDS PROCESSED = 5
TOTAL NUMBER OF BOOKS = 1194
```

Figure 8-2
Interaction at the
terminal—Example
8-1.

A convenient feature of the **INPUT** statement can be included in this program. That is, the message to be printed (line 2120) can be included as part of the **INPUT** statement. The statement

```
2120    INPUT "NEXT RECORD";N,T$,B
```

may be substituted for

```
2120    PRINT "NEXT RECORD";
2130    INPUT N,T$,B
```

In both cases, the question mark prompt will be on the same line as the message prompt. Notice that the message is followed by a semicolon rather than a comma. This operates in the same way as when used within a **PRINT** statement. The cursor is not tabbed over; it remains immediately following the question mark prompt.

EXERCISES

8.1 What is the difference between the basic form of the **INPUT** statement as used here and the **READ** statement:

8.2 What would occur if the book title

COBOL, THE ELEMENTS

were entered without using quotes as in Figure 8-2?

Use of Immediate Mode

The subject of the next module is program loops—the real heart of programming. Overall, if a program is carefully planned and modularized, problems associated with getting it running can be minimized. However, loops do tend to cause problems, especially for the careless beginner. One of the devices which is sometimes helpful in debugging a program is the immediate-mode facility of Basic. As we have learned, one distinction between commands and statements is that commands are executed immediately and statements later on during execution of the program. This is not exactly true as many of the statements can be entered at the terminal *without* a line number, thus causing them to be executed immediately (as if they were commands); hence the term *immediate mode.* Figure 8-3, for instance, is a direct dialog with the compu-

**Figure 8-3
Statements in the
immediate mode.**

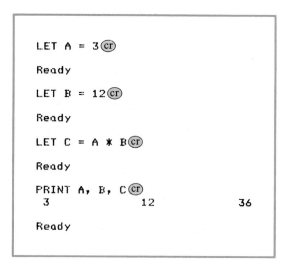

```
LET A = 3 (cr)

Ready

LET B = 12 (cr)

Ready

LET C = A * B (cr)

Ready

PRINT A, B, C (cr)
   3              12              36

Ready
```

ter. At first thought, this may appear to be of little value to us. However, it is important to recognize that whenever program execution is terminated, all variables contain their values at termination. Thus if a program terminates at the wrong point or gives incorrect results, we can inspect any variables in the program. To illustrate, assume that our program is calculating the mean of a data set and the program input statement is:

```
510     INPUT #1, N$, Q, A
```

Furthermore, the program has terminated on an error condition and we are suspicious of the input quantities and the internal loop variable I. We could then use the following immediate mode **PRINT** to get the desired values printed at the terminal:

```
PRINT I, N$, Q, A
```

This is a powerful and useful feature of the language.

INTERRUPTING EXECUTION Sometimes a program will become locked up in a loop and never break out (bad program logic). If the loop involves no input or output, we will see nothing happening at the terminal. With Basic, it is possible to stop the program and make inquiries. Some systems even allow the user to change variable values and then continue processing.

To illustrate, let us assume that a program requires a sequence of operations to be performed exactly 20 times. To handle this, we set up a simple counter and test in an **IF** statement as shown in Figure 8-4(a). In keeping with good structured principles, our loop consists of one entry point (line 500) and one exit (line 690). If this loop included input or output operations, we would see "activity" at the terminal. If it included no input or output, we would see nothing at the terminal as it executed. Now let us assume that we entered the wrong **GOTO** statement number at line 510 [Figure 8-4(b)]. This happens to be an especially bad error because the following will occur.

1. Execution of the loop will proceed as desired for the first 20 times through the loop.
2. When the value of I reaches 20, the relational expression in statement 510 will be true and execution will be transferred to statement 680. (Obviously this is an error; the **GOTO** should have been to statement 691.)
3. Execution of line 680 returns control to 500, and hence 510.
4. Since the value of I never changes, this will go on indefinitely.

Our program is now trapped in an infinite loop. Regardless of the operations normally performed within the loop, we will see nothing happening. This

Figure 8-4   **(a) Program loop. (b) Incorrect exit from program loop.**

```
500 REM ACCUMULATE LOOP          500 REM ACCUMULATE LOOP
510     IF I=20 THEN 691         510     IF I=20 THEN 680
520       I = I + 1              520       I = I + 1
           .                                .
           .                                .
           .                                .
680     GOTO 510                 680     GOTO 510
690 REM LOOP EXIT                690 REM LOOP EXIT
691     ... (next statement)     691     ... (next statement)


        (a)                              (b)
```

program will merely jump back and forth between lines 510 and 680. Now the question is, "What do we do about it?" Fortunately the designers of interactive systems thought of this possibility. Most systems include some means for the operator to terminate execution of a program from the keyboard. On many computers, it is done by depressing a key labeled "BREAK." Others use a combination of two keys: the CONTROL key and the letter C. This is called a *control C.* In any event, you should find out what your computer uses. Whether it is BREAK or CONTROL C, or something else, this action from the keyboard causes execution of the program to be terminated immediately and control returned to the command mode. Let us consider how a person might go about debugging the error in Figure 8-4(b). We will assume that execution has begun and that nothing appears to be happening at the screen. Following is a typical debugging sequence.

1. Stop execution of the program by depressing the appropriate key(s).
2. Determine the line at which program execution was terminated. Assume that execution terminated at line 680 (remember, in this case it will be either 510 or 680). Many computers will display a message such as:

   Break at line 680

   With some computers, you must request the computer to print the line number.
3. Upon finding out that we terminated at line 680, we type in the command

   LIST 680

   and the computer lists line 680 on the terminal. This does not tell us much and, upon looking at the program, we do not spot the error.
4. We type the immediate-mode statement:

   PRINT I

   and see that I has a value of 20. "Well," we conclude, "it should break out of the loop next."

If the computer which you are using allows execution of a suspended program to continue, then you would go on to the following step 5. Otherwise you might simply rerun the program.

5. We decide to continue execution of the program so we type in the command

   CONT

   which means continue. Even though we have listed part (or all) of the program and printed values in the immediate mode, execution will continue at the point of interruption. It will be as if we had never stopped execution.

6. But wait—bad news: It does *not* break out of the loop. After a few moments, we stop execution again.
7. This time, we enter the immediate-mode statement:

```
PRINT I
```

We see that the value of I is *still* 20, and this time execution stopped at line 510. At close inspection, we see the error.

The interactive programming capability of Basic gives the programmer powerful tools.

This example illustrates the dangers inherent in the **GOTO**. It is far too easy to use a wrong statement number reference with disastrous results. As we shall learn in Chapter 9, Basic includes an automatic loop control structure for the type of control illustrated by this example.

With the capabilities described in this chapter, the programmer can often spot errors very quickly that would otherwise be difficult to detect. But, these methods are no substitute for careful program design *prior* to coding and testing. All too often, the beginner has a tendency to get on the terminal and start poking around. Remember, an ounce of thinking is worth a pound of poking.

ANSWERS TO PRECEDING EXERCISES

8.1 The **READ** statement obtains data from the **DATA** statements that are included as part of the program. The **INPUT** statement displays a question mark prompt and awaits entry of the data from the keyboard.

8.2 The comma between COBOL and THE would be considered as separating the COBOL from THE ELEMENTS. In the statement

```
INPUT N,T$,B
```

the computer would place the word COBOL into **T$**, then attempt to put THE ELEMENTS (a string field) into the numeric variable **B**. An error would result. The use of quotes causes the **INPUT** to take everything within the quotes (including the comma) and place it in **T$**.

CHAPTER 9

Program Loops

OBJECTIVES

Control of loops is so important in programming that virtually all programming languages include features for automatic loop control. We have already seen this to a limited extent with the repeated execution of **GOSUB**s to processing routines. In this chapter, you will learn how to use the **FOR-NEXT** capability of Basic. You will study a simple loop and also a loop within a loop (called nested loop). The **FOR-NEXT** "tool" will be applied to searching a table of values for a particular entry. (Table searching is a common operation in programming.)

Basic Concepts of Loops

COUNTED LOOPS   Most of the sample programs in this book involve the repeated execution of a sequence of statements. For instance, a processing routine is executed repeatedly by a sequence beginning with an **IF** and ending with a **GOTO**. Exit from this repeated execution (program *loop*) has been achieved by detecting a trailer record that has indicated the end of the file. These have been relatively simple examples of the loop concept. This module deals with loops in a much more general way. The concept of the *controlled loop* involves performing a sequence of operations until a particular condition arises. This can range from detection of a trailer record to execution a predetermined number of times. The latter commonly occurs in programming and is called a *counted loop*. For instance, let us assume that we are to execute a **PRINT** exactly five times. The logic of such a loop can be illustrated by the flowchart of Figure 9-1. We can see that the loop is executed exactly five times before execution breaks out and that the structure corresponds exactly to the structured programming looping construct.

Figure 9-1
Flowchart of a
simple loop.

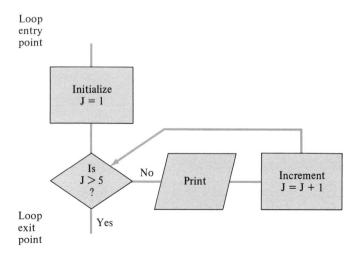

A sequence of statements to perform these operations (execute the loop exactly five times) is shown in Figure 9-2. The following commentary relates to this example.

1. The variable J is used as a counter (commonly called the *control variable*) to control the loop. Its value is initialized to 1 prior to entering the loop (statement 210).
2. The test for loop completion is made by statement 230 where J is compared with 5. When the condition is satisfied, execution is transferred to the loop exit point.
3. The *body* of the loop consists of the three statements 240, 250, and 260. These will be repeatedly executed.
4. Upon completion of each pass through the loop, the control variable J is increased by 1.

Printed output for this example is shown in Figure 9-2(b) where we see that the loop is executed exactly five times before execution breaks out.

Figure 9-2   (a) A counted loop. (b) Loop output.

```
200 REM LOOP ENTRY POINT
210       J = 1                        Initialize loop index J to 1
220 REM BEGINNING OF LOOP
230       IF J>5 THEN 281              Test loop index for exit condition
240           PRINT "TEST LINE"; J
250           PRINT                    Increment the counter
260           J = J + 1
270       GOTO 230
280 REM LOOP EXIT POINT               Body
281           PRINT "LOOP TERMINATED"  of the loop
    .
    .
    .
```

(a)

```
TEST LINE 1

TEST LINE 2

TEST LINE 3

TEST LINE 4

TEST LINE 5

LOOP TERMINATED
```

(b)

SINGLE-ENTRY/ Earlier in this book, the concept of a single-entry point to a loop and a single
SINGLE-EXIT exit point from the loop was stressed as fundamental to structured program-
PRINCIPLE ming. This means that a loop is always entered at the first statement of the
loop. For instance, in Figure 9-2 execution would never **GOTO** statement 250
from some other point in the program as illustrated in Figure 9-3. Entrance is
only via line 200.

Figure 9-3   Single
entry to a loop.

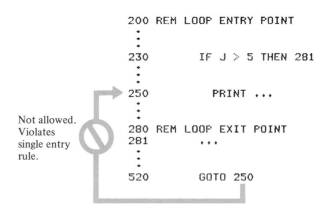

Exit from the loop likewise is always via the loop exit line (280 in Figure
9-2). Normally execution of a loop will continue under the sole control of the
loop control statement (line 230 in Figure 9-2). However, in some situations, it
is necessary to terminate a loop early. A calculation within a loop, for example,
might produce a result which makes further execution of the loop undesir-
able. Under these conditions, it is considered acceptable to jump to the loop
exit point from anywhere within the loop. However, exiting to any other point
outside of the loop is not in keeping with structured principles. These two
cases are illustrated by the samples of Figure 9-4.

EXERCISE

9.1 What would happen in the sequence of Figure 9-2 if each of the following
conditions occurred?
   a. The index **J** was initialized to 10 instead of 1.
   b. The test for **J** (statement 230) was **J** = 5 instead of **J** > 5.
   c. A value of 1 was subtracted from **J** rather than added in statement 260.
   d. Line 270 said **GOTO** 200.

Figure 9-4   (a) Valid exit from a loop. (b) Invalid exit from a loop.

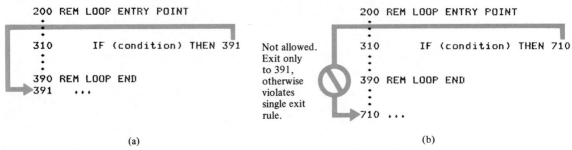

```
200 REM LOOP ENTRY POINT
    .
    .
    .
310         IF (condition) THEN 391
    .
    .
    .
390 REM LOOP END
391    ...
```

Not allowed.
Exit only
to 391,
otherwise
violates
single exit
rule.

```
200 REM LOOP ENTRY POINT
    .
    .
    .
310         IF (condition) THEN 710
    .
    .
    .
390 REM LOOP END
    .
    .
710 ...
```

(a)   (b)

THE FOR AND NEXT STATEMENTS Counted loops are so common in programming that Basic includes a special pair of statements which provide automatic control of the loop. The loop of Figure 9-2 is rewritten in Figure 9-5 using a **FOR-NEXT** loop. This loop will function in exactly the same way as that of Figure 9-2 and will produce the same output. Details of how the **FOR-NEXT** works are given in Figure 9-6. Upon entering the loop (the **FOR** statement at line 210), the control variable **J** is set to the initial value. Upon encountering the **NEXT** statement, it is increased by the increment of the **STEP** value. If the increment is 1, then the **STEP** may be omitted as in statement 210 of Figure 9-5. The test value (5 in this case) is the maximum allowable value for which the loop will be executed. When this value is exceeded, execution automatically continues to the statement following the **NEXT**.

GENERAL FORM OF THE FOR STATEMENT The general form of the **FOR** statement is:

FOR <var> = <expr> **TO** <expr> **STEP** <expr>

The examples on the next page further illustrate the characteristics of the **FOR** statement.

Figure 9-5   Loop control with the FOR-NEXT.

```
200 REM BEGINNING OF FOR-NEXT LOOP
210         FOR J = 1 TO 5
220             PRINT "TEST LINE"; J
230             PRINT
240         NEXT J
250 REM END OF FOR-NEXT LOOP
260         PRINT "LOOP TERMINATED"
    .
    .
    .
```

```
FOR J = 5 TO X+3
```

Note that the initial value need not be 1. Furthermore, the initial value, the test value, and the increment can all be expressions. If **X** contained 4, then this loop would be executed for values of 5, 6, and 7, or three times.

```
FOR P = 0 TO 13 STEP 2
```

In this case, the loop would be executed for values of 0, 2, 4, 6, 8, 10, and 12. Note that the index need not end up equal to the test value. The rule is that the loop will be executed as long as the index does *not* exceed the test value.

```
FOR A = -1.5 TO 2.4 STEP 0.1
```

Fractional quantities are allowable in the **FOR** statement. This loop would execute 40 times.

```
FOR C = 0 TO -5 STEP -1
```

It is possible to use a negative increment. Here the loop would be executed for values of **C** of 0, –1, –2, –3, –4, and –5 (six times).

EXERCISE

9.2 How many times would the loops controlled by each of the following **FOR** statements be executed?

a.   `FOR J = 3 TO 13`
b.   `FOR J = 3 TO 13 STEP 3`
c.   `FOR J = 5 TO -5 STEP -1`
d.   `FOR J = 0 TO 3*X-1`   (Assume X = 4.)

Figure 9-6   Details of the FOR-NEXT.

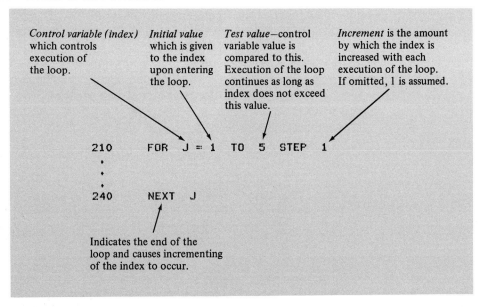

A FLOWCHART The counted loop example of Figure 9-2 includes user-prepared code to
REPRESENTATION perform the initializing, incrementing, and testing functions. Thus the flow-
OF THE chart of Figure 9-1, which shows the initializing and incrementing operations,
FOR-NEXT LOOP is quite appropriate. However, these operations are performed automatically
by the **FOR-NEXT**. Remember, the basic purpose of a flowchart is to define
what the programmer must do in writing the code. Thus it could be argued
that the initialization and incrementing (which are not explicitly done by the
programmer) should not be included as shown in Figure 9-1. An alternative
flowchart form for representing a **FOR-NEXT** loop is shown in Figure 9-7.
Here we see that the control details regarding the loop are included in a
separate description box. This carries all the detailed information necessary
in writing the **FOR** statement.

**Figure 9-7   Flowchart
representation of
FOR-NEXT.**

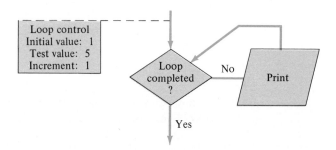

Programming Examples with FOR-NEXT

CALCULATING Inflation and the decreasing purchasing power of the dollar are a prime
A TABLE problem today. We continually read how $10 of goods today will cost us $11
or $12 next year, $13 or $14 the year after, and so on. Predictions such as
these are based on the expected annual rate of inflation. To illustrate, let us
assume that economists predict a 12 percent annual inflation rate. Then the
cost of purchasing $10 worth of goods in one, two, and three years would be
calculated as in the following.

The general form for the calculations is:

Cost next year = Cost this year × (1 + Inflation rate)

Current year: $10 purchases $10 worth of goods

Cost after 1 year = 10 × (1 + 0.12)
                 =$11.20

Cost after 2 years = Cost after 1 year × (1 + 0.12)
                   = 11.20 × 1.12
                   = $12.54

$$\text{Cost after 3 years} = \text{Cost after 2 years} \times (1 + 0.12)$$
$$= 12.54 \times 1.12$$
$$= \$14.05$$

Let us consider this as the basis for illustrating use of the **FOR-NEXT**.

Example 9-1

Prepare a program which will accept an annual inflation rate as input, and then calculate a 10-year table of the cost of $10 worth of goods related to the base year. The program must print appropriate headings and a termination message.

PROGRAM This problem is typical of many encountered in data processing; that is, a
PLANNING table must be computed and printed. A print layout form is shown in Figure
AND SOLUTION 9-8(a). A sample output using an inflation rate of 12 percent is included in
Figure 9-8(b).

Operations to be performed in this program involve:

1. Performing initial operations.
2. Accepting the inflation rate.
3. Computing and printing the cost repeatedly for years from 1 to 10.
4. Terminating execution.

Figure 9-8 (a) Print layout. (b) Sample output.

(a)

```
INFLATION TABLE          DATE: 26-APR
COST OF $10 WORTH OF GOODS

INFLATION RATE = 12%

    YEAR          COST
     1           11.20
     2           12.54
     3           14.05
     4           15.74
     5           17.62
     6           19.74
     7           22.11
     8           24.76
     9           27.73
    10           31.06

PROCESSING COMPLETE

Ready
```

(b)

The logic of this problem is relatively straightforward, as shown in the partial set of flowcharts of Figure 9-9. Here we see the looping sequence controlled within the process routine (as opposed to the main calling program). The description box clearly identifies the nature of the loop control. To the right of the flowchart, we see an indication of placement of the **FOR** and **NEXT** statements relative to the flowchart operations.

Figure 9-10 is a complete program for this example. Previous example programs repeatedly execute the process routine by way of a **GOSUB** in the main program. This executes the process routine only once, but the process routine itself involves a loop. This is not the only way to program this problem (see Exercise 9.4). It is interesting that the heart of the program consists of only a few lines (3020 to 3050). The bulk of the listing involves printing headings and needed "housekeeping" operations.

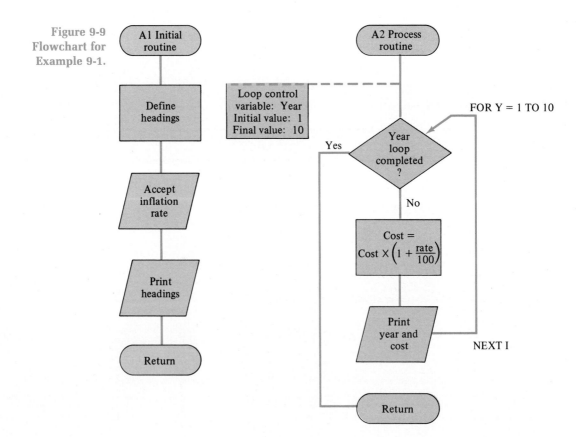

**Figure 9-9
Flowchart for
Example 9-1.**

Figure 9-10 Program
for Example 9-1.

```
100   REM INFLATION RATE - EXAMPLE 9-1
110   REM THIS PROGRAM CALCULATES THE PURCHASING
120   REM POWER OF THE DOLLAR OVER A 10-YEAR
130   REM PERIOD.  INPUT IS THE INFLATION RATE.
140   REM OUTPUT IS A TABLE OF THE AMOUNT REQUIRED
150   REM TO PURCHASE $10 WORTH OF GOODS RELATIVE
160   REM TO THE BASE YEAR.
170   REM   VARIABLES USED ARE:
180   REM      Y - YEAR
190   REM      R - INFLATION RATE IN PERCENT
200   REM      C - AMOUNT NEEDED TO MAKE '$10
210   REM            PURCHASE' FOR A GIVEN YEAR
220                                             REM
1000 REM MAIN PROGRAM
1010      GOSUB 2010
1011        ! INITIALIZE
1020      GOSUB 3010
1021        ! PROCESS
1030      GOSUB 4010
1031        ! TERMINATE
1040      STOP
1050 REM END OF MAIN PROGRAM
1060                                            REM
2000 REM INITIAL ROUTINE
2010      H1$ = 'INFLATION TABLE        DATE: \          \'
2020      H2$ = 'COST OF $10 WORTH OF GOODS'
2030      H3$ = 'INFLATION RATE = ##'
2040      H4$ = '  YEAR       COST'
2060      D$  = '   ##         ##.##'
2070          REM DEFINE HEADINGS
2080      INPUT 'WHAT INFLATION RATE DO YOU WISH'; R
2090      C = 10.
2100          REM INITIALIZE YEAR COST
2110      PRINT H1$, DATE$
2120      PRINT H2$
2130      PRINT
2140      PRINT USING H3$, R
2150      PRINT
2160      PRINT H4$
2170          REM PRINT HEADINGS
2180      RETURN
2190 REM END OF INITIAL ROUTINE
2220                                            REM
3000 REM PROCESS ROUTINE
3010 REM TABLE PROCESSING LOOP
3020      FOR Y = 1 TO 10
3030         C = C * (1 + R/100)
3040          PRINT USING D$, Y, C
3050      NEXT Y
3060 REM END OF TABLE PROCESSING LOOP
3070      RETURN
3080 REM END OF PROCESS ROUTINE
3090                                            REM
4000 REM TERMINATION ROUTINE
4010      PRINT
4020      PRINT 'PROCESSING COMPLETE'
4030      RETURN
4040 REM END OF TERMINATION ROUTINE
4050                                            REM
9999      END
```

EXERCISES

9.3 In statement 3030 of Figure 9-10, the new value of **C** is calculated as:

```
C * (1 + R/100)
```

The quantity within the expression is calculated during each pass through the loop. This is not very efficient. Explain why not and show what change might be made.

9.4 Control of the loop in Figure 9-10 is contained within the processing loop (the **FOR** statement at line 3020). Make the changes necessary to place the control in the main program. In other words, loop control should relate to the **GOSUB** at line 1020.

NESTED LOOPS   Frequently programming needs involve a loop completely within another loop. These are called *nested loops* and are easily handled with the **FOR-NEXT**. Example 9-2, which is an expansion of Example 9-1, illustrates this concept.

Example 9-2

This example involves inflation tables as in Example 9-1. However, the user is to key in a range of interest rates. For example, if the "beginning" rate is entered as 8 and the "ending" rate as 12, then complete tables must be produced for each of the rates 8, 9, 10, 11, and 12 percent.

This program will require an overall or *outer* loop which will execute for values of inflation rate ranging from a designated beginning value to an ending value (for instance, 8 to 12). For each of the inflation rate values, an *inner* loop (identical to that of Example 9-1) will execute 10 times. The logic of a loop included completely within another loop is relatively simple when approached on a step-by-step basis. We see this in the logical structure of Figure 9-11. In fact, this is the essence of structured programming: using the three basic structures to solve a problem. This concept is incorporated into the flowchart of Example 9-2 shown in Figure 9-12 on page 174. Note that the nature of each loop is carefully documented.

The program of Figure 9-10 has been modified in Figure 9-13 to include repetitious calculation of tables. With the use of indentation, the inner and outer loops are readily apparent. Each pass through the outer loop will cause entry into the inner loop (statement 3070), which will produce a complete table, including headings, for the current value of the rate **R**. We should note that each pass through the inner loop causes the variable **C** to be changed (this is the object of the program). However, for each new table, it must be initialized back to a value of 10 (see line 3040). By contrast, the rate remains constant within the inner loop. Thus, prior to entering the inner loop, an

Figure 9-11   The concept of nested loops.

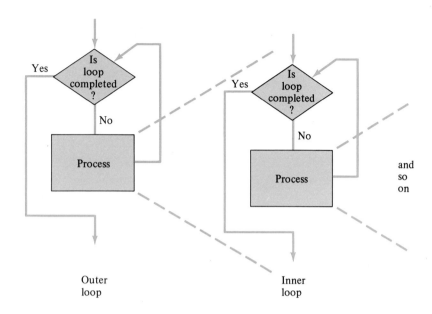

Outer loop   Inner loop

"inflation factor" **F** is calculated. This avoids the identical calculation for each pass through the inner loop. The value of this is evident if we compare line 3030 of Figure 9-10 with the combination of lines 3030 and 3080 in Figure 9-13.

EXERCISE

9.5 In your opinion, how many tables would be prepared (that is, how many passes through the outer loop) if the initial and final values entered were the same? What if the final value were smaller than the initial value?

Early Exit from a FOR-NEXT Loop

SEARCHING A TABLE   Frequently the needs of a program will require that a loop be executed a certain number of times. However, if a particular condition occurs, then the exit is to be made immediately. (This concept is depicted in Figure 9-4.) the **FOR-NEXT** loop allows this to be done. To illustrate, let us consider a simple example.

Example 9-3

This example is a greatly simplified version of an online information system. The user will enter a student number through a terminal and the computer will search a **DATA** table containing the student number, name, and grade-point average (GPA). Upon finding the student num-

**Figure 9-12
Flowchart for
Example 9-2.**

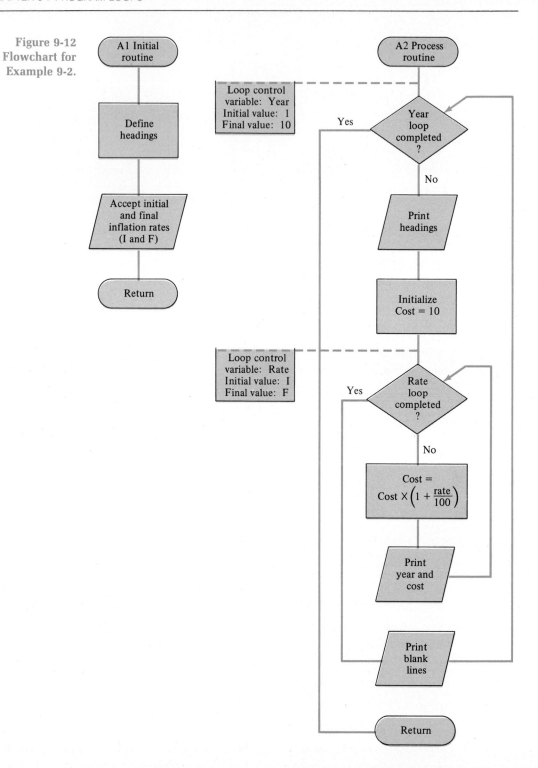

Figure 9-13   Program for Example 9-2.

```
100   REM INFLATION RATE - EXAMPLE 9-2
110   REM THIS PROGRAM CALCULATES A SERIES OF INFLATION RATE
120   REM TABLES.  SUCCESSIVE TABLES ARE CALCULATED STARTING
130   REM WITH A BEGINNING RATE AND ENDING WITH AN ENDING
140   REM RATE.   THE USER ENTERS THESE QUANTITIES INTO THE
150   REM VARIABLES "R1" AND "R2".
160                                                       REM
1000 REM MAIN PROGRAM
1010      GOSUB 2010
1011          REM INITIALIZE
1020      GOSUB 3020
1021          REM PROCESS
1030      GOSUB 4010
1031          REM TERMINATE
1040      STOP
1050 REM END OF MAIN PROGRAM
1060                                                      REM
2000 REM INITIAL ROUTINE
2010      H1$ = "INFLATION TABLE        DATE: \        \"
2020      H2$ = "COST OF $10 WORTH OF GOODS"
2030      H3$ = "INFLATION RATE = ##"
2040      H4$ = "  YEAR       COST"
2050      D$  = "   ##        ##.##"
2060      INPUT "ENTER THE BEGINNING AND ENDING INFLATION RATES";R1,R2
2070      RETURN
2080 REM END OF INITIAL ROUTINE
2090                                                      REM
3000 REM PROCESS ROUTINE
3010      REM   OUTER LOOP - CONTROLS INFLATION RATE INCREMENTS
3020      FOR R = R1 TO R2
3030          F = 1 + R/100
3031             REM FOR USE IN CALCULATION
3040          C = 10
3041             REM SET COST BACK TO INITIAL VALUE
3050          GOSUB 5010
3051             REM PRINT HEADINGS
3060          REM TABLE PROCESSING (INNER) LOOP
3070          FOR Y = 1 TO 10
3080              C = C * F
3090              PRINT USING D$, Y, C
3100          NEXT Y
3110          REM END OF INNER LOOP
3120          PRINT
3121          PRINT
3122          PRINT
3130      NEXT R
3140      REM END OF OUTER LOOP
3150      RETURN
3160 REM END OF PROCESS ROUTINE
3170                                                      REM
4000 REM TERMINATION ROUTINE
4010      PRINT
4020      PRINT "PROCESSING COMPLETE"
4030      RETURN
4040 REM END OF TERMINATION ROUTINE
4050                                                      REM
5000 REM PRINT HEADINGS ROUTINE
5010      PRINT H1$, DATE$
5020      PRINT H2$
5030      PRINT
5040      PRINT USING H3$, R
5050      PRINT
5060      PRINT H4$
5070      RETURN
5080 REM END OF HEADINGS ROUTINE
5090                                                      REM
9999    END
```

ber, the name and GPA are to be displayed. If no such student is found, the message

STUDENT *nnnn* NOT IN TABLE

will be displayed.

This problem involves searching a table for a particular entry, a common operation in programming. The table will be stored in a series of **DATA** statements, with each statement containing the student number, name, and GPA, such as the sample shown in Figure 9-14. Preceding the first student record is a separate **DATA** statement with the number of entries in this table. Thus the example table includes 37 entries; this value will be used to control the **FOR-NEXT** loop.

The logic of this problem solution is illustrated in Figure 9-15. Some points of importance which will be reflected in the program are:

1. To terminate processing, the user can enter a value of zero for the student number.
2. Whether or not the student number is found during the search is indicated by use of a string variable whose value is initially set to "NO." If the student number is found, this variable is given a value of "YES." Outside the loop, the variable is tested to determine what is to be printed.
3. If a student number is found, exit from the loop is immediate. Although this structure is not consistent with the three basic structured programming concepts, it is generally considered acceptable. In fact, some languages include a special **EXIT** statement for this purpose.
4. After each search of the table, which will involve **READ**ing the **DATA** statements, the **DATA** pointer must be "restored" to the first student. This is necessary so that each search will begin at the first entry in the table.

Figure 9-14   Student data table for Example 9-3.

```
5000 REM DATA TABLE FOR EXAMPLE 7-3
5005    DATA 37
5010    DATA 1572, 'BAKER ALICE',    3.62
5020    DATA 9713, 'COLUMBO ERNEST', 2.11
5030    DATA 4613, 'DICKEY SCOTT',   3.91
            .
            .
            .
5370    DATA 2218, 'ZENER DONALD',   2.88
9999 END
```

Figure 9-15   Flowchart for Example 9-3.

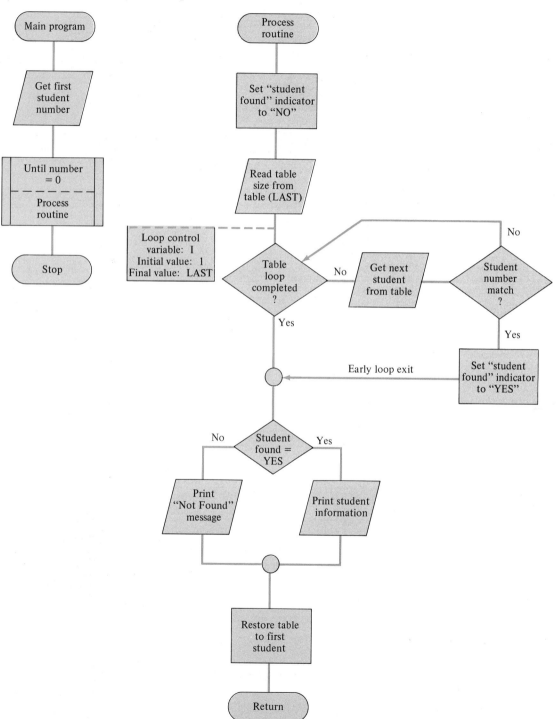

Figure 9-16   Program
for Example 9-3.

```
100  REM TABLE SEARCH - EXAMPLE 9-3
110  REM THIS PROGRAM ACCEPTS A STUDENT NUMBER ENTRY FROM A
120  REM KEYBOARD AND SEARCHES A TABLE FOR THAT STUDENT.
130  REM IF FOUND, THE STUDENT NUMBER AND G ARE DISPLAYED.
140  REM    VARIABLES USED ARE:
150  REM     S    - STUDENT NUMBER ENTERED FROM KEYBOARD
160  REM     F$   - SWITCH TO INDICATE WHETHER OR NOT
170  REM             STUDENT FOUND
180  REM     L9   - NUMBER OF ENTRIES IN TABLE
190  REM     N    - STUDENT NUMBER FROM TABLE
195  REM     N$   - STUDENT NAME
200  REM     G    - GRADE POINT AVERAGE
210                                                    REM
1000 REM MAIN PROGRAM
1010     INPUT "Student number (0 to terminate)";S
1011        REM GET FIRST STUDENT NUMBER
1020     IF S=0 THEN 1030
1021        GOSUB 3010
1022        GOTO 1020
1023           REM PROCESS UNTIL NO MORE STUDENTS REQUESTED
1030     STOP
1040 REM END OF MAIN PROGRAM
1050                                                   REM
3000 REM PROCESS ROUTINE
3020     F$ = "NO"
3021        REM   INITIALIZE F$ TO "NO"
3030     READ L9
3031       REM READ NUMBER OF STUDENTS IN TABLE INTO L9
3040     REM TABLE SEARCH LOOP FOLLOWS
3050     FOR I = 1 TO L9
3060        READ N, N$, G
3061          REM READ NEXT TABLE ENTRIES
3070        IF S <> N THEN 3100
3080           F$ = "YES"
3090           GOTO 3110
3091              REM STUDENT FOUND SO EXIT THE LOOP IMMEDIATELY
3100     NEXT I
3101       REM END OF TABLE SEARCH LOOP
3102                                                   REM
3110     IF F$ = "YES" THEN 3112 ELSE 3131
3111 REM  THEN
3112        PRINT N$; G
3120        GOTO 3141
3130 REM  ELSE
3131        PRINT "STUDENT"; S; "NOT IN FILE"
3140 REM  ENDIF
3141     PRINT
3150     PRINT
3160     RESTORE
3161        REM RESTORE THE DATA TABLE
3190     INPUT "Student number (0 to terminate)"; S
3200     RETURN
3210 REM END OF PROCESS ROUTINE
3230                                                   REM
5000 REM DATA TABLE FOR EXAMPLE 7-3
5005     DATA 37
5010     DATA 1572, "BAKER ALICE",    3.62
5020     DATA 9713, "COLUMBO ERNEST", 2.11
5030     DATA 4613, "DICKEY SCOTT",   3.91
            .
            .
            .
5370     DATA 2218, "ZENER DONALD",   2.88
9999     END
```

THE RESTORE
STATEMENT

As we learned in Chapter 2, the system forms a data pool from the entries in program **DATA** statements. As the program **READ**s through the data pool, the system maintains a pointer within the pool to keep track of the next value which is available. Although this pointer is handled automatically by the system, the programmer can set it back to the beginning of the data pool by use of the **RESTORE** statement. Execution of the **RESTORE** moves the pointer back to the beginning regardless of where it happens to be, and allows the **DATA** table to be read again from the beginning. This capability is needed in Example 9-3.

AN EXAMPLE
PROGRAM

The program of Figure 9-16 conforms to the logic of the flowchart in Figure 9-15. Points of note in this program are:

1. The variable **F$** is used as a *switch* to determine whether or not the student number is found. It is set to NO prior to searching in statement 3020. If the number is found, it is set to YES in statement 3080. Its value determines whether the message is printed by statement 3112 or 3131.
2. The comparison between the search student number and the table number is made in statement 3070. Note that the early exit (line 3090) is via the statement immediately following the **NEXT** statement.
3. Upon printing the appropriate output message, the **DATA** table is RE-STOREd at line 3160.

Further consideration of this program is via the following exercises.

EXERCISES

9.6 What would happen if statement 3020 were accidentally left out of the program in Figure 9-16?

9.7 The number of entries in the table is read into **L9** at line 3030. Note this is done within the process routine and is executed each time a new student number is entered. Since the number of table entries does not change, why not put this in the initialization routine where it will only be read once?

Rules Regarding FOR-NEXT Loops

Previous examples illustrate many of the features of **FOR-NEXT** loops. Let us consider a summary of these and other characteristics of the **FOR-NEXT**.

1. The control variable is "just another variable" in the program. Within the loop, its value can be used as that of any other variable. That is, it can be printed, used in a calculation, and so on. As a rule, it should not be changed—leave it for automatic control by the **FOR-NEXT**.

(However, some versions of Basic do allow it to be modified by the program within the loop.)

2. Upon exiting from a **FOR-NEXT**, the value of the control variable is unpredictable. For most versions of Basic, it will *not* remain at the last value used.

3. For positive **STEP** values, the loop is executed until incrementing the control variable would cause it to be greater than the final value. For negative step values, the loop is executed until incrementing the control variable would cause it to be less than the final value.

4. Entry to a **FOR-NEXT** loop is only through the **FOR** statement. *Do not branch into the body of the loop from outside the loop.*

5. Example 9-3 involves a nested loop (one loop within the other). There is no limit to the number of loops which may be nested within each other. However, care should be taken not to use the same variable as the control variable for two or more nested loops. Also, be certain not to overlap the ranges of two loops. Figure 9-17 illustrates correct and incorrect nesting of loops.

Figure 9-17   (a) Three-level nesting—VALID.   (b) Overlapped loops—INVALID

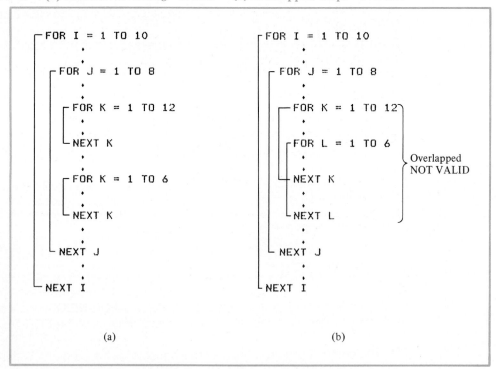

(a)   (b)

EXERCISE

9.8 What will be the value for the variable **A** in each of the following sets of nested loops, assuming that all loops run to completion?

```
a.  A = 0
    FOR I = 1 TO 10

      .
      .
      .

    FOR J = 1 TO 10
    A = A + 1
    NEXT J

      .
      .
      .

    NEXT I
```

```
b.  A = 0
    FOR I = 1 TO 10 STEP 2

      .
      .
      .

    FOR J = 7 TO 13
    A = A + 1
    NEXT J

      .
      .
      .

    NEXT I
```

```
c.  A = 0
    FOR I = 7 TO -2 STEP -1

      .
      .
      .

    FOR J = 0 TO 5

      .
      .
      .

    NEXT J
    A = A + 1
    NEXT I
```

```
d.  A = 0
    FOR I = 1 TO A

      .
      .
      .

    FOR J = 1 TO 9
    A = A + 1
    NEXT J

      .
      .
      .

    NEXT I
```

The WHILE and UNTIL Options of the FOR-NEXT

In many instances, we have situations in which we would like to have a loop continuously executed *until* a particular condition occurs. In others, we desire repetition *while* some other condition prevails. With the conventional **FOR-NEXT**, it is necessary to include an **IF** statement to test for the particular condition, and then execute an early exit. Some versions of Basic include special **UNTIL** and **WHILE** forms of the **FOR-NEXT**. For instance,

```
FOR K = 1 TO 20
```

will cause a loop to be executed until **K** reaches 20. On the other hand, the statement

```
FOR M = 1 UNTIL N = 9999
```

will cause this loop to be executed until the value for **N** becomes 9999. This may involve only one pass through the loop or many passes. If the value of **N** is 9999 upon executing the **FOR** statement, the loop will not be executed at all. This is a very useful feature. The general form of this version of the **FOR** is:

FOR <*var*> = <*expr*> [**STEP** <*expr*>] **WHILE** <*condition*>
FOR <*var*> = <*expr*> [**STEP** <*expr*>] **UNTIL** <*condition*>

The *condition* has the same structure as that used in the **IF** statement. Execution of the loop continues as long as the condition is true (**WHILE**) or is false (**UNTIL**). This is a powerful tool which provides the capability for implementing structured programming techniques. To illustrate its use, let us consider the following simple example.

Example 9-4

A loop is to be executed repeatedly until a particular condition is encountered. When that condition is detected, then processing is to be terminated after execution of the current pass.

Two program segments which illustrate these forms of the **FOR** are shown in Figure 9-18. Following are some important points relating to the examples.

1. The variable which forms the basis for the test (**L$**) must be given an initial value before entering the loop.
2. Although the control variable **K** is not used in this example, it will still be incremented by 1 each pass and is available for use within the loop. Upon exit from the loop, it will contain the last value.
3. The condition test is made when the loop is first entered and then only *after* the completion of each pass. Execution does *not* exit from the

Figure 9-18   The FOR-WHILE and FOR-UNTIL.

```
500    L$ = "YES"
510    FOR K = 1   WHILE L$ = "YES"
  •
  •
  •
560    IF (condition) THEN 570 ELSE 580
570        L$="NO"
580    ...
  •
  •
  •
600    NEXT K        End of loop

                    (a)
```

```
500    L$ = "YES"
510    FOR K = 1 UNTIL L$ = "NO"
  •
  •
  •
560    IF (condition) THEN 570 ELSE 580
570        L$="NO"
580    ...
  •
  •
  •
600    NEXT K        End of loop

                    (b)
```

loop the instant the value of, for instance, **L$** changes to "NO" at line 570. In many cases, this may result in an undesired pass through the loop.

If it were necessary in Example 9-4 to terminate execution of the loop *immediately* upon detecting the specified condition, then the segments of Figure 9-18 would not work. However, this need can be satisfied very readily merely by modifying the **IF** statement sequence beginning with line 560 as shown in Figure 9-19. Branching to the **NEXT** causes control to return to the **NEXT** at line 510. Since **L$** no longer has a value of YES, execution of the loop is terminated.

This technique can be used to advantage in the student inquiry program of Figure 9-16. Remember, in this example, the loop is to be executed

UNTIL the data table is exhausted

or   **UNTIL** the student number is found.

Figure 9-19   Terminating a FOR loop.

```
500    L$ = "YES"
510    FOR K = 1   WHILE L$ = "YES"
  •
  •
  •
560    IF (condition) THEN 570 ELSE 590
570        L$="NO"
580        GOTO 600
590    ...
  •
  •
  •
600    NEXT K        End of loop

                    (a)
```

```
500    L $ = "YES"
510    FOR K = 1 UNTIL L$ = "NO"
  •
  •
  •
560    IF (condition) THEN 570 ELSE 590
570        L$="NO"
580        GOTO 600
590    ...
  •
  •
  •
600    NEXT K        End of loop

                    (b)
```

Since the condition in this form of the **FOR** can be simple or compound, the table search portion of this program can be modified as shown in Figure 9-20.

Figure 9-20   Using the FOR-UNTIL in Example 9-3.

```
3050   FOR K = 1 UNTIL K>L9 OR F$="YES"
3060      READ N, N$, G
3070      IF S <> N THEN 3090
3080         F$ = "YES"
3090   NEXT K
```

The FOR as a Statement Modifier

Occasionally the programmer encounters a situation in which a single statement must be repeatedly executed a predetermined number of times. For instance, an output report might require 10 blank lines. The sequence of statements

```
500    FOR I = 1 TO 10
510       PRINT
520    NEXT I
```

can be replaced by the following single statement using a **FOR** modifier.

```
600    PRINT FOR I = 1 TO 10
```

Causes the preceding
statement to be
repeatedly executed.

The **FOR** modifier can assume any form allowed with the conventional **FOR** statement, for instance:

```
900    READ T, N$    FOR K = 1 UNTIL T=D
```

In statement 900, values will be read from the **DATA** pool until a value is read which is equal to the value stored in **D**.

ANSWERS TO PRECEDING EXERCISES

9.1 a. The condition at line 230 would immediately be true and the body of the loop would never be executed.

  b. The loop would be exited when **J** reached 5 rather than 6, thereby printing only for values of 1–4.

  c. The value of **J** would never exceed 5 (it would progress from 1 to 0, –1, –2, . . .). The loop would never be terminated; this is called an *infinite loop*.

  d. The value of **J** would continually be set back to 1 and the loop would never be terminated as in part c.

9.2 a. 11   b. 4   c. 11   d. 12

9.3 The rate **R** remains unchanged throughout the program, so the same thing is being recalculated each time. The following two statements inserted in Figure 9-10 would be more efficient.

```
2085     F = 1 + R/100
3030     C = C * F
```

9.4 Delete lines 3020 and 3050 (**FOR** and **NEXT**) from the processing routine and insert the following in the main program.

```
1020     FOR Y = 1 TO 10
1022        GOSUB 3000
1024     NEXT Y
```

9.5 The loop would be executed once if they are equal. Assume that the initial and final values were both 7. The control variable **R** would be set to 7 and compared with the final value of 7 before proceeding. Since the control variable does not exceed the final value, the loop would be executed. However, upon incrementing, the control variable would exceed the final value and so the loop would not be executed again.

  On the other hand, if the initial value exceeded the final value, the loop would not be executed at all. This results from the fact that the control variable **R**, upon first being assigned the initial value, would already have exceeded the final value.

9.6 To illustrate, assume that five inquiries were made from the terminal as follows:

  First inquiry—student not in table
  Second inquiry—student in table
  Third inquiry—student not in table
  Fourth inquiry—student not in table
  Fifth inquiry—student in table

Now we must remember that initially **F$** will be "empty" (will *not* be YES). Once a successful search is completed, then line 3080 will have placed YES into **F$**, which will never change. The output for these five inquiries will be:

First inquiry—not found message
Second inquiry—correct student information
Third inquiry—student information for last student in table since this will be the last one read in the unsuccessful search
Fourth inquiry—same as third
Fifth inquiry—correct student information

9.7 It is true that this count (number of entries in the **DATA** table) does not change. However, execution of the **RESTORE** moves the pointer back to the *beginning* of the data pool. Hence, at the beginning of each loop, the first available value is the header (value of 37 in this example). It must be read in order to "line up" with each student record that follows.

9.8 a.   100
    b.   35
    c.   10; the inner loop does not affect the value of **A**.
    d.   0; the outer loop will never be executed.

PROGRAMMING PROBLEMS

9.1 For counseling purposes, a college uses a personality test which provides scores in each of four categories. The data for each student is included in a record of a data file as follows (the trailer contains 9999 for a student number):

> Student number
> Student name
> Intrinsic motivation (IM)
> Self-enhancement (SE)
> Person orientation (PO)
> Goal deficiency (GD)

A program is to be written to locate students requiring counseling for personality problems. The criteria are as follows:

> IM > 40
> PO < 20
> GD > 40

The results for each "problem" student should be printed in the form of a bar graph as shown by the following example output.

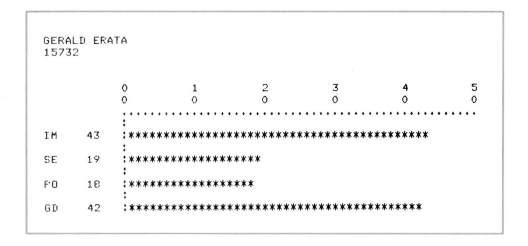

```
GERALD ERATA
15732


            0       1       2       3       4       5
            0       0       0       0       0       0
          :..........................................
          :
IM    43  :******************************************
          :
SE    19  :******************
          :
FO    18  :*****************
          :
GD    42  :*****************************************
```

9.2 For a manufacturing company, one objective of inventory control is to minimize the overall cost resulting from carrying inventory and setting up for new production runs. The term *economic order quantity* refers to the most economical quantity of a given item to produce in a single run for specified cost conditions; more explicitly, the economic order quantity may be computed as:

$$Q = \sqrt{\frac{2RS}{C}}$$

where: Q = economic order quantity
R = annual number of units required
S = setup cost per order
C = inventory cost to carry one unit for one year

A manager would like a program which will calculate tables such as the following.

```
ECONOMIC ORDER QUANTITY
UNITS REQUIRED:   200,000
INVENTORY COST:   0.030


  SETUP COST         QUANTITY

    12.00             12649
    12.50             12910
    13.00             13166
    13.50             13416
    14.00             13663
```

Input to the program will be:

Quantity	Example Values
R	200000
C	0.030
Beginning value of S	12
Ending value of S	14
Increment of S	0.5

Upon completing the table, the program should ask the manager whether or not another table is desired.

9.3 Modify Problem 9–2 to allow a range to be entered for both S and R and print a series of tables. Nested **FOR-NEXT** loops will be required for this.

9.4 Modify Problem 9–3 to print the results in a single table with the columns representing increasing values of S and the rows increasing values of C.

9.5 We are all familiar with the salesperson's approach of "for the low monthly payment of $20 you may have. . . ." This problem involves finding out what is behind "low monthly payments." The program to be written must:

1. Accept from the keyboard the amount to be borrowed, the annual interest rate in percent, and the number of months over which the loan is to be paid.
2. Calculate the monthly payment.
3. For each month, calculate and print how much was applied to interest and how much to the loan.
4. At the end of the report, print the total interest paid.

To calculate the monthly payment at the beginning of the program, use the following formula:

$$\text{Monthly payment} = \frac{i \times (\text{Loan amount})}{1 - (1 + i)^{-n}}$$

where i = monthly interest rate expressed as a decimal fraction. For instance, an annual rate of 18 percent would give:

$$i = (18/100)/12 = 0.18/12 = 0.015$$

n = number of monthly payments

To calculate interest relating to each monthly payment, use:

Monthly interest charge = Previous month balance $\times$ i
New balance = Previous balance – (Payment – Monthly interest charge)

An example of how the output should appear is as follows:

```
LOAN SUMMARY
    AMOUNT OF THE PURCHASE:   100.00
    ANNUAL RATE OF INTEREST:   21
    NUMBER OF MONTHS:   12

    MONTHLY PAYMENT BASED ON ABOVE:   $9.32

PAYMENT    PREVIOUS      AMOUNT OF     AMOUNT APPLIED      NEW
NUMBER     PRINCIPAL     INTEREST      TO PRINCIPAL      PRINCIPAL

1            100.00        1.75           7.57            92.43
2             92.43        1.62           7.70            84.73
.                .            .              .               .
.                .            .              .               .
.                .            .              .               .

TOTAL INTEREST PAID ON 100.00 LOAN = 11.73
```

Because of inherent "round-off" errors in numeric calculations, the last payment will probably not be exactly correct. In an actual environment, an adjustment would be made. Ignore this problem.

When processing is complete, the program should ask the user if another table is to be calculated.

9.6 A file contains examination score information for each student as follows:

Examination group number (integer)
Student number
Examination score

The file has been sorted such that the records in the file are grouped by their examination group number. (For instance, all students in examination group 17 will be together in the file, followed by all students in group 18, and so on.) The file is ended with a trailer having 9999 for the examination group number.

Write a program which will calculate the average for each group and print the group number and average.

Also keep a subtotal in order to calculate the overall average of all the scores. Upon completion, print the number of groups processed and the overall average. This program is oriented toward the use of the **WHILE** or **UNTIL** options of the **FOR** statement.

9.7 Expand Problem 9-6 to print each examination group average as a bar graph in the manner illustrated by the statement of Problem 9.1.

CHAPTER 10

Subscripted Variables and Arrays

OBJECTIVES

Processing of arrays of data is an important concept in all areas of computing. Often it is necessary to read a large data set into memory and save it for later processing. This chapter introduces the topic of subscripted variables. From it, you will learn the following.

1. The nature of subscripted variables in Basic and how they are used.
2. Techniques used in loading data into an array and searching the array.
3. How tables are handled and processed in Basic by use of two-dimensional arrays.

Basic Principles of Arrays

CALCULATIONS OF THE MEAN   Examples and techniques up until now have all involved the notion of reading a set of data values, operating on them, printing results, then reading the next set of data values, and so on. In other words, each data record is read, processed, and then discarded in favor of the next one. However, some applications require that the data values be read *and saved* for later processing. To illustrate this concept, let us consider the following example.

> **Example 10-1**
> An interactive program is required which will allow a user to enter a set of examination scores from the keyboard. The program is to calculate the mean (average) of the data set and determine how many test scores exceed the average. Assume that no more than 100 scores will ever be entered. The end of the data is to be signaled by entering a score of −1.

In this problem, it will be possible to perform the accumulating function (required for calculation of the mean) as the data is being entered. Then it will be necessary to "see" the data set a second time in order to compare each score with the mean. Obviously the principles which we have used up to this point are not well suited to such an operation. This brings us to the principle of *subscripted variables*.

THE NOTION OF SUBSCRIPTING   In mathematics, it is common practice to name a set of variables by the use of subscripts. For instance, assume that we have 16 different items which are similar in nature, such as monthly sales amounts for 16 salespeople. Rather than name them $a, b, c, \ldots, p$, which could be cumbersome, we might call them $a_1, a_2, a_3, \ldots a_{16}$. Thus, in referring to the seventh data point, we can speak of a_7, (which is called "a subseven" or simply "a seven") rather than g, which takes a moment to figure out. Furthermore we can speak of the data set a_i consisting of 16 elements. Technically we would refer to the data set a_i, where i ranges from 1 through 16. The collection of all *elements of the data set is commonly referred to as an array*. In speaking of the mean or average of the data set, it becomes much simpler to be explicit (an important requirement in using Basic), since we can write a simple formula for the mean:

$$\text{Mean} = \frac{a_1 + a_2 + a_3 + \cdots + a_{16}}{16}$$

As we can see, this form is a bit cumbersome when large numbers of quantities are involved. Following is another way of writing this—one which is suggestive of the way in which this type of operation is handled in programming languages.

$$\text{Mean} = \frac{\text{Sum of elements } a_i \text{ where } i \text{ ranges from 1 to 16}}{16}$$

SUBSCRIPTED VARIABLES IN BASIC   To this point in our studies, each variable named in a program reserves space for the storage of one value. Thus, for example, the variables **X**, **Y**, and **Z** would provide us with three "storage areas." Through use of the mathematical-type subscripting techniques, a single variable name can reserve space for many variables. Referring to Example 10-1, we will require space for up to 100 quantities. This is done by *dimensioning* the array in a so-called **DIM** statement as shown in Figure 10-1(a). This statement will cause the system to reserve storage for the 100 values which we may enter in Example 10-1. As we shall see, we will be able to refer to them as elements 1 through 100.*

As a general rule, all arrays in example programs in this book will be dimensioned in a **DIM** statement regardless of their size. However, if an array dimension is not to exceed 10 (for instance, **A(10)**), then it need not appear in a **DIM** statement. The system automatically assumes a dimension of 10 for any array not dimensioned. The same applies to two-dimensional arrays (described in a later section); the assumed size is 10 × 10.

In algebra, the subscripted variable takes a form such as a_3. In Basic, its form is identical to that in the **DIM** statement, as illustrated in Figure 10-1(b). Thus to read values into the first five elements of **A** (beginning with element 1), we could use the following sequence.

```
500     INPUT A(1)
510     INPUT A(2)
520     INPUT A(3)
530     INPUT A(4)
540     INPUT A(5)
```

*Actually space for 101 elements is reserved since Basic sets aside space for elements numbered 0 through 100. However, as a general rule, the element numbered 0 is not used since a counting sequence beginning at 1 is less confusing than one beginning at 0.

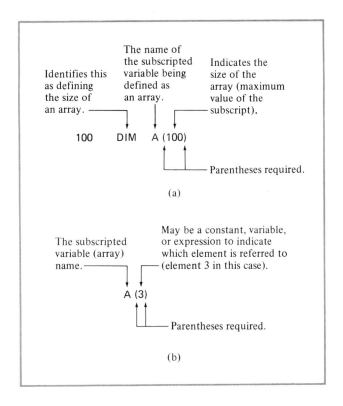

(a)

(b)

Figure 10-1 (a) The DIM statement. (b) A subscripted variable.

Obviously this "brute force" approach would leave something to be desired if we were to read 95 values instead of five. One of the beauties of subscripted variables is that the subscript, as used in a program, can be a variable or even an expression. Combine this with the **FOR-NEXT** and we have a powerful tool as illustrated by the following statements 600–620. If your system allows the **FOR** to be used as a statement modifier, then statement 700 will do the same thing as the sequence in 600–620.

```
600    FOR J = 1 TO 5          700      INPUT A(J) FOR J = 1 TO 5
610      INPUT A(J)
620    NEXT J
```

We can see that with the first execution of the **INPUT**, **J** will have a value of 1, and so statement 610 will be executed as if it were statement 500 in the previous sequence. With the second execution, **J** will be 2, which will give the same result as statement 510, and so on.

SELECTING ARRAY NAMES Since subscripted variables are, in fact, variables, the rules for selecting variable names apply equally to naming arrays. Furthermore arrays can be numeric or string ($). Thus **A**, **B9**, **C$**, and **X6$** are all valid for use as array names.

Processing an Array

PROGRAM PLANNING— EXAMPLE 10-1 In addition to the usual initialization and termination portions, Example 10-1 has *two* distinct and functionally independent parts. They are data entry and processing. We see this in the flowchart of Figure 10-2(a) and the hierarchy chart in part (b). In the data entry portion, the test scores are accepted from the terminal and stored into the array. In the process routine, the mean is calculated and the array is scanned to perform the required count.

READING AND STORING DATA VALUES— EXAMPLE 10-1 The logic of Figure 10-2 is reflected directly in the program of Figure 10-3. The following commentary relates to the data entry portion of this program.

1. In the data entry loop, reading of a valid exam score will cause the counter **C** to be incremented by 1 and **S** to be added to the accumulator. In statement 3030, the counter **C** is used as the subscript for saving the current score into the array **A**.
2. The array will not necessarily be "full." That is, if only 37 scores were entered, then only **A(1)** through **A(37)** would contain data values. Subscripted variables, like simple variables, initially contain values of 0. Thus **A(38)** through **A(100)** (and **A(0)**) will contain the value 0. The value stored in **C** "points at" the last element of **A**, which was loaded with a score.
3. The repetitious execution of the Data Entry routine is achieved by a **FOR-NEXT** sequence (lines 1030 –1034) with the final value being some exceptionally large number. Actual termination is controlled by the **IF** statement at line 1031.

EXERCISES

10.1 What would happen in the program of Figure 10-3 if the user entered more than 100 data values?

10.2 A programmer decides to put the counting statement at the end of the data entry routine. What would happen if the programmer changed statement 3010 to number 3035?

SEARCHING THE ARRAY The "second half" of this example involves calculating the mean and comparing it with each of the values stored in the array **A**. Actually we should note that this process of searching the array is virtually identical to that of searching the data table in Example 9-3 (Figure 9-16). In Figure 9-16, the maximum number of passes was controlled by the value read from the first entry of the data pool. In this example, the variable **C**, which was used as the index in the data entry routine, contains the subscript number of the last value loaded. (For instance, if 37 exams were processed, the value in **C** would be 37.) Thus this portion of the program would look at **A(1)** through **A(C)**. At this point, it is important to note the role of the subscript: it is only a "dummy" variable that defines *which*

Figure 10-2   Example 10-1. (a) Flowcharts. (b) Hierarchy charts.

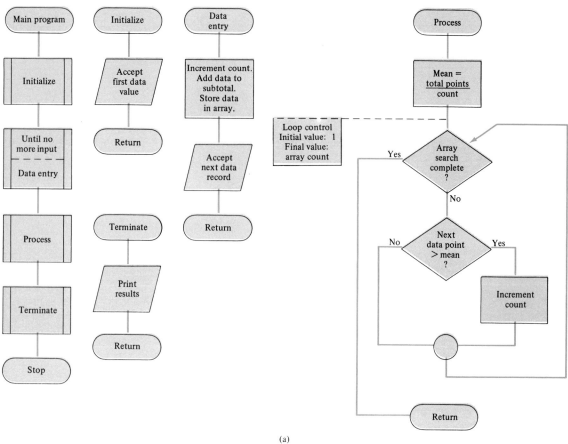

(a)

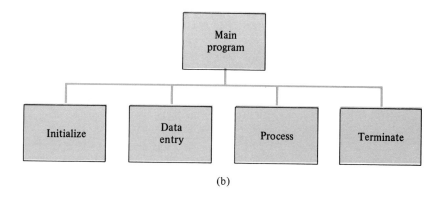

(b)

Figure 10-3   Program for Example 10-1.

```
100    REM EXAMPLE 10-1
110    REM CALCULATION OF THE MEAN
120    REM THE PORTION OF THE PROGRAM CALCULATES
130    REM THE MEAN AND STORES THE DATA VALUES
140    REM IN THE ARRAY A.
150    REM VARIABLES USED IN THE PROGRAM ARE:
160    REM      A - DIMENSIONED TO 100
170    REM      S - CURRENT SCORE
180    REM      C - COUNTER
190    REM      T - ACCUMULATOR FOR SCORES
200    REM      M - CALCULATED MEAN
210    REM      E - NUMBER OF VALUES EXCEEDING MEAN
300                                                  REM
1000 REM MAIN PROGRAM
1010      DIM A(100)
1011         REM DIMENSION THE ARRAY
1020      GOSUB 2010
1021         REM INITIALIZE
1030      FOR X = 1 TO 100
1031        IF S = -1 THEN 1040
1032        GOSUB 3010
1033           REM READ AND STORE INPUT VALUES
1034      NEXT X
1040      GOSUB 4010
1041         REM PROCESS
1050      GOSUB 5010
1051         REM TERMINATION ROUTINE
1060      STOP
1070 REM END OF MAIN PROGRAM
1071                                                 REM
2000 REM INITIALIZE ROUTINE
2010      INPUT "NEXT SCORE (-1 IF FINISHED)"; S
2020      RETURN
2030 REM END OF INITIALIZE ROUTINE
2031                                                 REM
3000 REM DATA ENTRY ROUTINE
3010      C = C + 1
3020      T = T + S
3030      A(C) = S
3031         REM COUNT, ADD TO SUBTOTAL & SAVE IN ARRAY
3040      INPUT "NEXT SCORE (-1 IF FINISHED)"; S
3041         REM ACCEPT NEXT INPUT
3050      RETURN
3060 REM END OF DATA ENTRY ROUTINE
3061                                                 REM
4000 REM PROCESS ROUTINE
4010      M = T/I
4011         REM CALCULATE THE MEAN
4020      REM   THE FOLLOWING LOOP COMPARES THE
4021      REM     MEAN TO INDIVIDUAL SCORES
4030      FOR K = 1 TO C
4040        IF A(K) <= M THEN 4050
4041          E = E + 1
4050      NEXT K
4060      RETURN
4070 REM END OF PROCESS ROUTINE
4080                                                 REM
5000 REM TERMINATION ROUTINE
5010      PRINT "NUMBER OF SCORES = "; C
5020      PRINT "MEAN = "; M
5030      PRINT "NUMBER EXCEEDING MEAN = "; E
5040      PRINT "PROCESSING TERMINATED"
5050      RETURN
5060 REM END OF TERMINATION ROUTINE
5070                                                 REM
9999      END
```

element of **A** is desired. Thus if **K** = 7 and **J** = 8, then all of the following refer to the same element of **A**—that is, the eighth one.

A(8)   A(J)   A(K+1)

The following sequence on the left, therefore, would print all scores which were entered, and the sequence on the right would print them in reverse order.

```
800    FOR X = 1 TO C          900    FOR X = C TO 1 STEP -1
810       PRINT A(X)           910       PRINT A(X)
820    NEXT X                  920    NEXT X
```

Note that the variable **C** used as the subscript in Figure 10-3 is used as a control variable in the **FOR-NEXT** loop here.

EXERCISES

10.3 Would the end result of processing in Figure 10-3 be any different if the array had been searched backward by changing statement 4030 to the following?

```
4030    FOR K = C TO 1 STEP -1
```

10.4 Considering the complete program of Figure 10-3, what changes would be required to allow the user the option of repeating the loop for another data set?

Table Searching

A TABLE SEARCH EXAMPLE One of the important uses of subscripted variables is for the storage of tables which must be searched for a particular value. Example 9-3 is a perfect example of this type of application. In that case, a data table is maintained in the program using **DATA** statements. For each student number which is entered, the **DATA** pool is searched. If a match is found, the desired information is printed; if not, an appropriate message is printed. This is commonly referred to as *table processing* and has wide use in data processing. As mentioned in Chapter 9, to use **DATA** statements for storing data (or a table) as part of a program is very restrictive and quite impractical in most cases. More commonly, table information, as well as data, is stored in separate files. The table file can then be opened, read into one or more arrays, and used for processing. To illustrate this type of usage, let us consider the following example.

Example 10-2
This example involves two input data files: one containing employee data and the other table information. Each record of the employee file (EMPDAT) includes:

Employee Social Security number
Employee name
Hours worked
Job code (<9999)

The last data record is followed by a trailer with a Social Security number field of 999999999. Each record of the table file (PAYTBL) includes a job code and the corresponding pay rate; the last table entry is followed by a trailer with the pay code field of 9999. Calculate the gross pay for each employee.

We should note that the employee record contains the hours worked, but *not* the pay rate. It does, however, contain a job code. Furthermore the table file consists of job codes and corresponding pay rates. Thus, for each employee, it will be necessary to search the table from the table file in order to obtain the pay rate for that employee. Overall this example is a typical batch-processing-type operation which is common in business data processing.

THE CONCEPT OF ARGUMENTS AND FUNCTIONS Most of us are quite accustomed to using tables. For instance, a store clerk will total the sales, then look up in a tax table the amount of tax corresponding to the purchase. Similarly, to find a person's telephone number, we scan the directory of names and, upon coming to the one of interest, we read the corresponding telephone number. Of importance in these examples is that both of them involve two types of data: something which is known and something which is unknown. In using the telephone directory, we know the name of the individual but we do not know the telephone number.

These table concepts are formalized in the job-code/pay-rate table shown in Figure 10-4. We can see that each entry in the table consists of two values: the *argument,* which we think of as the known quantity, and the *function,* which we think of as the unknown quantity. For example, if we wish to know the pay rate for the job code 225 (225 would be referred to as the *search argument),* we would scan the list of arguments to find that entry, then read across to obtain the corresponding function value of 5.10.

This type of operation is well suited to subscripted variables; let us see how it is implemented in Basic.

PROGRAM PLANNING— EXAMPLE 10-2 Interestingly this example involves no new concepts. We have used all of the basic tools in previous example programs. In reality, it is little more than a slightly different application (and combination) of principles used in preceding examples. Variations in this program include:

1. The pay-rate table will be read into storage and stored as part of the initialization process.

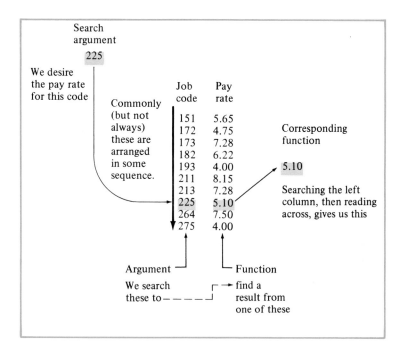

Figure 10-4   The principle of a table.

2. In the processing loop, for each record which is read, the search operation illustrated in Figure 10-4 is performed.

LOADING THE TABLE
Since each table entry consists of two quantities (argument and corresponding function), this example will require two arrays. The process of loading the table is virtually identical to the task of reading and storing test score values in Example 10-1 [see the flowchart of Figure 10-2(a)]. On referring to the problem statement, we see that there will be no more than 100 entries in the table. Thus, within our program, we would dimension for 100. But, what if the table file includes more than 100 values? If we try to store data into an array beyond the last-defined element, then an error occurs. In an actual application program, a check would normally be done and an error message printed if the table file exceeded the array size. However, in this example (for the sake of simplicity), if the table file includes more than 100 entries, then only the first 100 will be used.

SEARCHING THE TABLE
In searching the table, we must anticipate the possibility of a job code not being found in the table during the search. In Example 9-3, this was handled by using the variable F$ as a switch. Prior to entering the search loop, the switch was set to NO. If the desired entry was found in the table, the switch value was changed to YES. Then, upon exiting from the loop, appropriate action was taken, depending upon the value of the switch. This same techni-

que will be used in this program, but it will be implemented in a slightly different way—a simple variable **R1** will be used to hold the desired pay rate. Processing will be as follows:

1. Prior to entering the search loop, **R1** is given to a value of zero.
2. Within the loop, if the desired entry is found, then the table rate is placed in the variable **R1** and the loop exited. If it is not found, **R1** remains at zero.
3. Upon completion of the loop, appropriate action is taken, depending upon whether or not **R1** has a value of zero.

A PROGRAM— The complete program is shown in Figure 10-5. Here we see that this program
EXAMPLE 10-2 includes two input files. The table file is assigned to channel 2 and the data file to channel 1. The table is loaded in the routine beginning at line 6000 and processed in the routine beginning at 3000.

In the table load routine, the loop is controlled by the **FOR** statement:

```
6030     FOR I = 1 TO 101
```

It is extremely important to recognize the role the index variable I plays. First, it is used to store the code and rate into the proper elements of the arrays (lines 6060 and 6070). Second, its final value is used to define the table size (line 6110). The latter deserves special consideration. To illustrate, let us assume that our table file contains four table entries plus the trailer. Then the correspondence between the table record read and the value of I at the time statement 6040 is executed will be as illustrated in Table 10-1.

Table 10-1
Conditions
at Execution
of Line 6040

Record from Table File	Value of I
1	1
2	2
3	3
4	4
Trailer	5

We can see that the value of I is 1 *greater* than the number of entries in the table. Thus the table size is saved in the variable **T** as follows:

```
6110     T = I - 1
```

Great care must be exercised when the index variable is to be used after exiting from a loop. A situation in which the value ends up one increment too large is a common occurrence.

Accessing the rate in the processing routine is relatively straightforward.

Figure 10-5   Program for Example 10-2.

```
100   REM TABLE LOOK-UP         EXAMPLE 10-2
110   REM THIS PROGRAM FIRST LOADS A PAY RATE
120   REM TABLE THEN PROCESSES AN EMPLOYEE FILE TO
130   REM COMPUTE GROSS
140   REM VARIABLES ARE
150   REM ARRAYS
160   REM      C - JOB CODE (FROM PAYTBL FILE)
170   REM      R - PAYRATE (FROM PAYTBL FILE)
180   REM INPUT
190   REM      S$ - SOCIAL SECURITY NUMBER
200   REM      N$ - NAME
210   REM      H - HOURS WORKED
220   REM      C1- JOB CODE FOR EMPLOYEE
230   REM OTHER
240   REM      R1- PAY RATE EXTRACTED FROM TABLE
250   REM      P - CALCULATED PAY
260   REM      T - NUMBER OF ENTRIES IN PAYRATE TABLE
270   REM      C5, R5, I - OTHER WORK VARIABLES
280                                          REM
1000 REM MAIN PROGRAM
1010    DIM C(100), R(100)
1020                                          REM
1030      GOSUB 2010
1031        REM INITIALIZE
1040      FOR L = 1 TO 100
1041          IF S$="999999999" THEN 1050
1042          GOSUB 3010
1043      NEXT L
1044        REM PROCESS LOOP
1050      GOSUB 4010
1051        REM TERMINATION
1060      STOP
1070 REM END OF MAIN PROGRAM
2000 REM INITIAL ROUTINE
2010      OPEN "PAYTBL" FOR INPUT AS FILE #2
2020      OPEN "EMPDAT" FOR INPUT AS FILE #1
2040      GOSUB 6010
2041        REM READ AND STORE PAYRATE TABLE
2050      INPUT #1,S$,N$,H,C1
2060      RETURN
2070 REM END OF INITIAL ROUTINE
2071                                          REM
3000 REM **A2** PROCESSING ROUTINE
3010      R1 = 0
3020      FOR I=1 TO T
3021          IF R1>0 THEN 3060
3022            REM EXIT LOOP IF RATE FOUND
3023          IF C1 <> C(I) THEN 3040
3030              R1 = R(I)
3040      NEXT I
3050        REM END OF TABLE SEARCH
3051        REM  SUCCESSFUL SEARCH, R1 >0
3052        REM  UNSUCCESSFUL, R1 = 0
3053        REM
3060      IF R1>0 THEN 3071 ELSE 3101
3070 REM  THEN
3071          P = R1*H
3080          PRINT USING "\          \   \         \  ##.#   $###.##", S$, N$, H, P
3090          GOTO 3140
3100 REM  ELSE
3101          PRINT
3110          PRINT "JOB CODE"; C1; "NOT FOUND FOR EMPLOYEE "; S$
3120          PRINT
3130 REM  ENDIF
3140      INPUT#1,S$,N$,H,C1
3150      RETURN
3160 REM END OF PROCESSING ROUTINE
3170                                          REM
4000 REM **C1**  TERMINATION ROUTINE
4010      PRINT
4020      PRINT
4030      PRINT "PROCESSING COMPLETE"
4040      CLOSE #1
4050      RETURN
4060 REM END OF TERMINATION ROUTINE
4061                                          REM
6000 REM **B1**  LOAD PAY RATE TABLE
6010      INPUT #2, C5,R5
6020        REM READ FIRST RECORD
6030      FOR I = 1 TO 101
6040          IF C5=9999 THEN 6110
6050            REM EXIT CONDITION
6060              C(I) = C5
6070              R(I) = R5
6090          INPUT #2, C5,R5
6100      NEXT I
6110      T = I-1
6111        REM SAVE THE TABLE SIZE
6120      CLOSE #2
6130      RETURN
6140 REM END OF LOAD PAY RATE TABLE
6150                                          REM
9999    END
```

The key is in lines 3010 through 3040, which are shaded in Figure 10-5. In particular, the statements

```
3023    IF C1<>C(I) THEN 3040
3030       R1 = R(I)
```

are the essence of the search. The **IF** at line 3023 compares the value of the input job code (**C1**) with respective entries in the job code array **C**. When the equal condition occurs, the corresponding entry from the **R** array is stored in the simple variable **R1**. This serves two purposes: it causes termination of the loop and it makes the pay rate available for computation (line 3071).

EXERCISE

10.5 The statements in lines 6060 and 6070 seem unnecessary. Why not delete them and change 6010 and 6090 to the following?

```
INPUT #2, C(I), R(I)
```

Two-Dimensional Arrays

ROWS AND COLUMNS OF DATA

Many applications, both business and scientific, deal with tables which have rows and columns—in other words, *two-dimensional* arrays. To illustrate this concept, let us assume that we work for a company which manufactures four different models of "widgets." The shop in which the widgets are made includes five different machines, each of which is needed to make each type of widget. For production planning purposes, the management has summarized the time required by each model widget on each machine in Table 10-2.

Table 10-2 Product/Machine Summary (Minutes)

		Machine				
		1	2	3	4	5
Widget	1	23	6	18	6	2
model	2	17	4	21	5	3
	3	6	5	30	6	0
	4	17	4	22	6	4

Here we see that the table consists of four rows (model) and five columns (machine) arranged in a convenient, easy-to-use form. For instance, we can immediately see that model 3 requires six minutes on machine 4. In other words, we locate any item by its row and column. Using subscripting notation, we can refer to the time t for this particular model as $t_{3,4}$. Furthermore operations might be performed on entire rows or columns. For instance, the production manager would probably be interested in more information, such as, how much total machine time is required by each widget. This is easily obtained by summing the figures in each row, thus producing the following one-dimensional array.

55
50
47
53

These and many other operations are commonly performed on two-dimensional arrays. Let us examine how these are done in Basic.

TWO-DIMENSIONAL ARRAYS IN BASIC Exactly the same forms are used in Basic for two-dimensional arrays as for one-dimensional arrays. Table 10-2, for example, would require the following DIM statement.

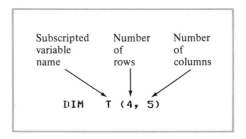

A two-dimensional array such as this is commonly used as consisting of rows 1–4 and columns 1–5. However, like one-dimensional arrays, it includes elements 0: that is, it consists of five rows—0 to 4, and six columns—0 to 5. In referring to a particular element, for instance, time required by model 3 on machine 4, we refer to:

T(3,4)

Similarly, if we are processing within a loop, we can use:

T(I,J)

In other words, the same rules apply to variables with one or two subscripts. The following example illustrates these principles.

Example 10-3
The production manager of Widget Corporation requires an interactive program to assist in production planning. It is to accept from the

keyboard the desired number of a particular model of widget, and then print the total number of hours required by each machine. Table 10-2 is to be included within the program in **DATA** statements as follows:

```
DATA 23,  6,  18,  6,  2
DATA 17,  4,  21,  5,  3
DATA  6,  5,  30,  6,  0
DATA 17,  4,  22,  6,  4
```

A sample of the dialog which our manager expects is shown in Figure 10-6. For each widget order, we see the total time required on each of the five machines.

Figure 10-6
Expected output for
Example 10-3.

```
WIDGET MODEL NUMBER? 4
QUANTITY? 12

MACHINE      TIME
    1         204
    2          48
    3         264
    4          72
    5          48


DO YOU WISH TO CONTINUE (Y OR N)?
```

A PROGRAM— As with Example 10-2, this program will consist of two basic components;
EXAMPLE 10-3 loading the table into the array and processing the array. In this example, loading the table is a bit trickier because of the two subscripts. As a rule, care must be taken to avoid becoming confused between the two. The actual load process itself is performed by the following sequence.

```
FOR I = 1 TO 4
  FOR J = 1 TO 5
    READ T(I,J)
  NEXT J
NEXT I
```

This sequence is based on the assumption that the table is included in the **DATA** statements in the same order as in Table 10-2. It is obviously important to vary the subscripts to correspond with the table in the **DATA** statements. Since **J** controls the inner loop, it will range from 1 to 5 while **I** is held constant. Then **I** will be incremented and the inner loop will be repeated. In other words, the subscript sequence will be:

(1,1), (1,2), (1,3), (1,4), (1,5), (2,1), (2,2), . . ., (4,4), (4,5)

The table load sequence is included in lines 320–360 of the program in Figure 10-7. This program is relatively short and straightforward. We see the calculation for each machine in the loop comprising statements 460–490. Details of this operation are described in Figure 10-8.

Figure 10-7 Program for Example 10-3.

```
100 REM TABLE PROCESSING - EXAMPLE 10-3
110 REM WIDGET CORPORATION PRODUCTION TIME SUMMARY PROGRAM
120 REM ACCEPTS WIDGET MODEL NUMBER AND NUMBER OF UNITS
130 REM REQUIRED AND PRINTS TOTAL HOURS FOR EACH MACHINE.
140                                        REM
200 REM DIMENSION ARRAY
210     DIM T(4,5)
300                                        REM
310 REM   THE FOLLOWING LOOP READS THE TABLE
320         FOR I = 1 TO 4
330           FOR J = 1 TO 5
340             READ T(I,J)
350           NEXT J
360         NEXT I
370 REM   END OF TABLE READ
380       Q$ = "Y"
390         REM SET THE LOOP CONTROL TO "ON"
400 REM MAIN PROCESSING LOOP
410       FOR A = 1 TO 1000
411       IF Q$<>"Y" THEN 550
412           REM EXIT THIS LOOP
420         INPUT "MACHINE MODEL NUMBER"; M
430         INPUT "QUANTITY"; Q
440         PRINT
450         PRINT "MACHINE    TIME"
460         FOR J = 1 TO 5
470         T1  =  Q * T(M,J)
480           PRINT USING "    #           ###", J, T1
490         NEXT J
500         PRINT
510         PRINT
520         INPUT "DO YOU WISH TO CONTINUE (Y OR N)"; Q$
530       NEXT A
540 REM END OF MAIN PROCESSING LOOP
541                                        REM
550         PRINT "PROCESSING COMPLETE"
551                                        REM
900 REM   TABLE ENTRIES
910         DATA 23,6,18,6,2
920         DATA 17,4,21,5,3
930         DATA  6,5,30,6,0
940         DATA 17,4,22,6,4
9999    END
```

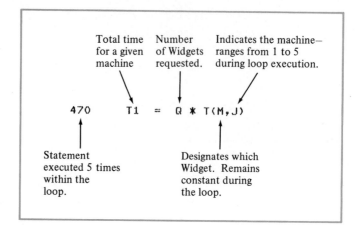

Figure 10-8
Calculation of time
required.

EXERCISES

10.6 Assume that the table has been entered in the **DATA** statements by columns rather than by rows, that is:

```
DATA 23,17,6,17,6,4,5,4,18,21,30,22,6,5,6,6,2,3,0,4
```

Modify the nested **FOR-NEXT** loops in lines 320–360 to reflect this change. Do not change the **DIM** statement.

10.7 Assume that the needs of the program required that the calculated times (line 470, Figure 10-7) be stored in an array. Define **T1** as an appropriate array and make the required modification to the program.

10.8 One important feature of interactive programs is the checking of data values which are entered. In Figure 10-7, there is nothing to prevent the user from entering a nonexistent value for a widget number such as 12. This would cause an error termination since the array dimension would be exceeded in statement 470. Write the necessary statements for preventing this occurrence.

ANSWERS TO PRECEDING EXERCISES

10.1 The last value would be ignored since the **FOR** loop will not execute more than 100 times.

10.2 The scores would be placed in the array beginning with element 0—A(0). In itself, this is not incorrect. However, changes would be required in the process routine in order to handle the data properly.

10.3 No.

10.4 The following modifications and additions to Figure 10-3 would be required.

```
1014     C$ = "YES"
1016     FOR M = 1 TO 10000
1018     IF C$<>"YES" THEN 1060
1020         GOSUB 2010   &
1021            REM INITIALIZE
1030         FOR X = 1 TO 100
1031            IF S = -1 THEN 1040
1032             GOSUB 3010
1033                REM READ AND STORE INPUT VALUES
1034         NEXT X
1040         GOSUB 4010
1041            REM PROCESS
1050         GOSUB 5010
1051            REM PRINT OUTPUT SUMMARY ROUTINE
1054         INPUT "Do you wish to process another data set"; C$
1056     NEXT M
1060     STOP
  .
  .
  .
2004         C = 0
2006         T = 0
2007            REM INITIALIZE ACCUMULATORS
```

Delete statement 5040

Note that nothing need be done with regard to elements of **A** since new values will be read into the array.

10.5 If there were fewer than 100 table values, then the trailer record would be read into the table. In this particular instance, it would cause no problem since subsequent searching of the table is controlled by the table size variable **T**.

10.6 Lines 320–360 would be as follows:

```
320      FOR J = 1 TO 5
330         FOR I = 1 TO 4
340            READ T(I,J)
350         NEXT I
360      NEXT J
```

10.7 The following statements would require the changes shown.

```
210      DIM T(4,5), T1(5)

470      T1(J) = Q*T(M,J)
480      PRINT USING "    #              ###",J,T1(J)
```

10.8
```
425      IF M>=1 AND M<=4 THEN 430
426         PRINT "MODEL MUST BE BETWEEN 1 AND 4"
427         GO TO 420

435      IF Q>0 THEN 440
436         PRINT "QUANTITY MUST BE GREATER THAN ZERO"
437         GO TO 430
```

PROGRAMMING PROBLEMS

10.1 The following file is used as input for several programming problems. A data file consists of statistical information (integer) stored one data value per record (line). The last data value is followed by a trailer record with a value of 9999. There will never be more than 100 data values in the file.

The data file is to be read into an array and printed as it is read. Then reverse the contents of the array elements. For instance, if 37 data values were read, then the array contents would be switched such that:

> X(1) is replaced by X(37)
> X(2) is replaced by X(36)

> .

> .

> .

> X(37) is replaced by X(1)

Print the array contents after the switch and check the results.

10.2 In statistics, the mean, which is simply an arithmetic average, is used to study data. However, it does not give the complete picture of a data set. For example, the two sets of

> 10, 50, 90
> 50, 50, 50

both have means of 50, but there is a significant difference between the two. Another entity in statistics which gives an indication of the data spread is *standard deviation*, calculated using the formula:

$$SD = \sqrt{\frac{\Sigma(x_i - \bar{x})^2}{n - 1}} \qquad i = 1, n \qquad \bar{x} = mean$$

Thus for the data points 10, 50, and 90, the standard deviation is:

$$SD = \sqrt{\frac{(10 - 50)^2 + (50 - 50)^2 + (90 - 50)^2}{3 - 1}}$$

$$= \sqrt{\frac{1600 + 0 + 1600}{2}}$$

$$= 40$$

Using the data file of Problem 10.1, calculate and print the number of data values, the mean, and the standard deviation. Note that other forms are available for calculating the standard deviation which are more compatible with conventional computational methods. Use the equation given here, however.

10.3 The sorting of a set of data into an ascending sequence (smallest first through largest last) is an important programming function. A simple technique is to compare the first element with the last. If the first is larger, then interchange the two. Repeat this with the second and the last, the third and the last, and so on. When completed, the last element will be the largest one. Now repeat the entire process using the next to last element, and the next to largest will be next to last. If this entire process is repeated the proper number of times, the array will be in sequence. Sort the file of Problem 10.1 using this method.

10.4 The input file for this problem consists of a data set followed by a 9999 trailer (call this the A set), followed by another data set, followed by its 9999 trailer (call this the B set). Assume that A and B will each consist of no more than 50 data values and that each is arranged in ascending sequence. Write a program to read these values into storage and merge the two sets into the single array C (which therefore may consist of up to 100 elements). The merging should be accomplished such that the elements in C are in ascending sequence.

10.5 Assume that the data values in the file of Problem 10.1 fall in the range 0–99. Write a program to determine how many values fall in each of the following 10 categories:

0–9	50–59
10–19	60–69
20–29	70–79
30–39	80–89
40–49	90–99

Define an array T consisting of 10 elements corresponding to the above 10 categories. Do not use a series of IF statements. In planning your solution, take some example scores, divide by 10, then throw away the fractional part (that is, *truncate* the result). For instance:

60/10 = 6.0, which yields 6 when truncated
63/10 = 6.3, which yields 6 when truncated
69/10 = 6.9, which yields 6 when truncated

Now compare this truncated result of the division with the category number.

In Basic, one way to cause truncation is by using the FIX function. For example:

```
Y = FIX(X/10)
```

will produce a truncated result in Y which is identical to the foregoing examples.

10.6 Expand Example 10-3 to request information as to how many of each widget model are to be processed. For example, an order may consist of three model 1's, five model 2's, and so on. Calculate the total time required on each machine for a complete order.

10.7 Problem 10.6 (and Example 10-3) are to be further expanded. Following the last DATA statement for the table is another DATA statement consisting of five entries. These are the cost-per-minute values of operating each machine. The program should now calculate, for an order of widgets, the cost of operating each machine and the total cost.

10.8 A teacher has decided to computerize a system for recording examination grades. Each class will consist of fewer than 100 students and the maximum number of exams given will be six. For the purpose of this program, students are identified by the student roster numbers, which are consecutive beginning with 1 (that is, 1, 2, 3, . . .). Exams similarly are numbered 1, 2, 3, ... After each exam has been graded, the score (0–100) of each student is stored as one record in a file with the following information.

Student roster number
Examination number
Examination score

The file will be preceded by a header record with the number of students in the class followed by the number of exams given. The last record will be followed by a trailer with 9999 for a student roster number.

Write a program to do the following.

1. Read the data into the array S(99,6).
2. Calculate the class average for each exam.
3. Calculate the total points for each student; the score received in the first exam is to be doubled in computing total points since it is the final exam. For instance, if four exams were given, then the total points would be

Total = (2 × exam 1) + exam 2 + exam 3 + exam 4

In planning your program, take into account that some students will not have taken all the exams for the course, and that there need not be one record for each student for each exam. However, every student will have taken the final exam.

Output is to include the averages for each of the six exams and the student roster number and total score for each of the students.

CHAPTER 11

Additional Topics

OBJECTIVES

The topics described in the preceding chapters form a good foundation for Basic programming. There are numerous other topics, however, that would be required to provide a broad, comprehensive knowledge of the language and how to use it. This chapter includes three of them: string manipulation, user-defined functions, and menu control. The important concepts which you will learn in this chapter include:

1. How to use the following statements and string functions.

   Statements   **LINE INPUT**
                  ON-GOSUB
   Functions   **ASC**
                  CHR$
                  STR$
                  VAL

2. How to search a string for a particular character or combination of characters and perform a variety of string operations.
3. The nature of the ASCII character set and control characters.
4. The topic of user-defined functions which allow the programmer to write functions for use in the program.
5. The use of a menu from which an interactive user is presented a list of options which can be performed within a single program.

String Manipulation

INTRODUCTION Chapter 6 provided us with a first insight into the handling of string data. The **LEFT$**, **MID$**, and **RIGHT$** string functions allow us to break out parts of a string (substrings). With the ordinary **LET** statement, we can create a new string by concatenating (adding together) two or more strings. These are relatively modest operations. In addition to these features, most versions of Basic include numerous other string-handling features. This section describes some additional capabilities and includes examples of how each is used.

STRING DATA The typical example in this book begins with a statement such as, "Each **IN STORAGE** record in a file contains an employee number, name, pay rate, and so on." Some of the fields may be numeric and others string. As long as we keep everything consistent between the data and our program, the computer differentiates properly. However, many applications involve string data which is simply text material. For instance, this book was first entered into a computer using a word processing system. Through use of word processing programs, it was possible to make needed changes, including some major shuffling. When the book is revised, the starting point will be the original manuscript stored in the computer. Within the computer, each line is stored as it was typed. For instance, if the typist entered the two lines:

THIS SAMPLE, EVEN THOUGH SHORT
ILLUSTRATES THE POINT.

then it would be stored within the computer file as illustrated in Figure 11-1.

Figure 11-1   Information stored on disk

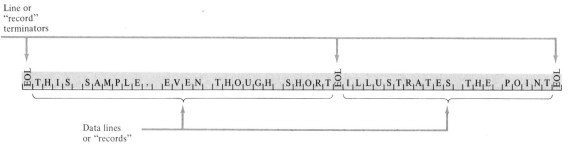

Each line which is entered is terminated by some type of "end-of-line" marker (EOL). The exact nature of the EOL depends upon the particular computer. In processing a file containing string data, we would most likely read lines (records) one at a time into a string variable and process them. For this operation, we need an input statement which will read an entire line into a string variable without being influenced by punctuation (that is, the comma). Most versions of Basic provide the **LINE INPUT** statement to perform this operation. (In some Basics, the statement is called **INPUT LINE**—check to see which it is on your system.)

EXERCISE

11.1 Study Figure 11-1 carefully. What problem would arise in reading the input lines with the **INPUT** statement as follows?

```
INPUT #3, L$
```

THE LINE INPUT STATEMENT   Whenever an entire line is to be read, the **LINE INPUT** (or **INPUT LINE**) statement is used. This statement reads the entire record or line and is terminated only when the line terminating EOL is detected. Thus the lines of Figure 11-1 would be read with the **LINE INPUT** as follows:

```
LINE INPUT #3, L$
```

Note that there must be only one string variable in the list of the **LINE INPUT**. The entire string, including commas if any, is placed in the string variable. In Figure 11-1, we see that the text in the first line consists of 30 characters. Thus the length of **L$** will be 30. (However, some versions of Basic also read the EOL code. If so, then it is necessary to get rid of this excess. You should check your system to see how it works.)

EXERCISES

11.2 A programmer included the following statement in a program and received an error message. Why?

```
340    LINE INPUT A$,B$
```

11.3 In response to the following statement, ABCDE was entered at the terminal. What is the length of **X$**?

```
400    LINE INPUT X$
```

SEARCHING A STRING One of many common operations in manipulating string data such as that shown in Figure 11-1 is searching for a particular substring. To illustrate some of these concepts, let us consider an example to print mailing labels from information stored in an address file.

Example 11-1

Each record of an address data file contains a person's name, street address, city and state, and Zip code. The following is a typical record.

AL JONES/4762 WINDY WAY/SAN FRANCISCO CA/99123/

Notice that each field is terminated by a slash character and that the city and state are treated as a single field. Every data record will be in exactly this format. The objective of the program is to print mailing labels. For each record, the program must:

1. Access each field from the record.
2. Print an address label for each person; for instance, the above would print as follows:

AL JONES
4762 WINDY WAY
SAN FRANCISCO CA   99123

Note that the Zip code is separated from the state by two spaces. Assume that the labels on which the addresses are printed are six lines in height. Some sample labels are shown in Figure 11-2.

Figure 11-2   Sample
labels—Example 11-1.

The process of scanning a record is illustrated by the example of Figure
11-3. This type of operation requires that a *pointer* variable be used which
allows us to keep track of where we are in the string. In the example of Figure
11-3, the pointer variable is **P**. As we see here, we require two "positions" in
order to access each field: the beginning and the end.

Figure 11-3   Scanning a string to obtain a substring.

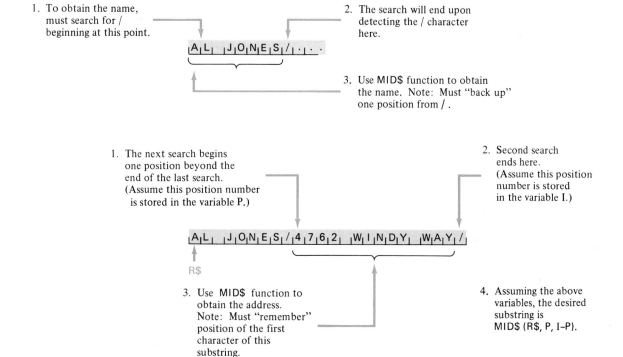

1. To obtain the name, must search for / beginning at this point.

2. The search will end upon detecting the / character here.

3. Use MID$ function to obtain the name. Note: Must "back up" one position from / .

1. The next search begins one position beyond the end of the last search. (Assume this position number is stored in the variable P.)

2. Second search ends here. (Assume this position number is stored in the variable I.)

3. Use MID$ function to obtain the address. Note: Must "remember" position of the first character of this substring.

4. Assuming the above variables, the desired substring is MID$ (R$, P, I-P).

The technique described in Figure 11-3 forms the GET SUBSTRING routine of Figure 11-4. The **FOR** statement (line 6010) uses a limit of 200, an arbitrarily large value. Since we are operating with "ideal" data, termination of this loop will always be via the **IF** at line 6020.

The process of scanning a string for a given substring (lines 6010 to 6030) is such a common operation that many versions of Basic include a special function to do it. Use of this function, usually called **INSTR**, is illustrated in Figure 11-5, which will produce the same result as the **FOR-NEXT** loop in Figure 11-4.

Figure 11-4   Program segment for Example 11-1.

```
3000 REM PROCESS ROUTINE
3010     P = 1
3011       REM SET SEARCH POINTER TO 1
3020     GOSUB 6010
3030     PRINT L$
3040     GOSUB 6010
3050     PRINT L$
3060     GOSUB 6010
3070     S$ = L$
3080     GOSUB 6010
3090     PRINT S$; " "; L$
3100     PRINT
3110     PRINT
3120     PRINT
3130     LINE INPUT #1, R$
3140     RETURN
3150 REM END OF PROCESS ROUTINE
3151                              REM
6000 REM GET SUBSTRING
6001 REM INPUT
6002 REM     R$- STRING TO BE SEARCHED
6003 REM     P - CHARACTER POSITION IN R$ TO BEGIN SEARCH
6004 REM OUTPUT
6005 REM     L$- "NEXT" SUBSTRING
6006 REM     P - UPDATED POINTER
6010     FOR I = P TO 200
6020       IF MID$(R$,I,1) = "/" THEN 6040
6030     NEXT I
6031       REM EXIT OF THIS LOOP IS VIA LINE 6020
6040     L$ = MID$(R$,P,I-P)
6050     P = I + 1
6051       REM MOVE POINTER TO BEGINNING OF NEXT WORD
6060 REM END OF GET SUBSTRING
```

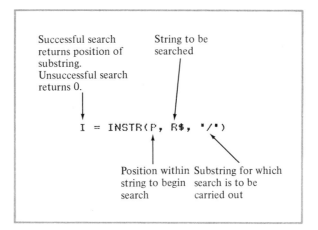

Figure 11-5 The INSTR function.

EXERCISE

11.4 What would occur in the GET SUBSTRING routine of Figure 11-4 if the programmer forgot to add 1 at line 6050 and simply placed the value of I into P?

Other String Processing Capabilities

THE ASCII CHARACTER SET To this point, our interest in string data has been fairly superficial. As we know, a string field can be whatever length the program requires. In dealing with a particular value, for example,

```
B$ = "EXAMPLE STRING FIELD"
```

we see it as written and recognize that it has a length of 20 (consists of 20 characters). We have given no consideration to the internal form in which it is stored. The most commonly used coding system in mini- and microcomputers is *ASCII* (American *S*tandard *C*ode for *I*nformation *I*nterchange). The ASCII set is a 7-binary-digit code with values which range from binary 0000000 to binary 1111111. The decimal equivalents of these values are 0 and 127. Thus the ASCII set consists of 128 characters (for a summary, see Appendix I).

The first 32 ASCII characters are special control characters. The rest are printable characters with which we are familiar: special characters, digits, uppercase letters, and lowercase letters. The decimal equivalent of the binary representation for each character is given in the ASCII table. For instance, the binary coding for the letter A (which is 1000001) has the decimal equivalent of 65. Although for most applications the programmer need not be concerned with these values, some operations do require reference to them.

EXERCISES

11.5 What is the decimal equivalent of each character in "23-Sept"?

11.6 What does the following ASCII coding represent?

66 97 115 105 99 45 80 108 117 115

THE ASC AND CHR$ FUNCTIONS

The result of executing the following is rather obvious to us by now.

```
200     A$ = "X"
210     PRINT A$
```

From the preceding section, we know that the ASCII code 88 will be transmitted to the terminal, which will in turn cause the letter **X** to be displayed. Another way of defining **X** in our program is by using its ASCII value in the **CHR$** function as follows:

```
201     A$ = CHR$(88)
```

The **CHR$** function allows us to define a 1-byte string by specifying its ASCII value. Needless to say, this is a clumsy way to define a character; statement 200 is preferred to statement 201. However, this capability is necessary for some types of operation.

The reverse operation, that of changing a single character to its ASCII value, is done by the **ASC** function (in some systems, it is called the **ASCII** function). Execution of the following statements would produce the results as shown.

```
A$ = "X"
B$ = "ANSWER"
PRINT ASC(A$),ASC(B$)

88                      65
```

We see in the case of **B$** that if the string quantity is longer than one character, only the first one is used.

EXERCISE

11.7 The variable **A$** contains a one-character uppercase letter. Write one or more statements to convert it to lowercase.

CONTROL CHARACTERS

Although ASCII includes 32 control characters, only a handful are commonly used in most programming applications. We will study only three of them: LINE FEED (10), FORM FEED (12), and CARRIAGE RETURN (13). We have already used the form feed to skip to a new page as follows:

```
PRINT CHR$(12);
```

This causes a character with an ASCII value of 12 to be transmitted to the output device. If the device is a printer, then a form feed results. A common practice is to define the form feed character as a string variable, and then use the variable whenever a form feed is required. For example:

```
120     F$ = CHR$(12)

3060    PRINT #2, F$
```

Each time a line of output is sent to a terminal, it is commonly followed by a pair of characters: the CARRIAGE RETURN and the LINE FEED. They produce the result which is implied by their names; that is, they return the cursor or print element to the beginning of the next line. Within a file, this pair of characters is commonly used to signal the end of the line (EOL).

THE VAL AND STR$ FUNCTIONS Converting numeric quantities stored as strings into numeric form (and the opposite) are common operations. For instance, let us assume that we have three string variables in our program and that they have been assigned values as shown in Figure 11-6(a). Here we see that these are valid numeric fields, but they have been assigned as string quantities. As string quantities, it is not possible to perform arithmetic on them. If necessary, however, they can be converted to numeric format as illustrated in Figure 11-6(b). Obviously the string field which is converted must be a valid number: It may contain digits, a sign, and a decimal point. Anything else will give an error. In each case of Figure 11-6(b), the numeric value will be assigned to the variable on the left of the equal sign.

Figure 11-7 The STR$ function.

```
Q$ = "125"           O = VAL(Q$)
R$ = "678.23         S1 = VAL(R$)
P$ = "-25"           P = VAL(P$)


        (a)                  (b)
```

The opposite operation, converting a number to a string, is just as easy. For example, in Figure 11-7, the quantities **X**, **N**, and **L1** are converted to

Figure 11-6 The VAL function.

```
X = 27              X$ = STR$(X)
N = 362.5           N$ = STR$(N)
L1 = -28            L$ = STR$(L1)


       (a)                 (b)
```

strings. Whereas each numeric variable occupies a fixed number of bytes in storage, when converted to string it occupies as many bytes as is required. In the examples of Figure 11-7(b), the lengths of **X$**, **N$**, and **L$** will be 2, 5, and 3 respectively.

To illustrate how these functions are commonly used, consider the following example.

Example 11-2

At one point in an interactive program, the user is required to enter a numeric field (digits only—no decimal point or sign). Within the program, the requirements are:

1. The quantity is read into the string variable **V$**.
2. The input field is to be checked to ensure that it consists only of digits.
3. A valid value is to be converted to numeric and stored in the numeric variable **V**. If **V$** contains any nondigit characters, then set **V** to –1.

Figure 11-8 is a routine to perform this operation. The **FOR-NEXT** loop of lines 7020 through 7070 processes the characters of **V$** one at a time. In statements 7030 and 7040, the ASCII value of each is checked to ensure that it is between 48 and 57 (the ASCII values of 0 through 9). Note how the variable **V** is used. It is first set to zero prior to the loop. If a nondigit is detected, its value is changed to –1. Then line 7090 (the actual conversion) will be executed only if **V** contains 0.

Figure 11-8   Converting from string to numeric—Example 11-2.

```
7000 REM CONVERT
7001 REM   THIS ROUTINE CONVERTS A POSITIVE NUMBER
7002 REM   STORED AS A STRING IN V$ TO NUMERIC IN V.
7003 REM   EACH CHARACTER IS CHECKED TO ENSURE THAT IT IS A DIGIT.
7004 REM
7005 REM   INPUT      V$ -- NUMBER IN STRING FORMAT
7006 REM   OUTPUT     V  -- INPUT CONVERTED TO NUMERIC IF VALID.
7007 REM                    SET TO -1 IF V$ NOT VALID NUMERIC QUANTITY.
7008                                         REM
7010    V = 0
7011       REM SET VALUE TO ZERO
7020    FOR J = 1 TO LEN(V$)
7030       D = ASC(MID$(V$,I,1))
7040       IF D>=48 AND D<=57 THEN 7070
7050             V = -1
7060             GOTO 7080
7061                REM IF NON DIGIT DETECTED THEN SET V TO -1 AND EXIT
7070    NEXT J
7080    IF V=-1 THEN 7100
7090       V = VAL(V$)
7091          REM PERFORM CONVERSION ONLY IF ALL DIGITS
7100    RETURN
```

EXERCISES

11.8 With the **VAL** function, if the string field contains a nonnumeric character (such as the letter **A**) or more than one decimal point, then an error occurs. Can you think of any equivalent error which might occur with the **STR$** function?

11.9 What would happen in Figure 11-8 if line 7010 were omitted?

User-Defined Functions

SINGLE-LINE FUNCTIONS The built-in functions available in Basic provide a convenient and powerful tool. The Basic language is further enhanced by the provision for the user to define functions. There are two broad categories of user-defined functions: those consisting of one line and those consisting of multiple lines. Let us first consider single-line functions.

Assume that we have a program in which it is necessary to calculate accumulated interest in several different places in a program using the formula:

$$I = P(1+r/100)^t - P$$

where P = principal
r = interest rate in percent
t = time in years

This is a natural situation for a subroutine in which we can transmit to the routine the values of P, r, and t and get back the value of I. The function gives us that ability. Every user-defined function must be identified as a function by the letters **FN** followed by the function name (any valid variable name). For instance, the following are valid function names.

FNA6$**—user-defined string function named **A6$
FNK—user-defined numeric function named **K**

Definition of the function requires the word **DEF** (define function), followed by the name and the arguments, followed by the definition of the operations. The desired interest function could be defined as shown in Figure 11-9. It is

Figure 11-9
Single-line function definition.

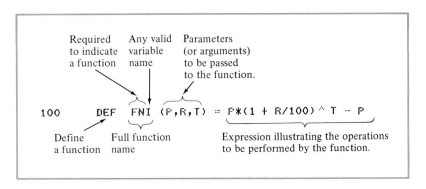

important to recognize that this definition represents a model of the function which indicates the operations to be performed. In itself, *it does not cause any calculations to occur.* For this, it must be used just as any other function, such as **SQR**. Let us assume, for instance, that in two different places in a program we must calculate the interest. At line 500, the principal, interest rate, time, and interest amount must be printed (the "input" values are stored in the variables **P2**, **R**, and **T2**). At line 820, the interest must be calculated for the principal **A**, rate **I9**, and time **T1**. The result is to be multiplied by 2 and stored in the variable **T9**. This is illustrated in Figure 11-10. Here it is *imperative* to recognize that the variables **P**, **R**, and **T** in the function definition (line 100) are *dummy* variables (also called *formal* variables). They are used to indicate the relationship between the argument list and the variables in the expression. That is, when statement 500 is executed, **P2**, **R**, and **T2** will effectively be substituted for **P**, **R**, and **T** in the function definition. (**P2**, **R**, and **T2** are commonly called *actual* variables.) Similarly, when statement 820 is executed, **A**, **I9**, and **T1** will be substituted.

Figure 11-10   A user-defined function.

```
100     DEF FNI(P,R,T) = P*(1 + R/100)^T - P
   .
   .
   .
500     PRINT P2, R, T2, FNI(P2,R,T2)
   .
   .
   .
820     T9 = 2.0*FNI(A,I9,T1)
```

Further points relating to user-defined functions are as follows: First, the number of arguments which can be used can range from zero to five. However, any call to a function must include the exact number of arguments as shown in the definition. Second, the function can be numeric or string as required by the programmer. That choice must be reflected in the function name selected.

EXERCISE

11.10 In using the interest function defined in Figure 11-10, a programmer became confused about the order of the arguments and wrote:

```
820     T9 = 2.0*FININTR(I9,A,T1)
```

Note that the principal amount and interest rate have been switched. Would this result in an error condition? What would happen?

MULTIPLE-LINE FUNCTIONS Although single-line functions are convenient for some applications, operations are commonly required which involve many more than a single line of code. To illustrate, let us assume that the interest calculation of the preceding single line involves several lines of checking to ensure that the data is within allowable limits. The definition would then appear as illustrated by Figure 11-11. Here we see that the function definition line includes only the function name and the argument list. The operations to be performed are defined in subsequent lines. The definition is ended by the **FNEND** statement.

Figure 11-11
General forms of a multiple-line function definition.

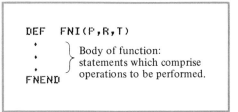

Multiple-line functions of this form are a very useful tool. Not all versions of Basic have this capability, however.

Example 11-3
A function for interest calculations is required which will calculate either interest or accumulated amount (principal and interest) using the following formula:

$$I = P(1 + r/100)^t - P$$
$$A = P(1 + r/100)^t$$

The function call must have the form:

```
FNI2(T$,P,R,T)
```

where **T\$** = value of *A* means calculate the amount *A*; any other value
means calculate the interest *I*
    P = principal amount
    R = rate in percent
    T = time in years
If any of the arguments *P*, *r*, or *t* are negative, return a value of zero.

CHARAC- The function definition and two examples of using it are shown in Figure
TERISTICS 11-12. The following commentary describes points of note relative to this
OF MULTIPLE- example, and to user-defined functions in general.
LINE FUNCTIONS

1. The function definition may be included at any point in the program. It
need *not* be defined before it is used (as we see in Figure 11-12).
2. The result is returned to the main program at line 6081 through a **LET**
statement in which the value is assigned to the function name
(*without* the argument list). This is the proper way to return the result.
3. In the first function call (line 360), values for principal, interest rate, and
time, together with the calculated interest, are printed. (Presumably
the input values to the function came from earlier statements in the
program.) Note that the first argument is the string value "I". This
indicates to the function that interest only is to be calculated (see line
6040).
4. The second function call (line 510) involves an interactive situation. Here
the user is allowed to key in the type of calculation required (interest
only or total amount) and the principal, rate, and time. Line 520
checks the value returned to ensure that all values entered were
valid.
5. The dummy arguments defined in the function (**T\$** and so on in this
example), are meaningful only within the function. If one or more are
modified in the function body, they will have no influence on the
equivalent variables is the call. For instance, if the value of **T** in the
function definition (lines 6000–6060) were changed, it would not
change the value of **Y1** (line 360) or of **Y9** (line 510) in the main
program.
6. Any variable used in the function body which is not defined as a dummy
argument is treated as simply another variable in the program. For
example, assume that in the main program of Figure 11-12 the
variable I is used to represent some type of interval which is incremented as follows:

```
810    I = I+1.0
```

This is an unfortunate choice of names since I is used as a working
variable in the function (line 6031). Upon execution of the function,

Figure 11-12   A multiple-line function—Example 11-3.

```
       ◆
       ◆
       ◆
  360      PRINT P1, I1, Y1, FNI2("I",P1,I1,Y1)
       ◆
       ◆
       ◆
  450      PRINT "YOU CAN GET THE INTEREST ONLY OR THE TOTAL AMOUNT."
  460      INPUT "DO YOU WANT INTEREST ONLY"; Q$
  470      C$="I"
  471        REM SET UP INITIALLY ASSUMING INTEREST ONLY
  480      IF Q$<>"YES" THEN 500
  490         C$="A"
  491            REM CHANGE TO TOTAL AMOUNT IF REQUESTED
  500      INPUT "PLEASE ENTER PRINCIPAL, RATE & TIME"; P9, R9, Y9
  510      S = FNI2(C$,P9,R9,Y9)
  520      IF S>0 THEN 540
  530         PRINT "PRINCIPAL, INTEREST & RATE MUST BE > ZERO."
  540         PRINT "PLEASE REENTER YOUR VALUES."
  550         GOTO 500
  551            REM REQUEST A NEW VALUE
  560         ...
       ◆
       ◆
       ◆
 6000 REM FUNCTION FOR INTEREST CALCULATION
 6010     DEF FNI2(T$,P,R,T)
 6020       IF P>0 AND R>0 AND T>0 THEN 6031 ELSE 6071
 6030 REM   THEN
 6031            I = P*(1 + R/100)^T
 6040            IF T$="A" THEN 6060
 6050               I = I - P  ◄──────── Deduct principal if
 6060            GOTO 6081                interest only
 6070 REM   ELSE
 6071            I = 0
 6080 REM   ENDIF
 6081          FNI2 = I
 6082            REM RETURN RESULT
 6090     FNEND
 6100 REM END OF INTEREST FUNCTION
```

the value from line 810 would be destroyed. Obviously care must be taken in selecting working variable names within the function which will not be likely to be used in the main program.

7. The function may be numeric or string as determined by the selection of the function name. The arguments may also be numeric and/or string and are totally independent of the function mode.

8. The main program should never branch into a function; execution must always be from the normal function call (as in statement 510). Similarly exit from a function must always be via the **FNEND**; do not simply **GOTO** a statement outside the function in order to exit from it. The single-entry/single-exit rule is a must in the case of functions.

Figure 11-13 (a) Flowchart for multiple selection. (b) Multiple selection using IFs.

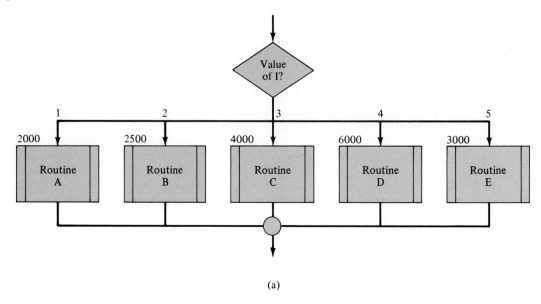

(a)

```
450    IF I<>1 THEN 460
451       GOSUB 2000
452       GOTO 511
460    IF I<>2 THEN 470
461       GOSUB 2500
462       GOTO 511
470    IF I<>3 THEN 480
471       GOSUB 4000
472       GOTO 511
480    IF I<>4 THEN 490
481       GOSUB 6000
482       GOTO 511
490    IF I<>5 THEN 501
491       GOSUB 3000
492       GOTO 511
500    REM OUT OF RANGE ERROR
501       PRINT "OUT OF RANGE IN GOSUB SELECTION"
502       STOP
510 REM CONTINUATION POINT
511    ...
```

(b)

Menu Control

THE ON-GOSUB
STATEMENT Occasions will sometimes arise in a program where one of several routines is to be executed depending upon a particular set of conditions at the time. For instance, let us assume that at a particular point in a program, one of five different routines is to be executed, depending upon the value of the variable I. The logic of this is illustrated by the flowchart segment of Figure 11-13(a). This is a commonly encountered structure in programming and is referred to as the *case* structure. Some structured languages include a special case statement specifically for this type of operation. Although most versions of Basic do not include such a statement, it can be simulated using a series of IFs as shown in Figure 11-13(b). Here, if I is 1, then the first condition test is false and the routine at 2000 is executed. Upon return from the routine, the case is terminated by transferring to line 511. If I is not 1, then execution proceeds to the test for 2 at line 460, and so on. If I is not within the acceptable range (1–5), execution is terminated at line 502.

For special cases such as this in which the test condition depends upon consecutive whole-number values, a special multiselection statement may be used. It is illustrated in Figure 11-14. Here we see that the control variable determines which statement in the list is selected. If I is 1, then the first statement is selected; if 2, then the second statement; and so on. Upon execution of the subroutine, encountering the **RETURN** will cause execution to continue at line 470.

We might ask, "What if the control variable has a value which is greater than the number of statement numbers in the list?" For instance, what if the value of I in statement 470 in Figure 11-14 were 6? The answer is that an error will occur. For this reason, whenever there is a doubt, a test should be made prior to the **ON-GOSUB**.

Figure 11-14   The ON-GOSUB statement.

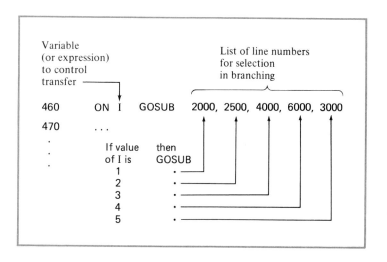

EXERCISE

11.11 Write an **ON-GOSUB** statement (and whatever else is necessary) to select the routine to be executed based on the variable **A** as follows:

Value of A	Line
1	1000
2	1700
4	2500
6	3000
7	4000
8	3000

A SIMPLE MENU EXAMPLE

It is very common for an application to require several different programs to do the job. For instance, a file-handling system might require one program to create a new file, another to add records, another to make corrections, and so on. In many instances, to use several different programs for one application is very clumsy. In fact, sometimes it is more convenient to integrate all of the functions into a single program then operate under control of a central module. To illustrate this concept, let us assume that our file-handling system is to (1) create a new file, (2) kill (delete) an existing file, (3) add records to an existing file, (4) delete records from an existing file, and (5) make corrections to records of an existing file. The selection of which function is to be performed is commonly handled by use of a *menu.* A menu is simply a list from which the user can make a desired selection. A menu approach to this problem is illustrated in Figure 11-15, which also includes a sample dialog. The key to this solution is use of the **ON-GOSUB** statement in line 2440.

Menu control of access to various components of a program is a commonly used technique. It is a convenient method for providing easy-to-remember access to numerous operations and is often used to control and/or limit access among users to particular operations.

Figure 11-15   A menu program.

```
      .         Open files and perform
      .         other operations common
      .         to all functions.
2320         C$ = "YES"
2330         FOR I = 1 TO 10000
2331         IF C$<>"YES" THEN 2470
2332            REM EXIT THE LOOP IF FINISHED
2340           PRINT "THIS IS THE FILE MAINTENANCE PROGRAM."
2350           PRINT "THE OPTIONS AVAILABLE TO YOU ARE:"
2360           PRINT "  1 - CREATE A NEW FILE"
2360           PRINT "  2 - KILL AN EXISTING FILE"
2370           PRINT "  3 - ADD RECORDS TO A FILE"
2380           PRINT "  4 - DELETE RECORDS FROM A FILE"
2390           PRINT "  5 - CORRECT AN EXISTING RECORD"
2400           INPUT "WHICH OPTION DO YOU WANT (1,2,...)";Q
2410           IF Q>=1 AND Q<=5 THEN 2440
2420              PRINT "OPTION MUST BE BETWEEN 1 & 5."
2430              GOTO 2400
2440           ON Q GOSUB 5010, 6010, 7010, 8010, 9010
2450           INPUT "Do you wish to perform more processing";C$
2460         NEXT I
2470

      .
      .
      .
5000 REM FILE CREATE ROUTINE
5010     ...
      .
      .
      .
5980     PRINT "FILE CREATION COMPLETED"
5990     RETURN
      .
      .
      .
6000 REM FILE KILL ROUTINE
      .
      .
      .
6990     RETURN
```

```
THIS IS THE FILE MAINTENANCE PROGRAM.
THE OPTIONS AVAILABLE TO YOU ARE:
   1 - CREATE A NEW FILE
   2 - KILL AN EXISTING FILE
   3 - ADD RECORDS TO A FILE
   4 - DELETE RECORDS FROM A FILE
   5 - CORRECT AN EXISTING RECORD
WHICH OPTION DO YOU WANT (1,2,...)? 1
   .
   .          (Creation dialog)
   .
FILE CREATION COMPLETE
Do you wish to perform more processing?
```

ANSWERS TO PRECEDING EXERCISES

11.1 Some lines contain commas which are part of the text. However, the **INPUT** statement will see them as delimiters. Consequently, when the first line shown in Figure 11-1 is read, **L$** will contain THIS SAMPLE. Everything beyond the comma and up to the end of line will be ignored since there is only one variable in the list of the **INPUT** statement. The next time the file is read, the string ILLUSTRATES THE POINT will be read. The **LINE INPUT** statement resolves this problem.

11.2 The **LINE INPUT** statement may specify only one string variable in its "list."

11.3 The length is 5. However, if your system also reads the EOL code, the length will be longer.

11.4 After accessing the name, the value stored in **P** would point to the slash character following the name. Upon entering the routine the second time, the **FOR-NEXT** would be terminated immediately, with **I** and **P** containing the same value. This causes a problem at line 6040 in which the **MID$** function would be saying "get −1 characters from **R$**." On some computers, this would cause an error condition. On others, it would return a zero-length string (commonly called a *null string*) and continue. The result would be an infinite loop. Try it on your computer to see what happens. You might include a simple counter which you print at the beginning of the routine.

11.5 50 51 45 83 101 112 116

11.6 Basic-Plus

11.7
```
B = ASC(B$)
B = B + 32
B$ = CHR$(B)
```

or

```
B$ = CHR$(ASC(B$) + 32)
```

11.8 There is no similar error condition.

11.9 The first time through **V** would contain 0 and so the routine would function properly. However, after that **V** would contain the result of the previous execution of the routine. If an invalid entry were detected at any time, then **V** would be set to −1 and would so remain. Then the routine would always act as if an invalid quantity had been entered.

11.10 The computer knows only by position. Thus, the first argument, which is the interest rate **I9**, would be used as the principal amount, and the principal, which is **A**, would be used as the interest rate. There would be no error but the results would probably be quite incorrect.

11.11
```
460      ON A GOSUB 1000,1700,9000,2500,9000,3000,4000,3000
  •
  •
  •
9000 REM DUMMY ROUTINE
9010    RETURN
```

PROGRAMMING PROBLEMS

11.1 This problem involves writing a subroutine to allow changes to be made to records in an address file. Input to the routine is via the array **A$**, which consists of the following elements.

A$(1) person's name (maximum length: 20)
A$(2) street address (maximum length: 20)
A$(3) city (maximum length: 14)
A$(4) state (length: 2)
A$(5) Zip (length: 5)

The routine is to display the values and ask if corrections are desired as illustrated in Figure 11-16. Note the use of hyphens (or underscores) when asking for the new field. Their number must be equal to the length of the field which is to be keyed in. This serves as a guide to the user.

Figure 11-16
Correcting a record.

```
1)   Name:      Alfred Jones
2)   Address:   123 Okay St.
3)   City:      Oakland
4)   State:     CA
5)   Zip:       94123

Line to be corrected (enter 0 if no more corrections)?
```

At this point, user enters 2 and hits RETURN.

```
2)   Address:   --------------------------
```

At this point, user enters new address and hits RETURN.

```
2)   Address:   --------------------------
                6251 Better Ave.
```

When user depresses RETURN, the computer displays the corrected record.

```
1)   Name:      Alfred Jones
2)   Address:   6251 Better Ave.
3)   City:      Oakland
4)   State:     CA
5)   Zip:       94123

Line to be corrected (enter 0 if no more corrections)?
```

At this point, user corrects another line or enters 0 to terminate this sequence.

If the input line is longer than allowable, then truncate it to the proper length. If shorter, then pad to the right with spaces to achieve the full length. If the user simply depresses the carriage return key without making an entry, then leave the original value unchanged.

Figure 11-17   Sample labels.

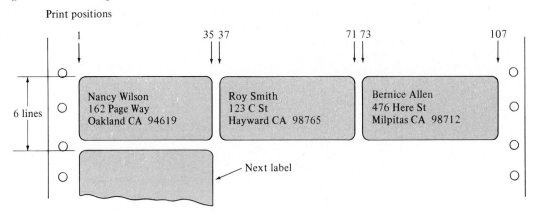

Print positions

11.2 Expand the address label routines of Example 11-1 to include the following.

1. Write a complete program; the data file to be processed is named ADDR. The last data record in the file is followed by a trailer with only the letters EOF.
2. With the exception of the first letter in each word and the state abbreviation, convert letters from uppercase to lowercase.
3. Print the labels "three across" as illustrated in Figure 11-17.

11.3 Text is stored in the file WORDS with no regard to formatting. Write a program which will write a new file with each line limited to 78 characters. (This corresponds to an 8½-inch page width with 1-inch margins and typing at 12 characters per inch.) The file will be terminated by a three-letter line containing EOF.

11.4 Many enhancements may be made to Problem 11.3. Three of them are:

1. Upon filling a page, progress to the next page to continue printing. An 11-inch page with printing at six lines per inch consists of 66 lines. Leaving 1 inch at the top and bottom margins gives 54 lines per page.
2. Print a page number at the bottom of each page. This number is to be printed in the center of the bottom margin.
3. If the first character in an input line is a space, then a new paragraph is to be started. Leave one line blank prior to the new paragraph, and then indent the new line five positions.
4. Never print the first line of a paragraph as the last line on a page.

Program one or more of these enhancements.

11.5 In interactive programs, it is quite common to request a user to enter some numeric response in answer to a question. For example, a menu program might require a numeric entry from 1 to 10; a quizzing program might ask for a question number from 1 to 75; and so on. In such instances, two different error conditions commonly arise. First, the quantity entered may not be numeric; second, the quantity entered may not be within the allowable range. This problem involves writing a function, which is illustrated by the following sequence of code.

```
300    INPUT "PLESE SELECT AN OPTION BETWEEN 1 AND 9"; N$
310    N = FNN9(N$,1,9,"Y")
320    IF N = -9999 THEN 300
```

The purpose of the function is to check to ensure that the number entered into **N$** is (1) numeric and (2) within the allowable range (this is a function option). Referring to the sample call of statement 310, the arguments of the function call are:

First argument (**N$**)—numeric quantity to be tested
Second argument (1)—smallest allowable value for the number
Third argument (9)—largest allowable value for the number
Fourth argument ("Y")—"Y" for "Yes, the range check is to be performed."
"N" for "No, the range check is not to be performed."

If the number is valid and within the range (if required in the particular test), then return its numeric value. If invalid, the function should print an appropriate error message and return a value of −9999.

APPENDIX I

The ASCII Character Set

The following table summarizes the 7-bit ASCII character set and includes the decimal equivalent of each character.

Decimal Value	ASCII Character	Common Usage	Decimal Value	ASCII Character	Common Usage
0	NUL	FILL character	16	DLE	
1	SOH		17	DC1	XON(CTRL/Q)
2	STX		18	DC2	
3	ETX	CTRL/C	19	DC3	X OFF(CTRL/S)
4	EOT	CTRL/D	20	DC4	
5	ENQ		21	NAK	CTRL/U
6	ACK		22	SYN	
7	BEL	BELL(CTRL/G)	23	ETB	
8	BS	BACKSPACE	24	CAN	
9	HT	HORIZONTAL TAB	25	EM	
10	LF	LINE FEED	26	SUB	CTRL/Z
11	VT	VERTICAL TAB	27	ESC	ESCAPE[1]
12	FF	FORM FEED(CTRL/L)	28	FS	
13	CR	CARRIAGE RETURN	29	GS	
14	SO		30	RS	
15	SI	CTRL/O	31	US	

Decimal Value	ASCII Character	Decimal Value	ASCII Character	Decimal Value	ASCII Character
32	SP	64	@	96	Grave accent
33	!	65	A	97	a
34	"	66	B	98	b
35	#	67	C	99	c
36	$	68	D	100	d
37	%	69	E	101	e
38	&	70	F	102	f
39	"	71	G	103	g
40	(	72	H	104	h
41	)	73	I	105	i
42	*	74	J	106	j
43	+	75	K	107	k
44	,	76	L	108	l
45	−	77	M	109	m
46	.	78	N	110	n
47	/	79	O	111	o
48	0	80	P	112	p
49	1	81	Q	113	q
50	2	82	R	114	r
51	3	83	S	115	s
52	4	84	T	116	t
53	5	85	U	117	u
54	6	86	V	118	v
55	7	87	W	119	w
56	8	88	X	120	x
57	9	89	Y	121	y
58	:	90	Z	122	z
59	;	91	[	123	{
60	<	92	\	124	| Vertical Line
61	=	93	]	125	}
62	>	94	ˆ OR ↑	126	~ Tilde
63	?	95	—OR←	127	DEL RUBOUT

APPENDIX II

Summary of Basic Statements

Conventions Used in this Appendix

In the interest of standardizing, certain conventions are used to represent general statement forms. They are as follows:

1. Items in lowercase are supplied by the programmer. The abbreviations used in this book are as follows:

   arg—argument or arguments used in a function call
   cond—conditional, which may be true or false
   const—numeric or string constant
   dim—dimension required in defining an array
   expr—arithmetic expression; may be a simple constant or variable
   filename—name of disk data file
   filenum—internal channel number for disk file reference
   list—list of variables, expressions, or constants
   ln—line number
   string—string variable or constant (enclosed in quotes)
   string var—string variable
   var—numeric variable

2. Items in capital letters (**LET**, **DATA**, etc.) must appear exactly as shown since they represent Basic keywords.
3. Angle brackets <> indicate required elements which are to be supplied by the programmer. For instance,

   ln **LET** <*var*> = <*expr*>

   Note: Line numbers on statements, although required, are not shown in angle brackets in the general form.
4. Braces [ ] indicate an optional element (that is, one which may or may not be included, depending upon the way in which the statement is to be used).

   ln **FOR** <*var*> = <*expr*> **TO** <*expr*>[**STEP** <*expr*>]

5. An element repeated twice followed by ellipses (periods) implies that one or more such elements may be included:

   DATA <*const*>, <*const*>, . . .

Differences for Apple II, IBM Personal Computer, and TRS 80 Microcomputers

Variations between the forms described in this book and the forms for the Apple II (Applesoft), IBM Personal Computer (DOS), and TRS 80 (TRSDOS) microcomputers are included with each definition. If, for a given statement form, there is no indication, then that form is consistent with each of the three microcomputers.

Summary of Statements

The following statement general forms each includes one or more example statements. For simplicity of reference, they are listed alphabetically rather than grouped by function.

CLOSE
> *In* **CLOSE** <*filenum*>, <*filenum*>, . . .

```
100   CLOSE #1, #2
120   CLOSE I
```

Apple:
> *In* **PRINT CHR$(4) (CLOSE** *filename*)

DATA
> *In* **DATA** <*const*>, <*const*>, . . .

```
920   DATA 25.3, 64, "STRING DATA"
```

DEF
> *In* **DEF FN**<*var (arg)*> = <*expr (arg)*>   single-line function
> *In* **DEF FN**<*var (arg)*>   multiple-line function

```
200   DEF FNC(R) = 2.0*3.14*R*R      (single line)
300   DEF FNC4$(A,B,C)               (multiple line)
```

Apple:
Limited to single-line numeric functions.
IBM:
Limited to single-line numeric or string functions.

DIM
ln **DIM** *<var (dim)>*, *<var (dim)>*, . . .

```
150   DIM A(20), B(10,15), C$(15)
```

END
ln **END**

```
9999   END
```

FNEND
ln **FNEND**

```
920 FNEND      End of multiple line function
```

Apple and IBM:
Not available

FOR
ln **FOR** *<var>* = *<expr>* **TO** *<expr>* [**STEP** *<expr>*]

```
370   FOR I = 1 TO 20
980   FOR J = N TO 0 STEP -1
```

FOR-UNTIL, FOR-WHILE
ln **FOR** *<var>* = *<expr>* [**STEP** *<expr>*]**UNTIL** *<cond>*
ln **FOR** *<var>* = *<expr>* [**STEP** *<expr>*]**WHILE** *<cond>*

```
650   FOR A = 1   WHILE X>0.0
790   FOR B = 3 STEP 4   UNTIL F$="F"
```

Apple, IBM, TRS 80:
Not available

GOSUB
ln **GOSUB** *<ln>*

```
280   GOSUB 750
```

GOTO
ln **GOTO** *<ln>*

```
370   GOTO 260
```

IF-THEN
ln **IF** *<cond>* **THEN** *<ln>*

```
800   IF X<0 THEN 270
900   IF X>0 OR Y=2*P THEN 990
```

Apple, IBM, and TRS 80 also include:
ln **IF** *<cond>* **THEN** *<statement>*
ln **IF** *<cond>* **THEN** *<statement>* *<:statement>* . . .

```
400   IF A>0 THEN PRINT "VALUE OKAY"
500   IF C=D THEN C=0 : PRINT : PRINT "C ZEROED" : PRINT
        (Note:  If condition true, all statements following THEN
        are executed; if false, all are ignored.)
```

IF-THEN-ELSE
ln **IF** *<cond>* **THEN** *<ln>* **ELSE** *<ln>*

```
690   IF X<0 THEN 720 ELSE 780
```

Apple:
Not available

IBM, TRS 80 also include:
ln **IF***<cond>***THEN***<statement :statement. . .>* **ELSE***<statement :statement . . .>*
Note: Either or both **THEN** and **ELSE** may be followed by one or more statements.

```
640   IF A=B THEN PRINT "CHECK" ELSE PRINT "NOCHECK"
650   IF P=0 THEN C=C+1 : PRINT C  ELSE PRINT : PRINT : PRINT "P<>0"
```

INPUT
ln **INPUT** [*literal,*] *<list>*

```
130   INPUT P,Q$
140   INPUT "WHAT IS THE MAXIMUM", M
```

INPUT
ln **INPUT #***<expr>*, *<list>*

```
150   INPUT #1, A,B,C
```

Apple:
Does not use file number designation (standard **INPUT** is used). However, input must have been switched from keyboard to disk previously. Refer to the Apple note on the **OPEN** statement.

LINE INPUT
ln **LINE INPUT***<string var>*
ln **LINE INPUT #** *<filenum>*, *<string var>*

```
460   LINE INPUT Q$
470   LINE INPUT #4, L$
```

Apple:
Not available

LET

ln **LET** <*var*> = <*expr*>

```
220   LET A = B*C + 25.0
240   A = B*C + 25.0
```

NEXT

ln **NEXT** <*var*>

```
490   NEXT J
```

ON-GOSUB

ln **ON** <*expr*> **GOSUB** <*list of line numbers*>

```
400   ON N GOSUB 500, 620, 700, 850
```

OPEN

ln **OPEN** <*filename*> **FOR INPUT AS FILE** <*filename*>
ln **OPEN** <*filename*> **FOR OUTPUT AS FILE** <*filename*>

```
100   OPEN "ABCXYZ" FOR INPUT AS FILE #1
110   OPEN F$ FOR OUTPUT AS FILE #2
```

Apple:
ln **PRINT CHR$(4)** "**OPEN** <*filename*>"

Notes:
1. It is not necessary to specify input or output.
2. The **OPEN** must be accompanied by a second statement which accepts input from the disk rather than the keyboard or diverts output to the disk rather than the screen. These are:

ln **PRINT CHR$(4)** "**READ** <*filename*>"   (For input)
ln **PRINT CHR$(4)** "**WRITE** <*filename*>"   (For output)

IBM, TRS 80:
ln **OPEN** "I", <*filename*>, <*filenum*>   (For input)
ln **OPEN** "O", <*filename*>, <*filenum*>   (For output)

Notes:
1. The TRS 80 does not allow the comma between the *filename* and *filenum*.
2. The IBM also allows use of the general form but the word **FILE** must be omitted.

PRINT

In **PRINT** *<list>*

```
250   PRINT A,B$,C
270   PRINT
```

PRINT

In **PRINT** #*<filenum>*, *<list>*

```
290   PRINT #1, X,Y,Z
```

Apple:
Does not use file number designation (standard **PRINT** is used). However, output must have been switched from screen to disk previously. Refer to the Apple note on the **OPEN** statement.

PRINT-USING

In **PRINT USING** *<string>*, *<list>*
In **PRINT** #*<filenum>*, **USING** *<string>*, *<list>*

```
330   PRINT USING M$
390   PRINT #4, USING '###.##      ###', A,I
```

Apple:
Not available

READ

In **READ** *<var>*,*<var>*, . . .

```
210   READ A,B$
```

REM

In **REM** *<message>*

```
100   REM   EXAMPLE
```

Note: The Apple, IBM, and TRS 80 all allow the line number of a **REM** to be used in a transfer statement (**GOTO** or **GOSUB**). They also allow a remark preceded by a colon to be included on the same line as a statement as illustrated by the following.

```
200 C = C + 1   :REM INCREMENT COUNTER
```

IBM and TRS 80:
The single quote can be substituted for **REM**. Such a comment can be on a separate line or on the same line as a statement.

```
210   ' THIS IS A REM
220   C = C + 1   ' INCREMENT COUNTER
```

RESTORE
In **RESTORE**

```
100   RESTORE
```

RETURN
In **RETURN**

```
900   RETURN
```

STOP
In **STOP**

```
900 STOP
```

APPENDIX III

Summary of Basic Commands

This appendix briefly summarizes the most commonly used Basic commands. As in Appendix II, differences between the general form and the three microcomputers—Apple, IBM Personal Computer and TRS 80—are appropriately noted. For any given command, if there is no notation regarding a particular microcomputer, then the form used by that microcomputer is identical to the general form.

CATALOG
Displays a list of files stored in the system.

Apple:
CATALOG D1 (or **D2**)—Specify drive 1 or 2 (DOS Command)

IBM:
DIR A: (or **B:**)—Specify drive A or B (DOS Command)

TRS 80:
DIR :0 (or **:1**)—Specify drive 0 or 1 (DOS Command)

CONT
Allows the user to continue execution of a program which has been temporarily interrupted by a **STOP** or by some type of user-initiated break.

DELETE
Allows the user to delete one line or a range of lines from a program in memory. If a range of lines is to be deleted, then separate the line numbers by a hyphen. For instance, to delete lines 100 through 220, enter **DELETE 100–220**.

Apple:
DEL *n* (Deletes line *n*)
DEL *n,m* (Deletes lines *n* through *m*)

Caution: **DELETE** is used to delete files from the disk (see the **UNSAVE** command in this appendix).

LIST
Causes the system to display the program in memory at the terminal. Has the following three forms:
LIST (List entire program)
LIST *n* (List line number *n*)
LIST *n-m* (List lines *n* through *m*)

LOAD   See **OLD**.

NEW
Clears the memory of any current program and allows the user to begin entering a new program.

OLD *filename*
Clears the memory and brings in the specified program (filename) from disk storage.

Apple:
LOAD *filename*

IBM and TRS 80:
LOAD *"filename"* (Note: quotes are required.)

RUN
Causes execution of the program currently in memory to begin.

SAVE *filename*
Causes the program currently in memory to be saved on disk under the name *filename. Use caution,* if there is already a program on disk with this filename, many systems automatically delete the existing one with no warning.

IBM and TRS 80:
Require quotes around the *filename.*

UNSAVE *filename*

Causes the program named *filename* on disk storage to be removed from the system.

Apple:
DELETE *filename*

IBM:
ERASE *filename*

TRS 80:
KILL *filename*

APPENDIX IV

Summary of Basic Functions

This appendix briefly summarizes the most commonly used Basic functions. As in Appendix II, differences between the general form and the three microcomputers—Apple, IBM Personal Computer, and TRS 80—are appropriately noted. For any given command, if there is no notation regarding a particular microcomputer, then the form used by that microcomputer is identical to the general form.

String Functions

ASC

```
Y = ASC(A$)
```

Returns the ASCII value of the first character in **A$**.

CHR$

```
Y$ = CHR$(A)
```

Returns a character string having the ASCII value of **A**. Only one character is generated by the function.

INSTR

```
Y = INSTR(N,A$,B$)
```

Causes a search of the string **A$** for the substring **B$** beginning at position **N** of **A$**. If **B$** is not found in **A$**, a value of 0 is returned to **Y**. If **B$** is found in **A$**, the beginning position in **A$** of the substring **B$** is returned.

Apple:
Not available

LEFT$

```
Y$ = LEFT$(A$,N)
```

Returns a substring (of length **N**) from the string **A$** beginning with the first character and ending with the **N**th character of **A$** (the left-most **N** characters).

LEN

```
Y=LEN(S$)
```

Returns the length of S$.

MID$

```
Y$ = MID$(A$,N1,N2)
```

Returns a substring of length **N2** from the string **A$** starting with character **N1** of **A$**.

```
Y$ = MID$(A$,N)
```

Note: Not available on all systems.
Returns a substring from **A$** beginning with the **N**th position through to the last position of **A$** (that is, from position **N** on).

RIGHT$

```
Y$ = RIGHT$(A$,N)
```

Returns a substring from **A$** beginning with the **N**th position through to the last position of **A$**.
Alternate form on some systems:
Returns the last **N** characters of **A$** (that is, same as **MID(A$,N)** above). Apple, IBM, and TRS 80 all use only the alternate form.

STR$

```
Y$ = STR$(N)
```

Returns a string of numeric characters representing the value of the numeric variable **N**. The **STR$** function is the inverse of the **VAL** function.

VAL

```
Y = VAL(N$)
```

Returns the numeric value of a string of numeric characters. If **N$** is not a valid numeric form (a sign and a decimal point are allowable), then an error condition occurs or a value of zero is returned (depending upon the system).

Other Functions

ABS

```
Y = ABS(N)
```

Returns the absolute value of N.

DATE$

```
Y$ = DATE$
```

Returns to current date.

Apple:
Not available

TRS 80:

```
DATE
```

FIX

```
Y = FIX(N)
```

Returns the whole-number portion of **N**. For instance, if **N** is 27.683, then 27 will be returned in **Y**.

TAB

```
TAB(N)
```

Moves the printing element (or cursor) to position **N** of the current record. On some systems, the first printing position is numbered 0; on others, it is numbered 1.

Apple, IBM:
The first position is numbered 1.

TRS 80:
The first position is numbered 0.

Index